The Asian Military Revolution

D0217074

Records show that the Chinese invented gunpowder in the 800s. By the 1200s they had unleashed the first weapons of war upon their unsuspecting neighbors. How did they react? What were the effects of these first wars? This extraordinarily ambitious book traces the history of that invention and its impact on the surrounding Asian world – Korea, Japan, Southeast Asia and South Asia – from the ninth through the twentieth century. As the book makes clear, the spread of war and its technology had devastating consequences on the political and cultural fabric of those early societies although each reacted very differently. The book, which is packed with information about military strategy, interregional warfare, and the development of armaments, also engages with the major debates and challenges traditional thinking on Europe's contribution to military technology in Asia. Articulate and comprehensive, this book will be a welcome addition to the undergraduate classroom and to all those interested in Asian studies and military history.

PETER LORGE is Senior Lecturer in the Department of History at Vanderbilt University, Tennessee. His previous publications include *War, Politics and Society in Early Modern China* (2005) and *The International Reader in Military History: China Pre-1600* (2005).

New Approaches to Asian History

This dynamic new series will publish books on the milestones in Asian history, those that have come to define particular periods or mark turning-points in the political, cultural and social evolution of the region. Books are intended as introductions for students to be used in the classroom. They are written by scholars whose credentials are well established in their particular fields and who have, in many cases, taught the subject across a number of years.

The Asian Military Revolution

From Gunpowder to the Bomb

Peter A. Lorge

Vanderbilt University, Tennessee

CAMBRIDGE UNIVERSITY PRESS
Cambridge, New York, Melbourne, Madrid, Cape Town, Singapore,
São Paulo, Delhi

Cambridge University Press
The Edinburgh Building, Cambridge CB2 8RU, UK

Published in the United States of America by Cambridge University Press,
New York

www.cambridge.org
Information on this title: www.cambridge.org/9780521609548

First published 2008

Printed in the United Kingdom at the University Press, Cambridge

A catalogue record for this publication is available from the British Library

Library of Congress Cataloging in Publication Data
Lorge, Peter Allan, 1967–
The Asian military revolution / Peter A. Lorge.
p.   cm. – (New approaches to Asian history)
ISBN 978-0-521-84682-0
1. Asia–History, Military.   2. Military art and science–History.
I. Title. II. Series.
DS33.7.L66   2008
355.0095–dc22
2007051673

ISBN 978-0-521-84682-0 hardback
ISBN 978-0-521-60954-8 paperback

Contents

Maps

Acknowledgments

This book would not have been written without the encouragement of David Graff. It was his idea that I write a book on gunpowder in Asian history, and he overcame my initial resistance to such a project. I can only hope that the end result does not disappoint him. My editor, Marigold Acland, provided further encouragement, and steered me through the very long process of book production. Her team of editors vastly improved my manuscript. I must also thank the three anonymous reviewers of the initial proposal, whose comments were so helpful. To the anonymous reader of the final manuscript, who caught so many errors, I can only say *dōmo arigatō gozaimashita*. My thanks also to my copy-editor, Carol Fellingham Webb.

I was also fortunate to receive timely criticism from Michael Charney and Lai-chen Sun that corrected many points in my chapter on Southeast Asia.

Having stretched so far to write this book, I am acutely aware of my shortcomings. Despite the kindly and scholarly efforts of several people, many of my mistakes remain.

Chronology

808	First mention of a mixture retrospectively understood to be gun-powder
Late 9th century	First possible use of gunpowder in warfare
Mid-10th century	First representation of a fire-spear
960–1279	Song dynasty
Early 11th century	Introduction of explosive gunpowder bombs in China
1044	First direct description of gunpowder published in the *Complete Essentials from the Military Classics* (*Wujing Zongyao*)
1127	Jurchen Jin capture the Song capital at Kaifeng
1132	First mention of a fire-spear, used at the siege of De'an
1221	First mention of iron-casing bombs, used during the Jurchen siege of Qizhou
Late 12th century	Invention of the rocket in China
1290	Earliest dated extant gun
13th century	Appearance of the true gun in China
1259	Koryo surrenders to Mongols
1274	First Mongol invasion of Japan
1281	Second Mongol invasion of Japan
1363	Battle of Lake Poyang
1368–1644	Ming dynasty
1400	Melaka established
1405–33	Zheng He's seven voyages
1467–77	Onin War
1511	Portuguese conquer Melaka
1526	First Battle of Panipat
1526–1857	Mughal empire
1543	Putative introduction of Portuguese firearms into Japan
1556	Second Battle of Panipat
1575	Battle of Nagashino

1592–3	First Japanese invasion of Korea
1593	Battle of Pyongyang
1597	Second Japanese invasion of Korea
1600	Battle of Sekigahara
1600–1867	Tokugawa Shogunate
1644	Shivaji sacks the Mughal port of Surat
1644–1911	Qing dynasty
1674	Shivaji has himself crowned king
1739	Nadir Shah invades the Mughal empire and captures Delhi
1757	Battle of Plassey
1782	Chakri dynasty established at Bangkok
1804	Qing court grants the name "Vietnam" to the ruler of Annam
1824	Myanmar conquers Assam
1824–6	First Anglo-Burmese War
1839–42	Opium War
1850–64	Taiping Rebellion
1852	Second Anglo-Burmese War
1857	Sepoy troops mutiny against their British officers
1868	Meiji Restoration
1876	Britain's Queen Victoria assumes the title Empress of India
1885	Third Anglo-Burmese War
1894–5	Sino-Japanese War
1904–5	Russo-Japanese War

Glossary

Arquebus	Term for a handgun originally derived from the early fifteenth-century word "*hackenbüchse*," or hook gun.
Ashigaru	Lit. "light-foot." Less heavily armored Japanese troops of the lowest martial class or commoners pressed into service.
Atakebune	A kind of early Japanese battleship-mounting cannon.
Ban	A South Asian rocket arrow.
Corning	A method of granulating gunpowder that affects its absorption of atmospheric water and its burn rate when ignited.
EIC	British East India Company.
Fire-arrow	Either an arrow packed with gunpowder and fired by a conventional bow in order set fire to a target, or a rocket, a projectile launched by the reactive force of ignited gunpowder.
Fire-ball	A container of low-nitrate gunpowder launched at a target to burn it.
Fire-spear	A spear with a tube filled with low-nitrate gunpowder affixed near its head.
Fire-tube	A tube filled with low-nitrate gunpowder.
Firingi	A South Asian field gun.
Gunpowder	A mixture of a nitrate (potassium, sodium, magnesium or calcium), sulfur, and charcoal.
Huoyao	Lit. "fire drug." Chinese term for gunpowder.
Jaza'il	Originally a *shaturnal* modified to fire from atop a wall, it later evolved into a sort of sniper rifle.
Mansab	Imperial rank.
Musket	Originally the name for a heavier form of arquebus that came to encompass most long-barreled, but unrifled, handguns.
Naginata	A polearm with a long, curved blade.

x

Saltpeter	Potassium, sodium, magnesium, or calcium nitrate.
Shaturnal	Light swivel gun mounted atop a camel or elephant.
Trace italienne	"Italian plan"; a form of gunpowder fortification pioneered in Italy, where it was known as "*Alla moderna*" or "modern plan."
Tufang	South Asian handgun.
Wokou	Also "wakou"; originally Japanese pirates who raided Korea and southern China. Over time these pirates included large numbers of Chinese.
Wujing Zongyao	*Complete Essentials from the Military Classics*, completed in 1044. A military encyclopedia that first recorded the recipe for producing gunpowder for military purposes.
Yari	A Japanese spear.
Zamīndārs	Local landlords or powerholders.
Zarb-zan	A South Asian field gun.

Introduction

> There seems little doubt that the composition of gunpowder has been known in the East from times of dimmest antiquity. The Chinese and Hindus contemporary with Moses are thought to have known of even the more recondite properties of the compound . . .
>
> Gunpowder has been known in India and China far beyond all periods of investigation; and if this account be considered true, it is very possible that Alexander the Great did absolutely meet with fire-weapons in India . . .[1]

Early modern warfare was invented in China during the twelfth and thirteenth centuries. It was during those two centuries of brutal warfare between the Chinese Song dynasty, the Jurchen Jin dynasty, and the rising power of the Mongols that guns, grenades, rockets, and other incendiary weapons fueled by gunpowder became regular and widespread tools of war.[2] These weapons were used extensively in siege and naval warfare by vast armies and navies, and gradually moved on to the open battlefield. Chinese soldiers were recruited, trained, and armed by the government, and organized into regularly ordered military units supplied by a bureaucratic logistics system, as indeed they had been for more than a thousand years. These troops were even housed in barracks and provided with regular medical care. The major sieges of the time revolved around cities with relatively low, thick walls, almost impenetrable to missiles, with circumferences measured in miles. True guns developed in this environment, and subsequently spread to the rest of Asia and the world.

---

[1] W. W. Greener, *The Gun and its Development*, Guilford, CT: Lyons Press, 2002 (reprint of the 9th edn published 1910; 1st edn 1881), 13.

[2] Joseph Needham slipped in including the eleventh century in his "real proving-grounds" for the wide military use of gunpowder, since war with the Jurchen did not begin until after 1125. See Joseph Needham, *Science and Civilization in China*, Vol. V, part 7: *Military Technology: The Gunpowder Epic*, Cambridge: Cambridge University Press, 1986, 16. My point here is more specific to the invention of early modern warfare as a whole, rather than simply gunpowder's regular use in warfare. The latter began in at least the eleventh century.

The French king Charles VIII led the first "modern" European army, invading Italy in 1494 with a force of infantry, cavalry, and gunpowder artillery, all paid from his treasury, thus ending the medieval warfare of the knights. Between this early period and the Revolutionary wars of Napoleonic France that ushered in national armies, Europeans adopted the articulated army units of Classical Rome, developed centralized state bureaucracies to supply those armies, and fortified major cities with low, thick walls able to withstand cannon. In Europe, at least, the association of modernity with guns is clear, though the precise relationship is still the subject of debate.[3] In China, as Geoffrey Parker noted, all of these elements, minus guns, existed before the Qin dynasty (221–206 BCE), and for him constituted a military revolution.[4]

Gunpowder played an important role in Asian history. This simple fact has usually been downplayed in Western scholarship on Asia, if not entirely denied, because the modern perspective on Asian history is that, before the arrival of Europeans, Asian military practice as a whole, and military technology in particular, was primitive and backward. European military superiority in the nineteenth century, at least with respect to technology, training, and tactics, led to an assumption that Asians had fallen behind because they were culturally non-military and racially inferior. Although the explicit racial argument has disappeared from recent Western scholarship, the cultural argument remains.

The cultural explanation of Asian technological inferiority is as pernicious as the racial explanation, since it denies Asia a military and political history before the arrival of the West. Technology is often portrayed as an objective measure of development, and its advancement as something that can be examined outside of politics. But the history of technology, particularly military technology, has been deeply inflected by nationalist sentiment. Early modern European superiority convinced many observers that Asian rulers had neglected military technology. Historians like Joseph Needham, who had done so much to establish China's primacy

---

[3] Michael Howard, *War in European History*, Oxford: Oxford University Press, 1976, 19–20, and Gunther E. Rothenburg, "Maurice of Nassau, Gustavus Adolphus, Raimondo Montecuccoli, and the 'Military Revolution' of the Seventeenth Century," in Peter Paret (ed.), *Makers of Modern Strategy*, Princeton: Princeton University Press, 1986, 32–63.

[4] Geoffrey Parker, *The Military Revolution: Military Innovation and the Rise of the West, 1500–1800*, 2nd edn, Cambridge: Cambridge University Press, 1996, 7.

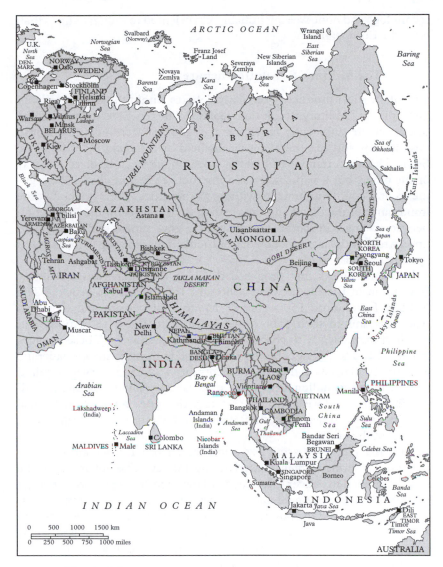

Map 1 Asia

in inventing gunpowder and cannon, felt they had to explain why a people who had been so precocious in technology fell so far behind. They argued that Asian regimes, with the possible exception of Japan, either did not value technology or were less militarily oriented than Europeans. This book will demonstrate that all major Asian regimes valued military technology and none was quantifiably less oriented to military affairs than were the Europeans.

The Military Revolution debate

One of the most productive scholarly debates within the field of military history is the "Military Revolution debate." The reactions to this ongoing discussion are sufficiently varied that it would be hazardous and unfair to describe any sort of general consensus held by the majority of scholars. Some scholars certainly feel that the question has been resolved one way or the other, but it is possible (and instructive) to adumbrate the arguments and counterarguments without taking sides. Fundamentally, the importance of the thesis and the ensuing debate rests on the connection between changes in warfare and changes in government and society, and upon whether the introduction of a particular technology produces only a specific response to it.

Michael Roberts first proposed the idea that there was a Military Revolution in Europe between 1560 and 1660 in a 1956 article, "The Military Revolution, 1560–1660."[5] Maurice of Nassau and Gustavus Adolphus shifted their shot-armed infantry to linear formations and required their cavalry to charge the enemy aggressively. These changes led ultimately to the early modern nation-state through the bureaucratic and structural needs of the army. A centralized bureaucracy was required to provide the standing army, now extensively trained and disciplined, with uniforms and weapons. The strategy that grew out of these tactical changes and the trajectory of the Thirty Years War dramatically increased the size of the army.

With the increased army size came much heavier demands on the populace in terms of men, material, and money. The apparatus of the state developed to deliver these goods to the army, along the way creating techniques of management and new institutions within the government. All of this enhanced the power of the state itself. Roberts' thesis provided a direct connection between the military, and the political and social changes that led to the modern state, thus making military history relevant to historians in other subdisciplines.

---

[5] Michael Roberts, "The Military Revolution, 1560–1660," originally delivered as his 1955 inaugural lecture at Queen's University Belfast. Initial publication as a pamphlet *The Military Revolution, 1560–1660* (Belfast: Marjarie Bajd, 1956), then reprinted with revisions in Roberts' *Essays in Swedish History* (1967).

Geoffrey Parker adopted and expanded Roberts' thesis, both chronologically and technically, by taking the period 1530–1710 as the time of
revolutionary change.[6] For Parker, the introduction of the *trace italienne*
(Italian plan) fortifications made battles irrelevant and sieges long and
difficult.[7] The *trace italienne* fortification was built with low and thick walls
to protect it against cannon, and angled bastions to provide defending
cannon overlapping fields of fire to prevent enemy troops from approaching. These new fortifications were also larger, requiring more money and
troops to create and maintain, and forced besieging forces to grow as well.
Where Roberts' revolution emphasized changes in drill and tactics, Parker
emphasized the changes caused by technology. Gunpowder and cannons
revolutionized warfare in Europe and, because of the economic, political,
and social demands of that revolution, changed the European states
themselves.

Parker's thesis has been attacked on a number of grounds, only two of
which concern us here.[8] Some scholars have argued that political factors
rather than technological ones were the cause of changes in warfare. This
is a critical chicken-and-egg problem, and one that this study directly
engages. In Asia, at least, it was political conditions that made the use of
guns possible. The second objection relates to the necessary effects of the
new technology. Did the technological changes necessitate growth in
army size, change in government operations, and so on, or did changes
in other areas cause those changes without particular respect to the
technology? Certainly in Asia, technology was not a driver of change,
but an indicator. These two problems obviously overlap. The first, however, concerns the political and social influence on warfare, and whether
governments and societies fashion modes of warfare in response to real or
perceived threats and cultural inclinations, or whether modes of warfare
are determined by technology, with governments and society forced to
accommodate them. The second problem is more technical, and confronts the issue of whether a specific technology requires a specific
response. John Lynn, for example, demonstrated that *trace italienne*

---

[6] Geoffrey Parker, *The Military Revolution: Military Innovation and the Rise of the West,
1500–1800*, 2nd edn, Cambridge: Cambridge University Press, 1996.

[7] I use the italicized Italian term "*trace italienne*" rather than the simple translation "Italian
plan" throughout to be consistent with scholarly convention. In Italy this kind of fortification was called "*alla moderna*" or "modern" plan. Some scholars now use the term "artillery
fortress" both to indicate that it was a phenomenon whose development was not restricted to
Italy and to emphasize the reliance upon artillery for the defense of the structures.

[8] These responses have been published in Clifford Rogers (ed.), *The Military Revolution
Debate: Readings on the Military Transformation of Early Modern Europe*, Boulder: Westview
Press, 1995.

fortifications did not require the vast increases in army size that Parker claimed they did.[9]

In contrast to early modern Europe, at least as Roberts and Parker have described it, there were a variety of responses to guns in Asia. This was true both before and after Europeans reached Asia. In some cases guns were paired effectively with cavalry, as the Mughals did, and in others they enhanced the infantry to the point of nearly rendering the cavalry obsolete, as in Japan. European historians have often, though not unanimously, assumed that European modern warfare was the one true path, a system that developed logically and inevitably from the nature of the advancing technology of guns. Since Europeans by their own definition were the most rational and logical of people, their mode of warfare was also the most rational and logical. Those who did not adopt it after seeing it were being deliberately irrational, or lacked the ability to advance their polity to the point where it could follow it. Yet European warfare in Asia was often highly unprofitable, involving vast expenditures to build and maintain *trace italienne* fortifications and colonial administrations that only profited a small number of merchants (while immiserating native populations and undermining local cultures). European imperialism as a whole was only rational for the narrow group of elites who were able to use the resources of their states to profit themselves economically and politically. Competition for glory among European nations led to political and ideological traditions that supported unprofitable military adventures around the world. Warfare in Asia did not materially benefit most Europeans, however, and may well have actually hurt them in the form of higher taxes, and resources diverted from domestic uses to foreign adventures.

Clifford Rogers has suggested that: "Henceforth it would be clear that the consequences of military innovation in early modern Europe belonged at least as much to World as to European History."[10] Rogers did not, presumably, intend to imply by this statement that it was only European developments in guns and their use in warfare that created a truly transformative revolution in world history. It is only that his frame of reference looks forward from early modern Europe for the roots of the modern world. Pulling the narrative framework back a little chronologically, it would be equally accurate to say that henceforth it would be clear

---

[9] John Lynn, "The *Trace Italienne* and the Growth of Armies: The French Case," in Rogers, *The Military Revolution Debate*, 169–99. But see Parker's response to Lynn in Parker, *The Military Revolution*, 169–71.

[10] Clifford Rogers, "The Military Revolution in History and Historiography," in Rogers, *The Military Revolution Debate*, 5.

that the consequences of military innovation in twelfth- and thirteenth-century China belonged as much to World as Chinese History. Without the Chinese revolution in warfare there could not have been a European revolution, no matter how it was constituted.

Western perspectives and the reality of gunpowder in Asia

The perspective of modern Western history and historians obfuscates a clear view of the Asian past. The current global dominance of Western technological, social, and economic systems has created a heuristic end point for the underlying Hegelian narrative of Western triumphalism, a point extensively discussed by Jeremy Black in *Rethinking Military History*.[11] Consequently, the modern bias in contemporary Western scholarship (which has spread to the rest of the world as well) insists upon focusing all attention on the formation of the modern world and "modernity." By directing attention to a time period rather than to a region, Western scholars can place the West at the center of any discussion, and subordinate backward Asia to Western history, without explicitly condemning Asian cultures and polities or arguing for a narrowly Eurocentric view of the world. Nevertheless, modern history is effectively a racist pursuit that not only elevates white Westerners above all others, but also actively denigrates Asian history.

Perhaps the strangest manifestation of the Eurocentric approach to the history of military technology is not the focus on the past few centuries, but the attempt to discern fundamental cultural roots in the distant past that have resulted in the perceived current Western dominance of the world.[12] This essentialism attempts to contrast ancient Greek logic and philosophy with the less rationally minded philosophies of the non-West. Modern science and technology, in this view, is a simple jump from ancient Greece to early modern Europe. Although historians of technology do not

---

[11] Jeremy Black, *Rethinking Military History*, London and New York: Routledge, 2004.

[12] Victor Davis Hanson is perhaps the most prominent current purveyor of this view, particularly with respect to Western warfare. Victor Davis Hanson, *The Western Way of War*, New York: Knopf, 1989, and many subsequent books. Hanson's views have been so thoroughly rejected that Stephen Morillo criticized John Lynn for spending too much time in his book explaining why they were wrong. See Stephen Morillo, 'Review of Kenneth Chase, *Firearms: A Global History to 1700* and John Lynn, *Battle: A History of Combat and Culture*,' *Journal of World History*, 15/4 (Dec. 2004), 525. David Landes has voiced a similar position with respect to economic history in his *The Wealth and Poverty of Nations: Why Some are So Rich and Some So Poor*, New York: W. W. Norton and Company, 1998. As with Hanson, critics have pointed out that Landes' descriptions of cultures and states outside of Europe and America are simply incorrect.

use this sort of simplistic approach to technological history, it is often present, implicitly or explicitly, in many popular histories that rely upon an earlier generation of scholarship.[13] Of course, this does not explain why gunpowder, guns, and rockets were invented in China, not the West.

The history of gunpowder spans pre-modern and modern history, and shifts focus from Asia as originator to receiver. Yet gunpowder's Asian history does not fit comfortably into any European schema of historical progression, and, consequently, the Asian side of the gunpowder story has been severely truncated or cloaked in the minutiae of purely technical history. The impression one is frequently given is that Chinese Daoists stumbled upon gunpowder while, ironically, searching for elixirs of immortality; not understanding the obvious uses of such a mixture, they used it only for fireworks.[14] It was only when gunpowder reached Europe that the potential of gunpowder to transform warfare was realized. Europeans then developed modern warfare and colonized Asia with its fruits. The pre-existing use of guns and gunpowder weapons before Europeans arrived, and the eager and smooth adoption of European guns into various Asian armies, is usually incorporated into the narrative of Asian backwardness. Although there were guns in Asia before Europeans, they were not very good.

A number of nationalisms are based upon the European narrative of gunpowder's history and the concomitant military relationship between the West and Asia. Technology has become the West's main prop to its claims of inherent superiority over the non-West, and the reason why the non-West should adopt Western culture. If advanced technology is particular to Western culture, then it is only by Westernizing that the non-West can obtain it. This argument collapses if Western technology can be adopted in isolation from the broader culture, or if other cultures can generate significant technology independently. Since gunpowder, guns, and rockets (not to mention the compass, paper, and movable type, among others) were invented outside of the West, Western culture is

---

[13] See for example Ian V. Hogg, *The Story of the Gun*, New York: St. Martin's Press, 1996, 12, where he asserts that the Chinese experimented with "various pyrotechnic compositions . . . but so far as we can ascertain, they never applied any of these compositions to the propelling of something out of a tube." He goes on to attribute the first mention of gunpowder to Roger Bacon, "a Franciscan friar, scientist and philosopher," in 1242. Notice that Hogg assiduously avoids using the term "gunpowder" with respect to the Chinese. Hogg's book accompanied a television show on the subject. Given that J. R. Partington's book on gunpowder, including information on the Chinese use of it, was published in 1960, and Needham's volume on the subject first appeared in 1986, Hogg's ignorance is impressive.

[14] See Landes, *The Wealth and Poverty of Nations*, 52–3, for a similarly ignorant assertion that the Chinese were more interested in incendiary devices than explosives.

clearly not a precondition for technological advancement. Europeans refined Chinese technology, and began fully to exploit the possibilities of that technology when their armies began to resemble Chinese armies in the sixteenth century. That is not to say that they somehow became "sinified," in the sense of actively copying Chinese practice, only that the technology came into its own when European warfare began to function like Chinese warfare.

Just as technology has served as an unreliable tool to prove Western cultural superiority, so too has the idea that many Asian polities were only able to form into states in response to Western colonialism. Once again, this idea is sustainable only when focusing on the modern world. Victor Lieberman makes a point of starting his discussion of the development of Southeast Asia in 800 in order to demonstrate that political development and state formation were well under way before the arrival of Europeans.[15] In Lieberman's extremely compelling formulation, the political consolidation of several Southeast Asian states developed in parallel with Western states, without any clear connections between them. What is important here is that a European presence was not necessary for state formation. Europeans believed that it was their arrival that created modern Southeast Asia since they had little knowledge or understanding of the pre-existing political trends.

Southeast Asia is something of a special case in Western historiography, since it lacks the politically asserted core cultural and political traditions of China, Japan, Korea, and South Asia (though see the discussion below for these terms). Yet if even the least consolidated Asian polities were gaining coherence and organization before the arrival of Europeans, then it is clear why Asians as a whole were so resistant to Western culture. It is also clear, then, that better guns were one of the few attractive things that Europeans brought to Asia. Guns were in widespread use in Asia and had already transformed Asian warfare before the arrival of Europeans. The use of guns in warfare was a marker of the level of political and military organization in Asia. Guns could not have been integrated into warfare without a certain degree of organization. The more organized polities were better able to avail themselves of the power of guns. When Europeans arrived with superior guns, it was the political state of Asian polities that determined their ability to absorb and deploy them.

This is not, however, a history of the decline of Asia from world leader to world follower in military technology. Nor is this a technological

---

[15] Victor Lieberman, *Strange Parallels: Southeast Asia in Global Context, c.800–1830*, Cambridge: Cambridge University Press, 2003.

history of the invention and diffusion of gunpowder and gunpowder weapons in Asia. The general outlines of that history are already known (and will be briefly recounted throughout the narrative), leaving the larger question of what effect that technology had still unanswered. It is not enough to locate and date the earliest appearance of a particular technology within a particular polity, or even simply to ascertain where and when that technology was invented, and if possible by whom. These are important pieces of information without which any subsequent discussion is impossible, but they do not explain how that technology was understood and used. What is critical to the discussion in this book is the impact gunpowder weapons, particularly guns, had on Asia.

Asia was a different place after the introduction of gunpowder, though the changes varied from place to place, and were mostly confined to the battlefield. There was no one "Asian" mode of warfare, nor a single response to gunpowder. Guns were incorporated into battle in ways consistent with the pre-existing culture. In and of itself, this varied response from different societies to the advent of not only early gunpowder and gunpowder weapons, but also later, more advanced weapons, disproves the notion that the introduction of firearms necessitated a particular military, political, or social reaction. Indeed, the easy adoption of guns by some societies was an indicator that the requisite military, political, or social environment already existed. Guns did not cause institutional change, or at least not irreversible institutional change. In Japan, for example, the shifting social makeup of soldiers at the end of the sixteenth century away from the samurai class was reversed in the early seventeenth century.

The political and social effects of new groups armed with guns entering into a particular political arena have often been mistakenly attributed to the gun itself. While guns gave these groups, for example the Mughals in the early sixteenth century, an advantage over their opponents, the resulting change outside the military environment was a result of the victorious groups' political program, not the guns. Well-armed and organized groups always had an advantage over their less well-armed or organized opponents even before the advent of guns. Guns were not an absolute advantage, though even early guns were effective, but a relative one whose effects depended on numbers, ammunition supply, and tactics. It was the system behind the guns that made them effective or not. Guns grew out of particular cultures and interacted with cultures in many different ways.

Defining Asia

The term "Asia" means different places to different people, so it is important clearly to define the scope of this book. In this section I will try briefly, and with a minimum of the painful etymological description so beloved of sinologists (myself included), to adumbrate the problems of terminology before describing the geographical and cultural boundaries that encompass and divide up the chapters that follow. These boundaries are meant to serve the needs of this book and cannot be said to represent real divisions between cultures that hermetically seal them off from nearby or even distant cultures. Indeed, much of the general thrust of this book is predicated on the constant flow of people, goods, and ideas throughout Asia and the world. Global trade long predated the European age of discovery.

Terms like "India," "South Asia," "Southeast Asia," and "East Asia" are not neutral in the current political milieu. The modern state of Pakistan, for example, is located on the Indian subcontinent, and might be considered part of South Asia, but is certainly not part of India. Even the term "China" is geographically unclear, as the People's Republic of China currently controls vastly more territory than the Chinese government of the eleventh century did, and lays further political claim to other lands it does not now control. It is, therefore, impossible to select terms that are wholly politically neutral. Worse still, the regional diversity of the Indian subcontinent and even China is entirely obfuscated by presenting the various empires that controlled those regions as culturally uniform and thus "naturally" coherent polities. How much more is this true of Southeast Asia, the most culturally diverse territory grouped together in this book? The chapter divisions in this book, China, Japan, South Asia, and Southeast Asia, can therefore only serve the convenience of the author, and do not support any contemporary political agenda.

Some readers may also wonder what happened to the "orient" and why this book was not titled: "The Oriental Military Revolution." Indeed, the very appearance of the word "oriental" as a serious geographic or cultural term triggers alarm bells for any American academic. The late Edward Said's *Orientalism* argued that the word "oriental" is a fundamentally pejorative term for certain parts of the non-Western world, not only indicating that they are inferior but also justifying Western colonization or domination of them.[16] Regardless of where one stands on Said's argument, it has carried the day and American universities and academics have systematically removed the word "oriental" from their vocabularies.

There is, however, another useful distinction to be made in the use of the terms "oriental" and "Asian" that is less emotionally charged. When Sir William Jones, Justice of the Supreme Court in Calcutta, founded the

---

[16] Edward Said, *Orientalism*, New York: Pantheon Books, 1978.

Asiatick Society in India in the late eighteenth century, his interest was in understanding Asia in Asian terms. The oriental approach, in contrast, was one whereby the East was explained to the West in Western terms.[17] British officials and officers later shifted from that Asian approach, inherently sympathetic to the culture they were ruling, to the oriental approach, where by they saw nothing good in Indian culture and actively sought to replace it with British culture.

In concrete terms, throughout this book "China" refers to all territory controlled by the current government of China; "Japan" refers to all territory controlled by the current government of Japan; "Korea" refers to all territory currently controlled by either the government of South Korea, or that of North Korea. "South Asia" encompasses the states of Pakistan, India, and Sri Lanka. "Southeast Asia" includes all the countries in the Association of South East Asian Nations (ASEAN).[18] These designations are not intended as political statements, nor are they necessarily fully reflective of the most recent international expressions of sovereignty. Taiwan, for example, is currently for all intents and purposes an independent sovereign state, but does not openly claim to be one, nor is it recognized as one, by most of the international community. Since the issue of Taiwanese independence does not directly concern us in this book, it has been included within China without intending that as a statement of support, intentionally or unintentionally, for the current government of China's position on Taiwan's status. These categories are only conveniences with any political implications purely accidental.

My most serious oversimplification of cultures is in relentlessly using the terms "the West" and "Europe" in the introduction and conclusion to refer to a monolithic intellectual and technological polity. A considerable amount of the scholarship on the Military Revolution in Europe is concerned precisely with the issue of which state developed which aspects of the Military Revolution at what time, and whether those developments were dependent on or independent of innovations in other states. Parsing those developments as they entered Asia would further encumber an already complex narrative. In most cases I have been specific about which European power supplied arms to a given state or conflict; it is in the more general discussions where the identity of individual European states has been elided in favor of the larger category of "the West" or "Europe."

---

[17] Hermann Kulke and Dietmar Rothermund, *A History of India*, 3rd edn, London and New York: Routledge, 1998, 226.
[18] These include Brunei, Myanmar (Burma), Cambodia, East Timor, Indonesia, Laos, Malaysia, Philippines, Singapore, Thailand (Siam), and Vietnam.

Gunpowder, guns, and technology

Technology is not an ahistorical or acultural artifact. Technology is created within a culture, and is as much a product of that culture and the time in which it was formed as a work of art, an idea, a work of literature, or any part of material culture. And just like all of those other cultural products, the use and effects of technology may differ from the original intention of its creator. Understood this way, the importance of Asian culture in the development of guns takes on a new meaning. Centuries of European superiority in gun and rocket technology have made the gun a quintessentially Western weapon, but it was originally a weapon of pre-modern China. Guns and rockets were designed for use by Chinese armies in the twelfth century. They were unmistakably weapons of war, invented and developed by a dedicated arms industry. In this section I will discuss the two main theories of why Europeans leapfrogged Asia in gun design, leaving the technical aspects of guns and gunpowder to the following section.

A considerable amount of scholarship on gunpowder has focused on who first invented it, and who first used it in true guns.[19] While determining this was quite important, the most frequent use of the information is to make larger arguments about the respective military and scientific values of a given culture. Thus China, where gunpowder, rockets, and guns were invented, but which Europe eventually surpassed in those technologies, is construed as scientifically precocious but militarily retarded. China failed to maintain its technological lead, and a similar failure throughout Asia to take advantage of the early exposure to that head start transformed precocity into a false dawn. Perversely, Asian improvements and adaptations of current (twentieth- to twenty-first-century) Western-developed technology are taken as further signs of lack of creativity.

While it is clear that the Chinese invented gunpowder and guns, and that they were available in Asia before the arrival of Europeans, it is less clear why further development of guns in Asia continued at such a slow pace compared with Europe. There are currently two, not entirely conflicting, explanations for why Europeans improved and developed firearms so much faster than the rest of the world. The first, proposed by Kenneth Chase, is that firearms developed faster in Europe because they

---

[19] J. R. Partington went a long way toward demolishing any of the myths of gunpowder's invention outside of China. This impressive work was ably amplified by Joseph Needham. J. R. Partington, *A History of Greek Fire and Gunpowder*, Baltimore and London: The Johns Hopkins University Press, 1999 (first published 1960); Needham, *Science and Civilization*.

were more useful in the military conditions that obtained there. Firearm development was comparatively slow in those parts of Asia subject to steppe nomad raiding because early gunpowder weapons were not very effective against that particular threat. Early firearms did not provide infantry armies with a significant advantage on the battlefield when fighting large numbers of fast-moving horse-archers because those early weapons were too slow and inaccurate. Since the main threat for sedentary armies bordering the steppe was steppe cavalry, there was little incentive in those societies to improve firearms. In Europe, by contrast, even early weapons were useful because they were effective against infantry armies and castles. The second explanation, proposed by Bert Hall, is that the practice of corning (granulating) gunpowder inadvertently opened up the path to further weapon development.

Stephen Morillo has criticized Chase's argument as too simply cause and effect, and suggested that the major difference between Chinese and European weapon development was economic. European rulers ordered weapons from private manufacturers who competed with each other to produce new and better weapons; Chinese governments manufactured their own firearms to bureaucratic specifications.[20] This may be somewhat true, though Chase does point out that firearms were often actually manufactured by private producers, and that the technical specifications of firearms were widely available in China. Ironically, the initial invention of the true gun and its widespread deployment occurred during the Song dynasty, when guns were manufactured exclusively by the government. There was actually less innovation during the Ming dynasty when production was usually in the hands of private artisans. Of course, Ming weapons were soon overtaken by European imports.

Bert Hall, in his extremely impressive book *Weapons and Warfare in Renaissance Europe*, argues, albeit, I think, obliquely, that one of the most important inventions in the progress of European firearm development was corning.[21] Corning was originally invented to overcome the spoilage of gunpowder manufactured with sodium, magnesium, or calcium nitrate saltpeter, rather than potassium nitrate saltpeter. In Asia, potassium nitrate was the most readily available form of saltpeter and, being less hygroscopic, was much less prone to being ruined by absorbing atmospheric water. In partially solving the problem of water absorption, however, corning also increased the power of the gunpowder, something that

[20] Morillo, 'Review of Chase and Lynn,' 525.
[21] Bert S. Hall, *Weapons and Warfare in Renaissance Europe*, Baltimore and London: The Johns Hopkins University Press, 1997. Hall is more forthcoming in his introduction to the 1999 edition of Partington's *A History of Greek Fire and Gunpowder*, xxvii–xxviii.

was initially seen as a problem, particularly for larger guns. Hall argues that the increase in power due to corning was a necessary step in creating effective handguns.

Matchlock arquebuses with long barrels and small calibers appeared in the middle of the fifteenth century in Europe. These weapons took advantage of the extra power of the corned gunpowder to achieve supersonic bullet velocity, which increased their range and killing power. Matchlock arquebuses developed in the commercial German urban centers possessed of both technological knowledge and commercial prowess.[22] Commercial competition and the need to defend urban centers from armies pushed up technological innovation and weapon production. It was not military logic, in the sense of battlefield demand, or even the "logic" of the technology itself, but probably commercial and political pressures that initiated these important advances in guns. It is worth noting, though it is not surprising, that these slow-firing weapons were used in the defense of walled settlements. Germany in the fifteenth century, like China in the twelfth and thirteenth centuries, was well provided with urban centers. Notwithstanding the value of matchlock arquebuses in hunting, handguns and guns evolved in and around cities.

Early gun terminology, particularly across cultures, can be confusing. In this book "gun" and "firearm" are the most general English terms, followed by "cannon" and "handgun." The latter term distinguishes guns that were fired while held in a person's hands, and was used in Europe in the fifteenth century (e.g. "coulverin à main"). Early in the fifteenth century the term "*hackenbüchse*" (hook gun) appeared, for a gun used from atop a defense wall and provided with a hook to absorb the recoil. This would develop into the English word "arquebus." "Musket" was a still later term for a particularly heavy form of arquebus. In contemporary usage, we speak of "small arms," firearms discharged while held in a person's hands, and "artillery," large-bore cannon too big to be carried. "Small arms" are further broken down into "handguns" or "pistols" and "rifles," though most modern firearms have rifled barrels. It would be anachronistic, however, strictly to separate early guns into small arms and artillery, since these modern distinctions were not yet fixed. Accordingly, gun terminology has been used as historically as possible throughout this book.

[22] Hall, *Weapons and Warfare in Renaissance Europe*, 95–100.

Hall may well be correct in his description of gun development in Europe, but if his argument that corning is necessary for handguns is true, then the Chinese may have had corning in the twelfth and thirteenth centuries, though this is highly speculative. As yet, there is no direct evidence that the Chinese corned their gunpowder before the arrival of Europeans, only circumstantial evidence. Early Chinese guns were handguns, very similar to the arquebus, and were initially used from fortification walls, though without the hook. Indeed, it is possible that Europeans received something like that form of the gun, whether a physical example or simply a description, in the transmission of the gun from Asia. Chinese gun barrels lengthened somewhat over time, though not consistently so, and it is unclear whether their projectiles achieved supersonic velocity before exposure to European arms. A fourteenth-century fire-tube was described as shooting a projectile five hundred yards, which would argue for corned powder and supersonic velocity of projectile.[23] Indeed, Joseph Needham believes the passage describing this weapon may have dated from as early as 1200, but he also thinks that multiple pellets were fired, and that the range is greatly exaggerated. Until more evidence is found, we are left with ambiguous passages and uncertain deduction. Yet if the Chinese did have corned gunpowder early on, then it must have been the particular conditions in Germany in the fifteenth century that brought the matchlock arquebus into being.

This brings us back to the question of why neither the Chinese nor any other group in Asia made as significant advances in gun technology as those in Europe. Certainly the evidence presented in this book supports Chase's thesis that guns advanced very slowly where the primary threat was steppe cavalry armies. Of course, some handguns were used in the field against steppe armies early on, and the Mughal army that descended from Central Eurasia into South Asia effectively combined guns with cavalry. But the cause and effect driver of technological change is difficult to sustain by itself when we acknowledge how many decades or even centuries it took to produce even the earliest weapons. Guns in their earliest forms were somewhat effective, though not in a revolutionary way. They were effective enough to be produced in ever-increasing numbers, and to spread across the world as the first chemical-powered weapons. The European, really German, creation of the matchlock arquebus was a very small, incremental improvement on earlier weapons that may have had nothing whatsoever to do with the push of culture or pull of military necessity.

---

[23] *Huolong Jing*, 18a, cited and page reproduced in Needham, *Science and Civilization*, 236–7.

Perhaps what this all adds up to is the differing intellectual positions that Chinese and non-Chinese (there was considerable firearms development in Turkey as well) had with respect to firearms in the fourteenth and fifteenth centuries. Gunpowder weapons had become a fairly mature technology, at least conceptually, in China, where a wide range of formulas and a broad variety of weapons demonstrated the full range of possibilities and limitations of the technologies involved. In Europe, by contrast, the technology was new and quickly demonstrated a narrow set of effective uses. Free from preconceived notions of what could be done, they set off with renewed creativity. Progress in China continued slowly, until the injection of European innovations nudged the technology slightly ahead. At that point, economic principles may well have come into play, whereby the costs of research and development were borne by Europeans, and China and the rest of the world bought the mature product.

As with the rulers in Southeast Asia during the eighteenth century, the influx of superior European weapons convinced Asian governments to rely upon the Europeans for the latest in gunpowder weapons. They chose to buy superior technology, and often reproduced their own copies of it, allowing them to keep up with the latest developments. Even where they adopted some European military organization or tactics, often by hiring European trainers, these remained fairly segregated from broader culture. Indeed, this pattern persists in much of the world today, where Western technology is adopted without the wholesale introduction or acceptance of Western culture. As we shall see in chapter 3, while there continued to be important advances in Chinese guns, most notably in their development of cannon and iron roundshot, in the fourteenth and fifteenth centuries, European weapons were somewhat better when they reached Asia in large numbers in the sixteenth century. Asia then became part of the European arms trading system, incorporating new advances as they became available. As a result, Asia was never more than a decade or two behind Europe in its weaponry.

The wealthy, mature, and stable societies of Asia, though subject to political developments and upheaval, gradually incorporated the new weaponry without great social change. Matters were much different in the poor, undeveloped, unstable societies of Europe. There the introduction of new weaponry coincided with a dramatic period of demographic and economic growth, and political consolidation. Asian polities absorbed European weapons without tremendous social or political upheaval because they were already familiar with guns; the gunpowder revolution had already happened. At least in Asia, guns were incidental to political and social changes outside of the military sphere. Guns neither initiated nor enabled larger changes. Economic, political, and social development preceded and laid the foundation for the invention and use of the gun, not the other way around.

The technical aspects of gunpowder

Gunpowder is a mixture of a nitrate (potassium, sodium, magnesium, or calcium), sulfur, and charcoal. In chemical terms, gunpowder can be defined as a low explosive or propellant.[24] An explosive is a substance, either a mixture or a single material, which can explode from its own energy. This explosive event is a sudden transformation of that substance which liberates energy, producing heat, and often, but not necessarily, gas. Explosives usually require a blow or spark to initiate the liberation of energy. The gunpowder referred to in this book would today be more usually called "black powder," to distinguish it from the propellant used in contemporary firearms. Contemporary firearms use a propellant based upon nitrocellulose, whether single, double, or triple-based, carefully calibrated for burn rate. Gunpowder does not actually explode, it burns, or deflagrates, and the expansion of the gases produced by that rapid burning can be used as a propellant under the right conditions.

Gunpowder functions as a propellant when the gases are confined in a casing with a single, narrow aperture. In the case of a rocket, the escape of gases through that aperture propels the entire casing in the opposite direction. In guns, a projectile occludes the aperture, and the gases force the projectile out of the aperture in order to allow the gases to expand. If the projectile does not fully or even mostly occlude the aperture, much of the force of the gases will escape around it. A tight fit places more force against the projectile, but it also strains the casing. If the projectile does not leave the aperture fast enough to relieve the pressure, then the casing itself will explode. This effect is directly exploited in the case of a bomb or grenade.

The earliest Chinese use of gunpowder was as an incendiary mixture, and this is reflected in its name, *huoyao*, sometimes translated literally as "fire drug." It would be, however, some centuries after its invention before the term *huoyao* was applied to the mixture. The Chinese gradually explored the explosive and propellant uses of gunpowder in containers over several centuries before inventing the true gun. Although early casings were made of paper or bamboo, stronger casings made of iron

---

[24] This discussion of the chemical definition and properties of gunpowder comes from Tenney L. Davis, *The Chemistry of Powder and Explosives*, San Pedro, CA: GSG and Associates, 1943, 1–11.

or bronze permitted the exploitation of much more powerful explosions. Stronger casings allow a greater build-up of force before either the casing shatters violently, the casing is propelled away from the jet of escaping gases, or a projectile is shot out of the aperture. In the case of a gun or rocket, the casing must be strong enough to withstand the initial sharp rise in pressure without shattering.

The burn rate of gunpowder is greatly affected by grain size. Larger grained powder burns faster than smaller grained because ignition propagates throughout the charge more quickly.[25] Fine powder packed in a tube will burn from one end to the other without igniting the entire charge, which is an advantage when used in rockets, but an obstacle in guns because the projectile will be ejected from the casing before most of the potential force of the gunpowder charge has been brought to bear. For these reasons, corned gunpowder with its larger grains was more powerful than gunpowder that had not been corned. It may well have been that the "bomb powder," as distinct from simple gunpowder, mentioned in China in the early twelfth century had been corned. Gunpowder is thus a general term for a substance whose qualities and performance can be manipulated for a wide range of purposes. It was not simply a matter of inventing or discovering the properties of the mixture of nitrate, sulfur, and charcoal and then exploiting them for military purposes.

What is a "revolution"?

Also important is the question of what constitutes a "revolution." There is no question that warfare changed markedly between 1500 and 1800 in Europe. But warfare also changed in Europe between 1200 and 1500, and 1800 and 2000. The debate very often turns on the definition of "revolution." A "revolution" is clearly more than a mere change, but in what way? Many of the objections to Parker's arguments concern the mechanisms of change rather than the fact of that change. A rather more serious objection to the idea that there was a revolution is that there is always change in warfare, and the "revolution" that Parker or Roberts describes was no different than any other change. Certainly any technology that was available in the late sixteenth century had precursors, and even infantry and cavalry tactics, or fortification designs, had been evolving beforehand. European society and military establishments were quite familiar with guns by the sixteenth century.

---

[25] Hall, *Weapons and Warfare in Renaissance Europe*, 81.

Over the course of a few centuries, guns drove out other forms of missile weapons in every area. The idea of the military revolution in Europe seems either to rely upon an oversimplification of what happened before the sixteenth century, or to posit a sort of "tipping point," to borrow a concept from complexity theory, where a particular product, brand, or way of doing something suddenly begins to predominate over its competitors, and that dominance reinforces further dominance. At the same time, the military revolution argument ignores the many smaller conflicts and raids that may, in fact, have constituted the bulk of military struggles in Europe. New gunpowder weapons were used in a wide variety of circumstances, and confining the consideration of their effects to only large, set-piece, state-to-state wars is deceptive. Moreover, even the development of new forms of set-piece battles continued to require infantrymen to arm themselves with bayonets to fend off cavalry and engage in hand-to-hand combat. What was truly revolutionary about guns was their ubiquity throughout all manner of conflict. Other kinds of missile weapons became objects of antiquarian, rather than practical, interest.

For the purposes of this book, a revolution has taken place if a new idea or device became ubiquitous and indispensable to an institution, society, or practice, particularly if the invention drastically altered previous functions. A revolution is a permanent change, rather than a temporary one. In this sense, parts of Asia underwent a military revolution before the arrival of Europeans. Guns and gunpowder weapons were an indispensable part of Chinese, South Asian, and Southeast Asian warfare before Europeans began selling their weapons. The adoption of European tactics or even conceptions of warfare is another matter. As an increasingly well-armed outside group, Europeans acted as many other, similar, groups had done in the past in attempting to shape Asian states and peoples to suit their own, rather than local, interests. The Asian response to this exploitation varied from effective resistance, to ineffective resistance, to accommodation, often simultaneously. Certainly European technology and tactics were a factor in European dominance, but the indigenous political and social milieus were more important. New guns were useful, but not revolutionary.

Conclusion

It has been argued that guns caused a military revolution in Europe, and that the technology led to a dramatic change in warfare that ultimately overtook the entire world. The reason guns did not cause this effect in Asia is that the social, institutional, military, and political frameworks that

Europe developed in order to take advantage of guns either already existed in Asia, or had proved unnecessary in exploiting the military potential of guns. Asian societies and cultures reacted differently to guns and, later, to the European mode of warfare. Yet much of this misses a very important point. If we return to the argument that technology does not develop outside of culture, that it is an artifact of culture, rather than something that exists in some objective world of invention, an interesting connection appears. Guns did not develop in China outside of its military environment, they developed within it. If we understand this basic origin, then it is clear that other cultures were faced with the challenge of how to react not just to guns, but to the Chinese culture that surrounded their use. Like any other piece of Chinese technology, the contextual framework was Chinese. The significance of the European military revolution was that European military practice, and possibly government institutions as well, became more Chinese before they could take full advantage of guns. Army size grew, fortresses became larger and harder to capture, and soldiers had to learn discipline and be supported by a bureaucratized logistics system.

European societies and armies did not, of course, consciously follow the Chinese military model in attempting to improve battlefield performance with guns. This is not surprising, given that few Asian polities followed the Chinese model, despite being much closer to its origins. Yet without the government institutions of imperial China, it was not possible to fight the way a Chinese imperial army fought. Of course, that was not the only effective, rational, or reasonable way to use guns in battle. Many Asian polities made extremely good use of guns without adopting the Chinese model of army organization or warfare. Many other groups both within Europe and outside of it used guns in very different ways than did the large state armies that the European Military Revolution thesis is built upon. Even if the states of early modern Europe proceeded along a particular path of development, the technology of guns did not require that.

The modern Western perspective is that Europeans developed the dominant world culture because of political and social developments in the early modern period, possibly initiated by changes in warfare. This position also informs contemporary Asian views of their own history. Something about Western culture led it to advance gun technology rapidly; in Asia it advanced much more slowly. Because of trade, however, Asia was never very far behind Europe in technology. Somehow the slight Asian lag in military technology has been conflated into a fundamental proof of the superiority of Western culture as a whole. The military, political, social, and industrial revolutions of Europe have produced a culture so dominant that no one else's history seems to matter, except to reinforce that notion. This idea persists despite many heroic attempts by scholars to dislodge this procrustean Western narrative.[26] The result has been that Asia is denied a military and political history in the West before the arrival of Europeans. The lack of this history in Western languages serves to reinforce further the idea of Asian backwardness.

The chapters of this book present some of the missing history of gunpowder in Asia, beginning with its invention and use in China (chapter 1). I then turn to Japan (chapter 2), before shifting back to China, and finishing out that chapter with the clash between Japan, Korea, and China in the late sixteenth century (chapter 3). From East Asia, I move to Southeast Asia (chapter 4), and then to a somewhat more extended discussion of South Asia (chapters 5 and 6). Before the conclusion I attempt to deal synthetically with the Asian experience of colonialism (chapter 7). In addition to the vast territorial scope of this book, the reader confronts an enormous chronological span, and a number of distinct cultures. Each culture and its mode of warfare are described both before and after the introduction of gunpowder and guns. I can only hope that this mass of history will not obscure my central argument that gunpowder and guns had a real and significant history in Asia even before Europeans arrived.

FURTHER READING

Jeremy Black, *Rethinking Military History*, London and New York: Routledge, 2004.

W. Y. Carman, *A History of Firearms from Earliest Times to 1914*, London: Routledge and Kegan Paul, 1955.

Kenneth Chase, *Firearms: A Global History to 1700*, Cambridge: Cambridge University Press, 2003.

Tenney L. Davis, *The Chemistry of Powder and Explosives*, San Pedro, CA: GSG and Associates, 1943.

W. W. Greener, *The Gun and its Development*, Guilford, CT: Lyons Press, 2002 (reprint of the 9th edn published 1910; 1st edn 1881).

Bert S. Hall, *Weapons and Warfare in Renaissance Europe*, Baltimore and London: The Johns Hopkins University Press, 1997.

Ian V. Hogg, *The Story of the Gun*, New York: St. Martin's Press, 1996.

---

[26] See for example Kenneth Pomeranz, *The Great Divergence: Europe, China, and the Making of the Modern World Economy*, Princeton: Princeton University Press, 2000; R. Bin Wong, *China Transformed: Historical Change and the Limits of European Experience*, Ithaca: Cornell University Press, 1997; Donald Lach, *Asia in the Making of Europe*, Chicago: University of Chicago Press, 1965. For the continuance of the Western triumphalist position see David Landes, *The Wealth and Poverty of Nations: Why Some are So Rich and Some So Poor*, New York: W. W. Norton and Company, 1998.

John Norris, *Early Gunpowder Artillery, c. 1300–1600*, Ramsbury, Marlborough: The Crowood Press, 2003.

Geoffrey Parker, *The Military Revolution: Military Innovation and the Rise of the West, 1500–1800*, 2nd edn, Cambridge: Cambridge University Press, 1996.

J. R. Partington, *A History of Greek Fire and Gunpowder*, Cambridge: W. Heffer and Sons, 1960.

Michael Roberts, *The Military Revolution, 1560–1660* (Belfast: Marjarie Bajd, 1956).

Clifford Rogers (ed.), *The Military Revolution Debate: Readings on the Military Transformation of Early Modern Europe*, Boulder: Westview Press, 1995.

1   China through the Yuan

Gunpowder and the gun were invented in China. And while knowledge of the former may have come about accidentally, the latter was unequivocally a weapon of war. The gun was created to kill people through an intentional exploitation of the properties of gunpowder. Of course, the gun was not the first or only weapon the Chinese invented to employ gunpowder for violent and destructive ends. A broad range of rockets, flamethrowers, grenades, smoke bombs, poison gas bombs, mines, and incendiary devices were also produced, demonstrating the ample resources in human ingenuity and materials expended in the interests of war. There was steady progress in the development of gunpowder weapons, with many new devices quickly applied on the battlefield. While in the eleventh century the Song dynasty had an established gunpowder-manufacturing bureau, and gunpowder weapons were included in a government-produced military manual, by the twelfth and thirteenth centuries gunpowder weapons were standard devices in sieges, battles, and naval combat. The true gun itself appeared in the mid-thirteenth century.

To the extent that gunpowder weapons played prominent, if not often decisive, roles in many twelfth- and thirteenth-century battles, there was a revolution in warfare even before the invention of the gun. The *Complete Essentials from the Military Classics* (*Wujing Zongyao*), finished in 1044, which currently ranks as the first text directly to describe the formula for gunpowder, was not, however, a pamphlet on new military devices and techniques; it was a compendium of all military knowledge up to that time. As such, it included both old and new materials indiscriminately mixed together. In this sense, it must be included in the military intellectual environment of the mid-eleventh century that also resulted in the compilation and publication of the *Seven Military Classics* (*Wujing Qishu*) in 1080. Both works were attempts to improve the Song dynasty's military performance by concentrating and formalizing all available knowledge of war.

The invention of gunpowder and gunpowder weapons did not, however, overturn the pre-existing military environment. In this chapter I will begin by briefly describing that environment, before turning to

Map 2 The Southern Song

the invention of gunpowder and early gunpowder weapons, and then concluding with an analysis of the effects of those weapons on Chinese warfare. Although I will argue that gunpowder did not revolutionize, or even have much effect upon, the political or institutional framework of Chinese government (and by extension the social structure), I will suggest that it did effect important changes in naval and siege warfare that favored both the Jurchen Jin and also the Song dynasty in their ultimately unsuccessful struggles with the Mongols.

Warfare in China before gunpowder

As I discussed in the introduction, Kenneth Chase has made a very convincing argument that the nature of warfare in China did not spur the development of new and better guns. Since early guns were not very effective against the threat of steppe armies, or at least not effective enough to shift dramatically the balance of military power between the steppe and sedentary polities, there was no particular urgency in improving guns. Chase points out that guns developed most rapidly and extensively in areas that did not face the threat of steppe cavalry.[1] At the same time, Chinese fortifications, particularly city walls, were formidable obstacles to artillery even in the twentieth century. What has not hitherto received much scholarly treatment in the discussion of gunpowder weapons in China is the effects those weapons had in siege warfare as anti-personnel and anti-equipment devices, and the even greater importance of those weapons in naval warfare. The major reason for this lacuna in the scholarship is the very secondary role these modes of warfare are perceived to have had in Chinese campaigns. This is a particular quirk of Chinese discussions of war even in the primary sources, and one that I will attempt to redress in this chapter after an overview of the more usual focus on steppe–sedentary war.

Even before the beginning of China's imperial age in 221 BCE, armies regularly numbered in the tens of thousands, and not infrequently exceeded a hundred thousand men. Sedentary Chinese civilization produced sufficient agricultural surpluses to support large armies, as well as cities and large-scale production of handicrafts. In relative terms, China was a wealthy place, particularly compared with the northern steppes. It was also a culture tied to the land, since agriculture provided the foundation upon which the population rested and sophisticated government relied. Control of the population made those large armies possible, allowing not only the drafting of a percentage of farmers in times of military need, but also the support of professional soldiers. This was possible because Chinese governments early on employed educated officials and clerks who were both literate and numerate. All households were registered, and the number of adult males, in particular, recorded for purposes of taxation, corvee labor, and military conscription. The government thus had a reasonably good idea of how much manpower it had at its disposal, and where it was.

The nomadic and semi-nomadic people occupying the steppe depended upon their herds for survival, leaving them very little margin above subsistence in good years, and leading to starvation in bad ones. Moreover, the population was limited by the availability of pasturage for herds, leading to a fairly low population density and overall population.

[1] Kenneth Chase, *Firearms: A Global History to 1700*, Cambridge: Cambridge University Press, 2003, 3–4.

Steppe people could produce their own necessities, but very little in the way of manufactured goods. While the steppe was not a wealthy place, its society was also not one tied to the land. This entirely mobile society possessed a disproportionately great military strength because every adult male rode a horse and used a bow in daily life. There was very little in the way of government since neither abodes nor people were fixed, and independence was fiercely defended. Leadership was exercised through personal ties reinforced by the distribution of luxury goods from superior to inferior, and booty gained in warfare.

The main product the steppe economy offered to the sedentary economy was horses, necessary for war and transportation, but seldom used in Chinese agriculture. Steppe products were therefore not critically necessary to the Chinese, while Chinese products like food, for survival, or luxury goods, for political uses, were critical to steppe people. Possessing so much inherent military force in any group of steppe horsemen, it was always tempting to raid the Chinese if trading failed to yield the desired goods. This has often been characterized as "traders and raiders" to simplify a more complex interaction. Steppe leaders were often employed along with their men to provide cavalry forces both within China, and to fight other steppe groups. The border area was also a porous region populated by multiethnic and multicultural transfrontiersmen whose loyalties and interests fit neither steppe nor sedentary paradigm.

Contrasting economies resulted in similarly different methods of, and attitudes about, war. Steppe armies were mobile and inclined to refuse battle unless they believed they could win. Clusters of horsemen rode around firing arrows to wear down opponents until they broke, at which point a ruthless pursuit would destroy anyone who did not get away. Standing and fighting was not valued as a demonstration of moral fortitude; a steppe army was willing to retreat before an advancing enemy until it became overextended and vulnerable. Fortifications could stymie a steppe army, however, as they seldom possessed the knowledge or equipment to capture them. A non-existent logistical system also strictly limited the ability of a steppe army, and its large cohort of horses, to remain in one place for very long.

Chinese armies were much less mobile, being primarily composed of infantry with a small cavalry component, and supported by a well-developed logistical system. Chinese campaigns focused on territorial acquisition, rather than the destruction of an enemy force (excepting bandit-suppression campaigns), and generally proceeded from position to position, with battles occurring in the struggle for control of those points. Consequently, sieges were frequent and regular, and direct clashes between opposing forces usual. An army was expected to stand and fight, with retreat likely to lead to the execution of the commanding general. Chinese armies used bows and crossbows, as well as spears and other close contact weapons. The crossbow had greater effective range and penetration than a bow, but the greater rate of fire of the bow made it extremely useful in combination with the crossbow.

Chinese cavalry operated in a similar fashion to steppe cavalry, though Chinese soldiers might be somewhat better armed and armored. Steppe cavalry was almost always mounted on better and more plentiful horses, came to the battlefield in greater numbers, and was of generally higher quality. The main Chinese advantage in terms of weapons was the use of the crossbow, both crew-served versions and hand crossbows. For example, a crew-served crossbow killed an important Liao general in an ambush in 1004.[2] And Song dynasty weapon manufacturers believed that the "wolf's tooth" crossbow bolts, which had barbed tips and shafts designed to break when someone tried to extract them, were the weapon most feared by the Liao.[3] Obviously, the crossbow did not obviate the steppe advantage in mobility and speed. Nonetheless, it is important to understand that land battles between Chinese and steppe armies began, and were often decided by, archery, whether mounted or on foot, with bows or crossbows.

Unlike steppe warriors, however, Chinese soldiers could not transfer skills from their daily life into military activity; they had to be trained to use weapons and fight as units as a separate practice. Chinese farmers did not usually own weapons, and were at times forbidden to do so. Archery was not a pastime for yeoman farmers, though in unsettled times villagers could and did arm and train for self-defense, and build walls around their settlements. These walled villages were quite effective in driving off small groups of steppe raiders or bandits. Larger armies could overwhelm local defenses, as when successive Mongol invasions swept through northern China in the thirteenth century, destroying everything in their path. Desperate central governments drafted these local self-defense forces into the regular army as the only pool of already trained men.[4]

The one area in which some ordinary skills bled over into the military realm was the navy. Every dynasty that wanted to create a Chinese empire extending south of the Yellow River had to build a navy. A competent navy could block or disrupt any campaign that crossed the Yellow, Huai,

[2] *Song Huiyao Jigao: Bing*, Taibei: Xin Wenfeng, 1976, 7/12a–13b.
[3] *Song Huiyao Jigao: Bing*, 26/36b.
[4] Huang K'uan-chung has written a series of articles on local defense forces now conveniently collected in *Nansong Difang Wuli*, Taibei: Dongda Tushu Gongsi, 2002.

or Yangzi rivers, as well as many smaller bodies. Moreover, the logistics of large Chinese armies made water transport of supplies a priority. Zhou Shizong had the waterways and locks repaired when he embarked on his campaign going north of the Yellow River in 959, having learned the value of water transport and a navy in his earlier campaign against the Southern Tang.[5] Naval combat in China was heavily dependent upon missile fire, with boarding and hand-to-hand combat usually playing a supporting role.

Fire was a devastating weapon in pre-modern naval combat, particularly when launched from a distance. Of course, fire attacks could be launched without gunpowder, but gunpowder-enhanced missiles were far more effective and precise vehicles than fire ships and flaming oil slicks. Naval combat was also highly technical, and a capable sailor was at a tremendous advantage over an incompetent sailor. It took the Mongols half a century to conquer the Southern Song because the Song navy defended the Huai River line so effectively. Incendiary gunpowder weapons were a critical part of the Song navy's arsenal.

Another critical aspect of warfare in China that made great use of incendiary gunpowder weapons was siege warfare. The walls of Chinese fortifications were built of tamped earth, usually thicker than it was high, which was gradually faced with brick over the course of the Song dynasty.[6] They were thus completely fireproof, and highly resistant to battering. Small, private fortifications were rare and unimportant for anything beyond local feuding. Villages not only fortified themselves against bandits and small raiding bands, but also built refuges in the mountains. Without any reliable means to smash through fortifications, sieges were usually decided by starvation or escalade. Attempts to break through gates were even more costly than those scaling the walls, though gates and the structures surrounding them were flammable. Almost everything necessary to besiege or defend a fortification beyond the earth walls and the moat was made of wood, from the poliorcetic machines, to the mantlets, fascines, ladders, and towers. Like naval warfare, siege warfare became highly technical once it progressed beyond a simple blockade or a direct rush over the walls.

Not only were Chinese walls highly resistant to battering, with extremely few successful sieges accomplished by breaking through the walls, but because those walls encompassed cities they were also quite expansive.

---

[5] For the repair of the canals and locks see Sima Guang, *Zizhi Tongjian*, 294.9594, Beijing: Zhonghua Shuju, 1992.

[6] Huang K'uan-chung, "Songdai chengguo de fangyu sheshi yu cailiao," *Dalu Zazhi*, 81/2 (1990), 1–23.

A besieging force had to be large enough to surround a wall many miles in circumference, punctuated by a number of heavily fortified gates, and usually protected by a moat. Failure to cordon off the city entirely allowed relief forces to resupply the city, and the need to disperse forces broadly enough to cover all approaches left those forces vulnerable to attack from inside and outside. The besieging army also had to keep itself supplied, which was a daunting task given the tens of thousands of men involved and attacks on its own supply lines. Consequently, the success or failure of sieges was a function of the success or failure of the broader field campaign taking place over the horizon. This was characteristic of many of the campaigns that created the great empires in Chinese history. Sieges were part of campaigns, sometimes even the key to the success of a given campaign, but an individual siege or battle was seldom decisive.

A successful dynastic army had to possess a number of specialized skills to unite northern and southern China militarily. It had to defeat other armies in the field over a wide variety of terrain and weather conditions, control and span rivers, and systematically reduce forts and cities spread over vast distances. The last two requirements also necessitated an effective logistics system capable of sustaining sieges and naval operations. Navies could not usefully forage on the river for food, and ships needed regular maintenance. Even the Mongols were forced to develop or take over the highly bureaucratized logistics systems that supported Chinese armies. Khubilai Khan, it must be remembered, moved his capital south into China in order to harness its productive capabilities in his steppe struggles. The Mongols absorbed captured soldiers with the technical knowledge of siege practice, and ultimately constructed a navy as well, manned by Chinese sailors.

Having established a dynasty and conquered northern and southern China, an imperial army needed to shift its focus to dealing with border threats. Northern steppe peoples presented the most serious border threat, with their incursions ranging in severity from mere annoyance to existential crisis. An imperial army therefore had to defeat, or at least manage, the threat of steppe incursions from the north. This was not a purely military problem, however, as it involved a considerable diplomatic component if it was to work at all. The main difficulty for a Chinese army was actually campaigning into the steppe. Peter Perdue has estimated the maximum campaign reach of a Chinese army venturing into the steppe before the second half of the eighteenth century at about ninety days.[7] Most Chinese armies were also too slow to catch a steppe

---

[7] Peter Perdue, *China Marches West*, Cambridge, MA: Harvard University Press, 2005, 40.

army and force it to fight even if they could have extended their reach. From the perspective of the steppe–sedentary military balance, steppe armies could always raid sedentary areas, but sedentary armies could not effectively raid the steppe.

Early gunpowder weapons could not substantially overturn the structural geo-strategic reality of the steppe–sedentary military balance. The existing paradigm turned on the issues of mobility and logistic reach, not striking power when battle was joined. Even in the Han dynasty, a Chinese army that retained its cohesion could fend off steppe cavalrymen in the open field as long as its supply of crossbow bolts held out. Forced on the tactical and strategic defensive, sedentary armies had to cede the initiative to steppe forces, and try to prepare to repel incursions once they occurred, rather than carrying the fight into the steppe. Combat remained a decidedly long-range affair, with hand-to-hand fighting taking place only after one force had broken, or when a steppe force was trapped against an obstacle. Even though early guns might considerably outrange bows, they were subject to the same difficulties of limited ammunition, slow rate of fire, and an elusive enemy that mitigated the advantages of the crossbow. They were also difficult to use from horseback. These limitations were less important in sieges and naval warfare.[8]

Gunpowder weapons would not ultimately resolve the steppe–sedentary military balance in favor of the sedentary empire. As we shall see in chapter 7, the productive power of sedentary China was only able to overcome the military power of the steppe in the eighteenth century under a dynastic house, the Qing, which was itself of steppe origin, and then only after decades of determined political, diplomatic, and military efforts. Yet if we were to compare the general characteristics of warfare in China before and after the introduction of gunpowder weapons, even including the period after European weapons came into widespread use, the picture would be very much the same. Both infantry and steppe cavalry field armies were often large, numbering in the tens of thousands, and sometimes exceeding a hundred thousand. These armies were usually well trained, capable of volley fire with arrows, and supported by extremely capable bureaucratic logistical systems, excepting purely steppe forces.[9] There were few private fortifications, the vast majority being directly subordinated to the bureaucratic state, in the form of either army forts or fortified towns and cities. The defensive walls, built of solid

---

[8] Chase, *Firearms*, xiv–23.
[9] The *Wujing Zongyao* clearly describes training troops in volley fire. See for example Zeng Gongliang, *Wujing Zongyao*, 2/19a and 2/20a, vol. III in *Zhongguo Bingshu Jicheng*, Beijing: Jiefangjun Chubanshe, 1988.

packed earth and proportionately thicker than they were high as we have seen, often exceeded ten miles in circumference around a large city.

As we turn to the consideration of gunpowder and the individual gunpowder weapons developed in China leading up to the true gun, it is clear that Chinese warfare throughout this period resembled the early modern European warfare that Geoffrey Parker proposed came into being subsequent to the Military Revolution, minus the cannons and handguns. At the same time, however, these new gunpowder weapons were used extensively in China, demonstrating that they were valued additions to the arsenals of armies. There was a revolution in warfare in as much as an entirely new class of weapons was invented, used, and adopted as a regular part of military activity. These weapons were the ancestors of most of our contemporary battlefield weapons, and were wholly unknown to people in previous times. What we shall see in the early history of gunpowder's use on the battlefield is the unprecedented development of entirely new ideas of weaponry and technology.

Gunpowder

The first mention of what we would call gunpowder appeared in 808, combining six parts sulfur to six parts saltpeter to one part birthwort herb (which provided the necessary carbon).[10] About a half-century later, a Daoist alchemy manual warned against some thirty-five dangerous mixtures, one in particular demonstrating a similar knowledge of gunpowder: "Some have heated together sulfur, realgar (arsenic disulphide), and saltpeter with honey; smoke [and flames] result, so that their hands and faces have been burnt, and even the whole house burned down."[11]

These mixtures grew out of a very long tradition of alchemical experimentation usually tied to certain schools of Daoism that sought elixirs of immortality or the means to transmute one material into another. While all of our early evidence for alchemical mixtures is tied to Daoists, this may be a historiographical artifact produced by the better preservation of texts tied to that school of thought (in all its varieties). There were also medical specialists, among others, interested in the effects of various substances and compounds on materials and bodies. We should not,

---

[10] This formula is contained in the *Taishang Guaizu Danjing Mijue* by Qing Xuzi dated to the third year of the Yuanhe period of the Tang dynasty. Cited in Liu Xu, *Zhongguo Gudai Huoyao Houqi Shi*, Zhengzhou: Daxiang Chubanshe, 2004, 263.

[11] *Zhenyuan Miaodao Yaolue*, contained in the *Daozang*, 917/3a, cited and translated in Needham, *Science and Civilization*, 111–12.

therefore, find too much irony in the search for immortality or the ability to turn lead into gold resulting in a weapon so fundamental to war.

The three components of gunpowder were known for some time before the ninth century. Charcoal was known to any civilization that had fire; sulfur and saltpeter were recorded in the *Pharmacopoeia of the Divine Agriculturist* compiled during the Han dynasty. All early formulae for gunpowder included a wide variety of other substances. Some of these substances were included to produce poisonous smoke, but many were there for reasons that are not clear. The first use of gunpowder in warfare, as an incendiary weapon, may have taken place as early as the late ninth century, though this is speculative.

By the Song dynasty, gunpowder was manufactured in the government arsenal. Although there were particular restrictions on workers inside the arsenal, they worked there for life, that is, in all other ways the government statutes and bureaucratic structure surrounding it were quite ordinary. Only officials above a certain rank had access to the written materials pertaining to the gunpowder manufacturing, and the information was not widely disseminated. Of course, most government information was restricted, both by design and by the inadvertent difficulties of distributing information in pre-modern times.

In contrast to the restrictive rules on information pertaining to gunpowder, the *Complete Essentials from the Military Classics*, the earliest extant discussion of gunpowder in a military context, was compiled to improve the dynasty's military performance. Begun in 1040, with a preface from 1044 (the text reportedly took five years to complete), it was presumably intended to spread a wide variety of military knowledge more broadly throughout the government. Zeng Gongliang, the chief compiler, was not a general, but an official, and as with other manuals produced during the Song dynasty, his intended audience was other officials. But by the time the text was made available, if it ever was, the war with the Tanguts that had partly prompted its compilation was over. It would be another three decades before the Song would begin campaigning in an attempt to destroy the Tanguts. Gunpowder played no role in these contests, and so the place of the *Complete Essentials* in Song history is unclear.

Gunpowder was regularly manufactured for use as a weapon in the eleventh century, but technical knowledge of its manufacture was a state secret. This is not to say that no one outside the Song government knew about gunpowder, only that the information was not widely available. All that would change in the twelfth century, when warfare, particularly siege and naval warfare, became widespread throughout China. During the relatively peaceful eleventh century, the components for the dawn of a new age in warfare waited, barely acknowledged.

Fire-spears, fire-tubes, and the true gun

The idea of using fire as a propellant, whether of the spear itself or of smaller projectiles, developed out of the fire-spear and the fire-tube. A commensurate rise in nitrate content in the gunpowder seems to have accompanied these developments, though the evidence for a gradual rise is slight. The rocket and the fire-spear shared similar forms and nomenclature, leading Jixing Pan and others to confuse the two by reading several ambiguous passages in grammatically valid, but erroneous, ways that set the invention of the rocket slightly earlier than the evidence warranted.[12] Quite a number of earlier scholars were very concerned about the invention of the rocket, an idiosyncratic interest to be sure given that rockets were of very limited value in warfare in pre-modern times. The fire-spear, by contrast, was a far more important device, since it was the basis of not only rockets, but also the true gun. Accordingly, I will first discuss the fire-spear and the fire-tube, before turning, briefly, to the rocket in the section that follows.

The fire-spear (or fire-lance as Needham would have it) first appears in representation in a Buddhist wall painting at Dunhuang dated to the mid-tenth century. A demon in military dress is attempting to distract the meditating Buddha by directing a jet of flame erupting from a tube attached to a pole. This early evidence for the weapon is not followed by other mentions until 1132, at the siege of De'an. Needham may well be correct in suggesting that fire-spears were not produced in sufficient quantities to warrant mention in texts like the *Complete Essentials from the Military Classics*, but the lacuna is nonetheless startling. Indeed, the device pictured seems more like a fire-tube (*huotong*), which I will discuss below, than a fire-spear.

A more conservative reading of the evidence might be that the fire-spear had not progressed beyond the experimental stage when the *Complete Essentials from the Military Classics* was compiled between 1040 and 1044. The device held by the demon in the Dunhuang painting is somewhat different than the later fire-spear in that it is not a spear with a fire-projecting tube attached, but simply a short pole with an attached tube. The difference is significant because a spear with a limited duration flame-projector is still a weapon once the projector runs out of fuel.

By the time the fire-spear is mentioned in 1132, its existence requires no comment, since the author clearly assumed that his reader knew what it was. When the Jurchen Jin attacked the city of De'an, Chen Gui

---

[12] Jixing Pan, "On the Origin of Rockets," *T'oung Pao*, 73 (1987), 2–15.

successfully held out for seventy days before finally managing to drive off the besiegers. Chen prepared his defenses:

We also used bomb powder and long poles of bamboo to make more than twenty fire-spears. Also striking spears and swords with hooks at the ends, many of each. It took two men to handle each one. These things were got ready to use from the ramparts whenever the assault towers with the flying bridges approached the city.[13]

Particularly in light of our previous discussion, it is important to note that the fire-spears were constructed on site, and that they used "bomb powder" and bamboo poles which required two men to manipulate. The exact descriptions used raise some very intriguing questions that we may not be able to resolve with the available information. Why is "bomb powder" (*huopao yao*) specified, rather than simply "gunpowder" (*huoyao*)? Presumably, "bomb powder" was different from other kinds of available gunpowder, though in what way we do not know. Alternatively, since Chen Gui was in some sense jury-rigging new weapons from the components of other weapons, in this case bombs, it may be that another name for gunpowder was "bomb powder." Were bamboo poles used because they could function as the tubes containing the powder? This is likely, though later fire-spears used other material for the gunpowder tube and also had a spearhead for fighting. The items described in this passage are clearly specialized siege equipment, so the two-man fire-spear is idiosyncratic.

Fire-spears were decisive in breaking the siege of De'an, but these were different weapons than the two-man fire-spears. Li Heng, the Jurchen general, surrounded De'an, and started building flying bridges, filling in the moat, and making a great tumult near the city. Chen Gui led the defense, and was wounded in the foot by a catapult, but the siege really became critical as the food ran out. Chen maintained troop morale by using his personal funds to supply the troops. After seventy days, Li Heng sent a messenger indicating that he would raise the siege if they sent him a maiden. Chen refused, despite the entreaties of his commanders. Instead, he led a sally from the west gate with sixty men carrying fire-spears, and with the aid of a "fire ox" incinerated the Jurchen flying bridges. Li Heng lifted the siege and withdrew.[14]

Chen Gui was obviously a commander of extraordinary ability and character, and the siege of De'an demonstrates the strengths and weaknesses of fire-spears. His earlier fire-spears were unable to destroy the

---

[13] Chen Gui, *De'an Shoucheng Lu*, 4/6a, cited and translated in Needham, *Science and Civilization*, 222.

[14] Tuo Tuo, *Songshi*, Beijing: Zhonghua Shuju, 1990, 377.11643, cited in Needham, *Science and Civilization*, 222.

Jurchen flying bridges from the ramparts of the city, though they did slow down the progress of the assault towers. The Jurchen besiegers were incapable of going through or over the walls, or through the gates, after more than two months of work. When Chen launched his attack, his most immediate threat was low supplies, though he realized by Li Heng's odd offer to raise the siege in return for a token gift that the Jurchen army was in similarly bad straits. Morale had reached a critical point for both sides, and Chen's destruction of the Jurchen siege equipment caused a complete collapse of Jurchen morale. Having suffered such a severe setback after such a long siege, it was impossible to contemplate continuing. What is so impressive about Chen Gui's performance was not only that he timed his attack so well, but also that he could overcome the fire-spear's lack of range and speed by waiting until his opponent's vulnerable resources were close and fixed enough to destroy.

Even in Chen Gui's remarkable feat the fire-spear was used as a device for destroying equipment, rather than as a hand-to-hand weapon. This is not surprising given the short, perhaps five minutes', duration of the jet of flame. About a century later, at the siege of Guide in 1233, a Jurchen force armed with fire-spears ambushed a Mongol force. This time the Jurchens were fighting defensively against the Mongols, on small boats in the canals around the city. In the confined area of the canals, on boats at night, with the Mongols caught in front and rear, the fire-spears were devastating close-range weapons.[15]

The fire-spear developed as a functional battlefield weapon from the early twelfth to the early thirteenth century. Whatever prototype forms it had in the tenth century were not regularly weaponized and distributed to the army, nor was the knowledge of how to make them widely available, until the twelfth century. Fire-spears played no significant role in the defense of the Song capital in 1126–7, but only a few years later they played a critical role at the siege of De'an. Knowledge of this weapon, both how to make it and, just as significantly, how to use it on the battlefield, was not widespread in the early twelfth century, even at the capital. Very few people may have known the possibilities presented by gunpowder's capabilities; ordinary soldiers might have known how to use bombs, grenades, and smoke bombs, without being aware of what the powder inside a bomb would do when ignited inside a tube with an open end. This knowledge would have spread very quickly during the intense period of warfare that began after the fall of the Song capital in 1127.

---

[15] Tuo Tuo, *Jinshi*, Taibei: Dingwen Shuju, 1995, 116.2548, cited in Needham, *Science and Civilization*, 226.

The next major improvement to the fire-spear was crucial in the development of the gun. People began to realize that the jet of flame produced by the tube of gunpowder had sufficient force to shoot small projectiles with enough energy to enhance the personnel-wounding effects of the flame. It is only because these weapons came to be used against people, rather than for attempting to batter down walls, that adding bits of metal or pottery shards to the packed gunpowder made any sense. We see here an intellectual evolution whereby gunpowder came to be understood as a propellant, as well as an incendiary mixture. By the early thirteenth century, shrapnel of various kinds was regularly added to the gunpowder of a fire-spear.

The tube of most fire-spears at that time was usually made of layers of paper or sections of bamboo, about two feet long. It was therefore not only light in weight, but also cheap. Perhaps more surprisingly, both paper and bamboo tubes were also reusable. The fire-spear could thus be easily manufactured, and its capabilities added to pre-existing spears. The major limitation of the fire-spear was not so much the range of its flame, as the duration. A fire-spear was an enhanced polearm, not a missile weapon like the bow or crossbow. This use of gunpowder as a propellant would not lead to the gun, however, because the fragile tubes were limited in the amount of pressure they could withstand, the projectiles used did not occlude the tube opening sufficiently to exploit the sudden discharge of built-up pressure, and the weapon was not conceived of as a missile arm.

While the fire-spear demonstrated the possibilities of gunpowder to carry a projectile, it was the parallel development of the fire-tube (*huotong*) that would lead more directly to the metal-barreled tube. The fire-tube was a bamboo tube with a handle at the base that initially operated in exactly the same manner as the fire-spear, minus the spear. This separation of the fire-tube from a functioning hand-to-hand weapon was important for two reasons: first, it emphasized the independent value of a chemical-based weapon and, second, it left the user in dire need of a hand-to-hand weapon. The latter problem was solved when an iron barrel was fixed to the handle, rendering the spent weapon a still usable club. Indeed, the first mention of an iron-barreled fire-tube emphasizes this point:

The Bandit-striking Penetrating Tube: Use iron to make a barrel three feet long with a handle two feet long. Infantry use this. In one discharge the pellet is able to strike a bandit at a distance of three hundred paces (five hundred yards). This tube can also be used to hit bandits. This one device with two uses is the most advantageous.[16]

---

[16] *Huolong Jing*, 18a, cited and page reproduced in Needham, *Science and Civilization*, 236–7. My translation.

Needham dates this particular section of the text, the *Fire Dragon Classic* (*Huolong Jing*), to the first half of the fourteenth century, but believed that the quoted passage is "probably as old as 1200." He also discounts the range of the projectile as a gross exaggeration, asserting that the flames carried only twenty or thirty feet. This would be consistent with the previous fire-tubes and fire-spears, so Needham also believes that the bandit-striking penetrating tube did not fire a single pellet, but rather a large number of them.[17] The language is ambiguous, since either the singular or plural is possible, though the accompanying drawing seems to show a spray of particles. Analyzing the drawing is problematic, since not only is it possible that the drawings come from a different period than the text, it is also a grave mistake to "read" the image as if it were a photograph. The images themselves are presumably from the fourteenth-century version of the text, though Needham is not explicit about this. If the weapon fired a single projectile out of an iron barrel with sufficient occlusion of the barrel and a high-enough nitrate mixture of gunpowder, then five hundred yards might well be possible as a lethal range. It would be terribly inaccurate, of course, and it would probably date more toward the middle or end of the thirteenth century, than the beginning of it.

Near-constant warfare starting in the first quarter of the twelfth century led to the development of a wide variety of fire-spears and fire-tubes in the early twelfth through the mid-thirteenth century. At some point during the thirteenth century, the true gun with a metal barrel, high-nitrate gunpowder, and firing a single projectile was invented, but this did not drive out all of the other weapons, or cause a sudden shift in military practice.[18] Fire-spears and fire-tubes gradually shifted from specialized siege equipment or naval weapons to battlefield anti-personnel weapons. But the precursors to the true gun, and the true gun itself, were weapons born of siege and naval warfare, and then transferred to the open field. The power of first Jurchen, and then Mongol, cavalry forced the Song off the open field and into fortified cities or on to rivers to stop their advances. In time, all sides gained knowledge of these weapons, and first the Jurchen and then the Song advantage in siege and naval warfare was negated by the Mongols. Warfare would never be the same.

The rocket

The rocket was not a very effective weapon in its earliest forms, or indeed until well into the nineteenth century if one is being charitable. This

---

[17] Needham, *Science and Civilization*, 234–6.
[18] For the emergence of true cannon see ibid., 288–306.

changed dramatically in the twentieth century, particularly the second half of the twentieth century, prompting many modern scholars to spend a perhaps unwarranted amount of effort determining when the first rocket was invented, and whether, in fact, the Chinese could once again claim primacy. The Chinese did, it seems, invent the rocket some time in the late twelfth century, and it quickly, in pre-modern terms, spread to the rest of the world. "Arrows of China" are mentioned in Syria about 1280, the *ban* reached South Asia some time in the fourteenth or fifteenth century, and rockets are mentioned at the Battle of Chioggia in Europe in 1380.

Needham expressed some surprise that Europeans did not make more military use of rockets after they obtained the technology: "But for some reason or other, probably the early and rapid development of gunnery in Europe, rockets played no great part in warfare after that, being mainly confined to firework displays."[19] At the same time, of course, he also lamented the fact that the evidence for rockets is so patchy because they are seldom mentioned in Chinese battle accounts. Rather obviously, the inaccuracy and limited payload of pre-modern rockets led the Chinese as well as the Europeans to use them mostly for firework displays. It was really only in South Asia, as we shall see in chapters 4 and 5, that the *ban* held a long-standing, if generally ineffective, place in warfare.

There is some difficulty in separating the terminology for fire-arrows from that for rockets, since both could be referred to as "fire-arrows" (*huojian*). Ironically, the earlier form of fire-arrow, an arrow enhanced with either extra flammable material or gunpowder and ignited before being launched by a bow or crossbow, was an extremely effective weapon in siege and naval warfare. Although the extra weight diminished the range of these missiles, launched in large numbers they could accurately strike many targets. The rocket, by contrast, a missile powered by the gases escaping the aperture of a tube of ignited gunpowder, was unlikely to hit anything it was pointed at. In the unlikely event that a rocket did strike a hostile target, it might inflict some damage with its arrowhead, or with a small payload of gunpowder.

The rocket most probably grew out of the fire-spear, and in this sense, the fire-spear is the ancestor of both guns and rockets. By reversing the gunpowder tube, the projecting fire became a propulsion system instead of a weapon. Although fins and wings were added to stabilize and direct rockets, their trajectory remained erratic. Multiple-rocket launchers were devised to enhance striking power and the likelihood of striking a target,

---

[19] Ibid., 517.

but it is hard to find mention of their use outside of military manuals. Unlike fire-spears and grenades, and even old-fashioned fire-arrows, rockets were hard to use in sieges, and positively dangerous to use on ships (the jet of flame projected back toward the launcher). In the field, they were wholly ineffective against mobile squadrons of cavalry, and only slightly more useful against even massed infantry. Ultimately, what is most remarkable about rockets in pre-modern times is that anyone even imagined that they had a use outside of firework displays.

Bombs and grenades

Projectiles using low-nitrate gunpowder were effective vehicles for incendiary attacks, but would not cause an explosion. These fire-balls (*huoqiu*) were containers of low-nitrate gunpowder thrown by trebuchet with the intention of directing fire attacks on to enemy targets. This was a useful and effective weapon that, though actual explosive bombs came into use in the first half of the eleventh century, continued in use beyond the seventeenth century (or at least continued to be mentioned in military manuals). The *Complete Essentials from the Military Classics* contains descriptions of both fire-balls and grenades/bombs. The distinction between a grenade and a bomb is modern; pre-modern Chinese sources do not separate explosive projectiles by size or delivery system (with the exception of occasional references to the "hand bomb," *shoupao*). Accordingly, I will use "bomb" as the overall term to describe these explosive projectiles.

Two changes in design made fire-balls into bombs: increasing the percentage of saltpeter, and placing the mixture in a rigid receptacle capable of temporarily containing the expanding gases when ignited. The bomb exploded when the force of expanding gases exceeded the ability of the receptacle to contain them. This happened very quickly, and a much stronger explosion could be achieved by using a stronger receptacle. The thunderclap bomb (*pili huoqiu* or *pili pao*) described in the *Complete Essentials from the Military Classics* used a bamboo receptacle. The anti-personnel effects of the explosion were enhanced by the addition of shrapnel to the gunpowder mixture inside the receptacle. This was more important when the receptacle was bamboo or wood, rather than iron. Given the apparent timing of the development of the bomb with its added shrapnel, it is possible that this contributed to the practice of putting shrapnel in the gunpowder tube of fire-spears to enhance their anti-personnel abilities. If this is the case, then there must have been considerable cross-fertilization between early gunpowder weapons leading up to the invention of the true gun.

Thunderclap bombs were used in the defense of the Song capital when the Jurchen attacked in 1126–7. Despite the use of such a powerful weapon, Song defenses were ultimately overwhelmed and the capital fell. The main reason the defenses failed was insufficient troops to man the walls, so the effect of the bombs is hard to measure. Yet even these early weapons were obviously useful. It may well have been that the supply of bombs was still limited, and the most effective tactics for using that small number had not been worked out. The supply of weapons directly affects their use, and at least one account of the siege indicates that the original commander of the defenses was reluctant to expend his artillery ammunition and bombs. He was sacked, and the new commander, Li Gang, ordered the soldiers to fire at will. Li, who recounted the incident, may have felt justified in his actions, but he may have also been incompetent.[20]

The final step in the development of the bomb came with the use of an iron receptacle. This required a higher percentage of saltpeter in the gunpowder to shatter the casing, and resulted in a much more powerful explosion. The first mention of a gourd-shaped, cast iron bomb is at the Jin siege of the Song city of Qizhou in 1221, though the name "thunder-crash bomb" (*zhentianlei*) was not recorded until a naval battle in 1231. By 1257, a Song official was complaining that the arsenals of two cities facing the Mongol border, which should have had "several hundred thousand iron bombshells," had only 85 in one of the cities, along with 95 fire-arrows (or rockets), and 105 fire-spears. He also pointed out that in other places one arsenal produced one or two thousand iron bomb-shells a month, and that ten to twenty thousand at a time were sent to some major cities.[21] We see here not only the rapid adoption of an effective weapon, but also a revolutionary change in military practice requiring the mass manufacturing of the new weapon.

Conclusion

From a modern perspective, with twenty-twenty hindsight, the development of gunpowder weapons seems not only slow, but also myopic. How could the Chinese not have immediately seen the potential for gunpowder as a chemical propellant for the true gun? Progress was initially slow, both as the properties of gunpowder were gradually understood and as

[20] Li Gang, *Jingkang Chuan Xinlu*, 2/13ab, cited and translated in Needham, *Science and Civilization*, 165.
[21] The official was Li Cengpo in his *Kezhai Zagao, Xugao Hou*, 5, 52a, cited and translated in Needham, *Science and Civilization*, 173–4.

the conception of what could be accomplished with it changed. The intellectual component is important, because it required the acceptance of a completely new idea in weaponry: the explosion. These new weapons and new ideas did not develop in a vacuum; they emerged in the wars of the twelfth and thirteenth centuries. Those wars created the modern panoply of weapons: guns, bombs, grenades, and rockets.

Were we to look at the pace of invention, from vague knowledge of a pyrotechnic mixture in the ninth century, to the creation of the true gun in the thirteenth, we would see a gradually increasing rate of experimentation and deployment. The greatest increase in the rate of invention took place during the wars of the twelfth and thirteenth centuries, as knowledge of gunpowder became widespread and production of all the materials involved increased. It was not just the scope and regularity of war during these centuries that drove the development of gunpowder weapons, however; it was also the nature of that warfare. Unlike the relatively peaceful eleventh century, or the more turbulent tenth century, most major campaigns during the twelfth and thirteenth centuries were decided through sieges and naval battles. This echoes Carlo Cipolla's argument that the development of guns in Europe was spurred by placing them on ships, where the problems of weight, and thus mobility, were greatly diminished.[22] In China, the open field weakness of early gunpowder weapons was avoided by using them on ships and fortifications.

Gunpowder weapons developed in a particular military milieu, and they remained the product of that cultural matrix. The Song army was a professional force, paid and armed by the government, trained to fight in bureaucratically structured units, capable of volley fire, supplied by an effective bureaucratic logistical system, and commanded by officers promoted by the government. It was, to our modern eyes, a modern army, albeit one armed with pre-modern weapons. Its opponents were initially less "modern" and certainly less professional, but nonetheless extremely effective in the open field. The military power of steppe cavalry armies was impressive, and their inherent mobility was often more than a match for even the most disciplined infantry force. Fortifications and rivers negated that power to the point where even a steppe cavalry-based army like that of the Jurchen Jin fell back to city defenses once it lost to the Mongols in the field.

It would take many more centuries before a disciplined infantry force armed with handguns could not only defend itself, but also destroy a purely cavalry force out of hand. In the interim, the new gunpowder

---

[22] Carlo Cipolla, *Guns, Sails and Empires: Technological Innovation and the Early Phases of European Expansion, 1400–1700,* New York: Pantheon, 1966.

weapons temporarily tipped the balance of power in favor of the besieged, rather than the besieger. The Jurchen were forced to acquire the new technology in their struggle with the Song regime, though they never managed to develop a navy strong enough to defeat the Song navy. The Mongols were similarly forced to acquire gunpowder technology, and to build a navy, in order to defeat the Song. It was the Mongols' ability to build a navy strong enough to contest the Huai River defenses that allowed their other initiatives, diplomatic, military, and personal, to break through Song defenses and force the dynasty to capitulate. And it is no accident that the final defeat of the last remnants of Song power came in a naval battle off Yaishan in 1279.

In Europe, by contrast, new gunpowder weapons shifted warfare in favor of the besieger, a difference that requires some explanation. Medieval European castle walls were relatively high and thin (to prevent escalade), constructed of stone facings with rubble infill. Chinese walls were low and thick, built of hard-packed earth, with the later addition of brick facing. Even a very limited siege train of early cannon could quickly knock holes in a European castle's walls. Moreover, those walls were not strong enough to support their own cannon, though they were able to permit the use of handguns. The defensive response to cannon in Europe was to build relatively low and thick walls of packed earth, which could both withstand the force of cannon balls and support their own, defensive cannon. Chinese wall-building practice was, by happenstance, extremely resistant to all forms of battering. This held true into the twentieth century, when even modern explosive shells had some difficulty in breaking through tamped earth walls. One of the reasons the Communist Chinese regime tore down Beijing's old city walls was specifically to prevent the old city from forming a defensive position that might be used to resist the government itself.

The shifts in warfare explain why there was no sense in the eleventh century that warfare had changed significantly in any respect. New weapons had been developed and used without causing an obvious rupture with past practice. The main reason for this lack of emphasis on the effect of the new weapons on warfare was that they had not, in fact, caused much difference. There were few major sieges and almost no naval combat whatsoever in the eleventh century. Although the Song dynasty was wealthy and technologically advanced in the eleventh century, and some have speculated that it was on the verge of an industrial revolution, this did not translate into an overwhelming military advantage because, on the one hand, they had not yet combined all of their available technologies into the most effective weapons and, on the other, they were not involved in any conflicts in which those weapons would have been decisive. All the components for guns, bombs, and rockets existed in the eleventh century, but it would take two centuries of sieges and naval battles to bring these weapons into being.

Mongol rule over much of Eurasia probably hastened the spread of China's new weapons to the rest of the world. Early gunpowder weapons were not difficult to make for a knowledgeable person with access to the right materials. Most craftsmen could duplicate example weapons. The Mongols brought their artillerymen with them from China and Central Eurasia as they campaigned west. It was now up to the rest of the world to react to the Chinese military revolution.

FURTHER READING

Kenneth Chase, *Firearms: A Global History to 1700*, Cambridge: Cambridge University Press, 2003.

Xu Liu, *Zhongguo gu dai huoyao huoqi shi*, Zhengzhou, Henan: Daxiang chu-banshe, 2004.

Peter Lorge, *War, Politics and Society in Early Modern China, 900–1795*, London and New York: Routledge, 2005.

Joseph Needham, *Science and Civilization in China,* Vol. V, part 7: *Military Technology: The Gunpowder Epic*, Cambridge: Cambridge University Press, 1986.

Joseph Needham and Robin Yates, *Science and Civilization in China,* Vol. V, part 6: *Military Technology: Missiles and Sieges*, Cambridge: Cambridge University Press, 1994.

Peter Perdue, *China Marches West*, Cambridge, MA: Harvard University Press, 2005.

Yingxing Song, *Tiangong Kaiwu*, Taibei: Shijie Shuju, 1962.

2   Japan and the wars of unification

Unlike the other Asian polities discussed in this book, Japan emerged as a modern, militarily powerful nation in the late nineteenth and early twentieth century. It avoided the plague of Western colonialism that so badly disrupted many societies around the world, and handily absorbed the technological developments of the Industrial Revolution. But in most respects Japan's reaction to the introduction of firearms was similar to the rest of Asia. Firearms were revolutionary in Japanese warfare, becoming indispensable weapons for armies soon after the Portuguese introduced them in 1543.[1] They fit extremely well within the already missile-oriented mode of Japanese warfare. The Portuguese arquebus, and the far more widely available Japanese reproductions of it, became prominent at just the time when Oda Nobunaga began to unify Japan. Toyotomi Hideyoshi completed that unification, and the coincidence of the introduction of new military technology and political change seems to imply causality; we shall see that this was not the case, in the same way that Japan's avoidance of the full effects of colonialism was due not to culture, but to geography and economics.

It was political and social development that allowed the arquebus to be taken up and used effectively, not the technology that initiated political and social development. Indeed, both Hideyoshi and the man who truly gained the benefits of Japan's unification, Tokugawa Ieyasu, successfully altered the direction of social development exactly contrary to where the technology seemed to drive it. Despite the increasing use of arquebuses by non-samurai, a pattern that would naturally suggest a power shift as the means of warfare were placed in non-samurai hands, those outside the warrior class were ultimately disenfranchised. For reasons of politics and security, a clear distinction was made between warrior and non-warrior,

---

[1] Delmer Brown, "The Impact of Firearms on Japanese Warfare, 1543–98," *The Far Eastern Quarterly*, 7/3 (May 1948), 236–53. The "first" introduction of firearms certainly predates the Portuguese and is difficult to date reliably. See Brown's extensive footnote on the issue on pages 236–7.

Map 3 Japan

and weapons forbidden to those outside of the former class. The resulting structure was stable for two and a half centuries.

The arms and armor of Japanese warriors were not static over the centuries, nor were the origins of the warriors themselves. Warrior rule over Japan itself developed out of the Gempei War (1180–5), which gave birth to the *bakufu*, the Shogun's government located in Kamakura. Even this apparent ascendancy of warriors was not complete until the destruction of the Kamakura *bakufu* in the fourteenth century. In order to understand the impact of guns on Japanese warfare, we must first appreciate the evolving nature of Japanese society and government, and the way in which warfare and warriors affected them. This consideration will show how the new technology participated in a process of ongoing change, rather than suddenly shattering a rigid, long-standing framework. The effect of the arrival of representatives of the West in the nineteenth century, which will be discussed in chapter 7, was much more shocking.

I begin this chapter by tracing the rise of warrior rule in Japan, laying out not just its political and social aspects, but also the methods and modes of warfare that it entailed. This background will serve as the basis for discussing the impact of the Mongol invasions of Japan in the thirteenth century, the Onin War, with its subsequent century of turmoil, leading up to the unification of Japan in the mid-sixteenth century, and the role of pirates in fifteenth- and sixteenth-century Japan. Hideyoshi's invasions of Korea will be dealt with in the following chapter, leaving me to conclude with Tokugawa Ieyasu's ultimate victory at the Battle of Sekigahara, the establishment of the Tokugawa *bakufu*, and a discussion of how that regime kept control of the guns in its own hands.

The rise of warrior rule[2]

The Heian period (794–1185) saw the rise of the professional warrior class, the *bushi*, as the main military service providers of the imperial court. This marked a shift of the court away from reliance on conscript peasant soldiers, toward, or more precisely, back to, the militarized provincial gentry. At the beginning of the eighth century, in response to fears of an imminent attack by Tang dynasty China (618–907), which had recently invaded Korea, the Japanese imperial court adopted the Tang military system of recruiting farmers and training them for military service. This military system would also bolster the central government against provincial threats to its power. Since it was impossible both to be a farmer and to practice the skills of shooting a bow while riding a horse, these troops were infantrymen. Unfortunately for the imperial court, cavalry was the dominant arm in Japanese warfare at the time, so it was necessary to buy the services of trained men from the provincial strongmen and centrally located aristocrats who maintained both the horses and the skills to use them in combat.

As the Tang and regional threats to the court faded, so too did the need for the large units of infantry raised from the farmers. They were abolished

---

[2] This discussion of the rise of warrior rule in Japan is based upon Karl F. Friday, *Hired Swords: The Rise of Private Warrior Power in Early Japan*, Stanford: Stanford University Press, 1992, and William Wayne Farris, *Heavenly Warriors: The Evolution of Japan's Military, 500–1300*, Cambridge, MA: Harvard University Press, 1992.

entirely in 792, leaving behind the cavalry of the provincial strongmen. Martial skills were no longer taught to the farmers by the central government, they were passed down privately among the warrior class. Provincial strongmen and lower-level central aristocrats advanced themselves through military prowess and the ability to deliver trained military men to the central government. The central government, in turn, used its ability to sanction the use of violence, provide rewards, and generally confer legitimacy on actions as the main lever of control. Similarly important was the competitive environment for those military services. The power of any particular strongman was balanced by the power of other strongmen. All the court needed to do was declare one a rebel, and legitimate the actions of others in suppressing him. Although this allowed, even promoted, the development of militarily strong provincial forces, the system worked remarkably well until the late twelfth century.

Competition among provincial strongmen engendered a considerable amount of regular skirmishing in the countryside. Since martial skills were privately developed, they were also frequently used in the service of private interests. Ambushes and small-scale fighting were the rule, with larger clashes much more rare. The armament of these warriors was initially cumbersome, with improvements over time increasing mobility and effectiveness. Although the samurai would be defined by the "way of the sword" in the Tokugawa period (1600–1867), prior to that the class of professional warriors continued to practice the "way of the horse and bow."

Japanese horses were not, however, very good.[3] They were small, weak, and had limited stamina. *Bushi* could not expect their mounts to gallop around for very long, thus limiting the range and duration of battle. The solution to the weakness of horses on the steppe was to bring more than one horse to battle, but this option was not available to the Japanese because there were fewer horses available overall. Japanese bows began as simple wooden staves, and gradually gained laminates of bamboo first on the outside face, then the inside face (early thirteenth century), then on the two sides (fifteenth century). Of course, a mounted archer could carry only a small number of readily available arrows, further limiting the duration of any mounted combat. The bow remained the primary combat weapon until the arquebus replaced it in the sixteenth century. *Bushi* shot from horseback or on foot until they ran out of arrows, or their string broke. They never willingly set aside the bow in favor of another weapon.

---

[3] In addition to the sources mentioned above, this section draws heavily from Karl F. Friday, *Samurai, Warfare and the State in Early Medieval Japan*, New York and London: Routledge, 2004.

This focus on missile warfare is important to keep in mind when we turn to the adoption of the arquebus below.

Despite the dominance of the bow on the battlefield, the Japanese sword took on great significance early on. Japanese swords remain some of the finest blades forged in human history, and the literature on them and theories regarding their development is correspondingly extensive. Here it is important simply to note that they did develop in style (length, curvature, blade profile) over the medieval period, and that they were extremely difficult to use effectively on horseback against an opponent on horseback. Even to behead a fallen opponent required dismounting, taking a two-handed grip, and landing a carefully aimed blow to the neck. This was time consuming, and might leave one vulnerable to other opponents. The sword was, however, the weapon of an individual, not of a group. Similarly, the *naginata*, a polearm with a long, curved blade like the Japanese sword, was a weapon for individual combat. By contrast, the spear, in particular the *yari* that became prominent in the late fifteenth century with the rise of infantry, was designed to be used by groups of men standing in formation.

Japanese armor was built up from small iron lamellae, 7–8 cm long by 3–4 cm wide, laced together into larger plates. These were combined together to form an extremely effective suit that offered good protection from arrows and swords. Indeed, it was virtually impossible for an arrow or sword to penetrate the plates, requiring an attacker to target the small areas of vulnerability under the arms, the face, and lower neck. Most non-lethal wounds were received in the arms and legs (an arrow or sword wound to the armpit, face, or neck would usually be fatal). Full suits of armor were also extremely expensive, and many *bushi* and virtually all infantrymen used simpler forms of it. *Bushi* usually supplied their own armor and weapons, placing a considerable economic burden on the professional warrior, while at the same time providing him a means to distinguish himself as a member of that class. A full suit of armor was a luxury good, and ownership of a set demonstrated conspicuous consumption.

The modes of Japanese warfare were determined not by the available technology alone, but by the entire cultural and political apparatus sur-rounding the use of violence. Violence was one of the main ways that *bushi* established themselves as a separate class. It was not fighting by itself that made one a *bushi*, but fighting in a particular manner, and fighting other *bushi*. Battles reinforced the existing structure of society because they were fought in a way that did so. For many centuries, the *bushi* and their provincial lords remained skilled with weapons, but politically naïve. The imperial court and its aristocrats effectively manipulated and balanced the competing strongmen against each other, even as those strongmen gained in power. Yet over time these men learned enough from their patrons, and indeed were intertwined with them closely enough, to form political ties able to challenge imperial power. The Kamakura *bakufu* demonstrated that the provincial strongmen were now politically capable of taking a greater share of power. They did not completely do away with the imperial court, and the rise of warrior rule created a dual government structure that continued to evolve.

The Mongol invasions

The two Mongol invasions of Japan, in 1274 and 1281, hold a position of much greater significance in modern Japanese history than these rather desultory affairs warrant. An examination of them does, however, allow us to look at fighting styles, the effects of a limited use of gunpowder weapons, and the difficulties of comparing the effectiveness of weapons, tactics, and military organization outside of the context of strategic and logistical planning. These issues directly confront not only the question of why new technology is or is not adopted by a given army, but also how our modern misunderstandings of past events color our conception of how and why events transpired as they did. In short, it is impossible to make sense of the past when we don't know what actually happened.

It took the Mongols some three decades first to intimidate and then to subjugate the Koryo regime that ruled Korea. Koryo fought back diplomatically and militarily, with considerable success, before finally surrendering in 1259. Much of Khubilai Khan's interest in attacking Japan may well have been to use the invasion as a way of tightening control over Korea. His initial letters to the Japanese court were only somewhat threatening, however, and mostly sought friendly contact, with implicit diplomatic submission to the Mongol court. If such contact were established, then there would be no need for resort to arms. The Japanese court was well aware of the history of Mongol–Koryo interaction, and likely understood that such a submission, no matter how minor, would lead to increasing demands by the Mongols. In any case, the Japanese simply did not respond to repeated letters and envoys.

While the Kamakura *bakufu* warned local warriors in Kyushu, the southernmost of Japan's large islands, to be prepared, Khubilai ordered the construction of a thousand ships in 1268. A rebellion broke out in Koryo in 1269 as a result of Mongol ship-building and provision demands, which was not put down until 1271. It would, in fact, take until 1273 to root out the last vestiges of this insurrection. The problem with Koryo, from the Mongol point of view, was that it was a secondary theatre. Far more resources were devoted to defeating the Southern Song, and to struggles with other Mongol leaders. The fleet Khubilai ordered built to defeat the Southern Song navy was nearly ten times as large, and was placed under the command of his best generals. Of course, the prize at stake was far grander: southern China in the thirteenth century was one of the wealthiest parts of the world, if not the wealthiest.

The Mongol force that sailed for Japan on April 21, 1274 had few if any Mongols in it, with the troops drawn from the State Farm army (part-time soldiers who also farmed state-assigned land) and Jurchen soldiers, the latter probably being steppe cavalrymen. Including the sailors, the total number of personnel was 15,000 men, traveling in 900 warships, large and small.[4] They were defeated by a force of anywhere from 2,300 to 5,700 Japanese, with the lower figure more likely.[5] In terms of the size of the force that actually made it to shore, however, neither side appeared to be markedly superior in number or fighting skill over the other. Japanese organization was poor, as was anything resembling unit coordination. The Mongol army was hobbled by limited intelligence, relatively few horses (Mongol armies in the steppe figured six horses per man as the standard), difficult terrain, poor leadership, and a very restricted line of retreat. Indeed, the Mongol force arrived with none of the advantages that had carried them to victory on the continent. The strategic and tactical mobility of their fluid and ruthless style of warfare was simply impossible. They relied upon the qualities of their troops to win out from a weak position. When this failed, they were forced back on their boats. Contemporary accounts, which were very concerned with the influence of divine forces, made no mention of a large storm driving off the Mongols.

The Mongol army made some use of bombs or grenades during fighting, and the Japanese noted the Chinese practice of coordinating groups of soldiers arrayed in formation by the use of gongs and drums. Japanese tactics were more driven by the desire for personal glory, and the very real

---

[4] Toghto (ed.), *Yuanshi*, Beijing: Zhonghua Shuju, 1976, 8.154. I cannot find Conlan's "8,000 Koreans" in the text, Thomas Conlan, *In Little Need of Divine Intervention*, Ithaca: Cornell University Press, 2002, 263.

[5] Conlan, *In Little Need of Divine Intervention*, 261–3, is highly skeptical of any number much beyond a few thousand on each side. His concerns are reasonable, but the sources could easily be correct from the central government's perspective without being intentionally dishonest exaggerations. For example, if all of the men actually participating in any aspect of the invasion were included, porters, sailors, etc., the number of fighting men actually setting foot on Japanese soil would drop to Conlan's numbers quite quickly. Moreover, the Mongol fleet clearly suffered great difficulties in getting troops on to the shore and back. It is possible that they were never able to land all, or even most, of the amphibious force.

rewards the warriors expected from the *bakufu* for performing provable acts of valor. Most of the initial cavalry skirmishing, however, gave way to a longer-range archery duel. As casualties mounted, and no more than a tenuous beachhead had been achieved, the commander of the Mongol force, who had himself already been wounded in the face by an arrow, ordered a withdrawal. Very little damage had been done to the Japanese, particularly where they had some fortified positions to bolster their defenses. The value of fortified positions was so clear after the Mongol fleet departed that the *bakufu* ordered the construction of a wall around Hakata Bay where they had landed, and at other important sites.[6]

The 1274 invasion showed that a Mongol army could get to Japan, but that a small force could neither establish a stable position nor do enough damage to intimidate the local government. If we recall the regular Mongol practice of repeated destructive raids designed to force submission and erode a state's ability to resist future raids, then the 1274 invasion seems in keeping with Mongol procedure. The Mongol force gathered some intelligence, something they appeared to be desperately lacking, and perhaps felt that they had made the point to the Japanese leadership that they could, in fact, attack Japan if they chose to do so. It became clear to the Japanese that the Mongols could reach Japan, and that they would likely do so again, but they had good reason not to be more than seriously concerned about the prospect. The limited use of bombs had been notable, but not revolutionary. There was no apparent technological superiority, tactical superiority, or even numerical superiority on shore. If the Mongol threat was not imaginary, and needed to be prepared for, it was also unlikely to destroy the government.

A second invasion in 1281 was larger but achieved even less. Some modern Japanese scholars have estimated this Mongol force at 100,000 strong, but Chinese sources offer no more than the possibility of 33,000 soldiers and 2,000 horses. It is unclear whether a Korean force of 10,000 soldiers and 15,000 sailors in 900 warships should be added to this number or was already part of it.[7] This force only succeeded in briefly occupying some small islands off the coast before low supplies forced it to withdraw. Its forays onto Kyushu were stymied by the new wall around Hakata Bay, and walls in other landing places. Chinese sources report that a great wind dispersed the fleet, which had already been ordered to withdraw, and that only 10 or 20 percent of it managed to return. The Mongol armada was

---

[6] Ishī Susumu, "The Decline of the Kamakura *Bakufu*," in Kozo Yamamura (ed.), *The Cambridge History of Japan*, Vol. III: *Medieval Japan*, Cambridge: Cambridge University Press, 1990, 138–40.

[7] Toghto, *Yuanshi* 11.228.

simply incapable of landing a large enough force to defeat even the forward defense line of the Japanese. Part of the armada had sailed about a hundred miles to reach Japan, but a large part had sailed nearly five hundred miles. Whatever gunpowder weapons had been brought to bear were insignificant in the face of these adverse logistical conditions.

Although the failed invasions were virtually insignificant events on the continent, they placed enormous stress on Japanese society. Japanese warriors fought for spoils, usually the lands of the men they defeated, and the great effort to repulse the Mongols yielded nothing in this regard. The *bakufu* struggled for decades to reward the warriors of Kyushu for their efforts. And while the Mongol court could set aside the events of 1274 and 1281, Khubilai's successor declining to send another invasion, in Japan the threat remained a very real possibility for years to come.[8]

The invasion of Japan did not connect the Japanese to the great revolution in warfare that had taken place on the continent over the preceding two centuries. This demonstrates how shallow that revolution was, and how confined it was to naval and siege warfare in central and southern China. Guns and bombs were not yet standard weapons for continental field armies, and there is no mention of their possible presence on board the Mongol navy because the naval encounters were not described in the sources. Recent archaeology has, however, discovered gunpowder residue in containers found in the wrecks of some Chinese riverine warships from the invasion.[9] Gunpowder weapons were available without being used in sufficient numbers to cause much damage. It would be another century before guns would be introduced to the Korean court to help against Japanese pirates, and another three centuries before the Japanese themselves would begin to incorporate guns into their armies.

The Onin War (1467–77)

The Onin War marked the final collapse of even the pretense of central authority under the Kamakura *bakufu*, and ushered in the Japanese Warring States period (1467–1568).[10] Widespread warfare created a

---

[8] For the political and economic effects of the Mongol invasions see Kyotsu Hori, "The Economic and Political Effects of the Mongol Wars," in John W. Hall and Jeffrey P. Mass (eds.), *Medieval Japan*, New Haven and London: Yale University Press, 1974, 184–98.

[9] James P. Delgado, "Relics of the Kamikaze," *Archaeology*, 56/1 (2003), 36–41.

[10] Various dates have been used for the end of the Warring States (*Sengoku*) period. Here I have used 1568, when Oda Nobunaga took control of Kyoto on November 7 and made Ashikaga Yoshiaki Shogun. Others have used 1603, when Tokugawa Ieyasu became Shogun (March 24), or 1605, when Ieyasu retired, or even 1615 after the Tokugawas' successful siege of Osaka Castle.

degree of social mobility as the political struggle demanded more and more military resources. Without a dominant political actor, warlords all over Japan felt free to pursue their ambitions for greater power, or even to become the new dominant power. From the point of view of military developments, the first important change was the return to the extensive use of infantry, which laid the groundwork for the adoption of arquebuses in the sixteenth century. As the response to the Mongol invasions demonstrated, cavalry were less useful than infantry in entrenched positions or confined spaces. Japanese warriors had changed their way of fighting to oppose the Mongols, but reverted back to their cavalry-centered methods when fighting each other. This continued to be the case until street fighting in the confines of Kyoto, the capital, forced warriors on to foot.

The spread of war outside of the capital, and the more generalized breakdown of the pre-existing political order, vastly expanded the total number of men involved in fighting and gave rise to increasing numbers of sieges. Given the limited number of horses available in Japan, let alone the changing nature of warfare, the growth in army size virtually mandated that infantry play a greater part in campaigns. The rise of infantry, in turn, opened the door to advancement for less wealthy members of the warrior class, and even men from outside the warrior class. This was something of a social revolution, but guns had nothing to do with it.

The Warring States period was brought to a close by an escalating series of campaigns fueled in no small part by the growing population and economy of the sixteenth century. As army size increased, the quality of individual soldiers decreased. Armies took on larger numbers of *ashigaru* (lit. "light-foot," less heavily armored troops of the lowest martial class or commoners pressed into service) and untrained men to add mass to their formations, allow them to maintain sieges, and extend their range of operations. Cavalry and well-trained samurai still played an important part in operations, if sometimes for no reason other than the military culture of the commanders, but minimally trained infantry grew in significance. Commanders and political leaders developed the administrative, strategic, and tactical means to raise, pay, supply, and deploy these armies, which had now moved well beyond the small bands of elite troops skirmishing on horseback. Without these changes in warfare, or indeed before they had taken place, guns and handguns could not be effectively used in battle.

As we have seen, guns and handguns had been available in East Asia for three centuries before Portuguese and Portuguese-style arquebuses became important in Japanese warfare. The growing role of poorly trained infantry now provided the demand for the new weapons. The introduction of Portuguese arquebuses to Japan is traditionally dated to 1543, by which time the Warring States period had long been under way. These weapons spread rapidly throughout the country as warlords contending for power sought any advantage over their rivals. But since no individual warlord or even faction had a monopoly over the new weapons, any advantage was relative rather than absolute, and also likely transitory. What the new weapons did was make lower-quality infantrymen much more effective in battle. Good strategy and tactics were still critical, however, in combining the arquebus into the existing modes of fighting in a useful way. Not surprisingly, possibly the most skilled general in this regard was Oda Nobunaga, the man who went so far in unifying Japan. It was not that he used handguns, but that he used them well, as can be seen at the Battle of Nagashino.

Takeda Katsuyori besieged Nagashino Castle on June 19, 1575 with about 15,000 men.[11] Oda Nobunaga and Tokugawa Ieyasu soon arrived to relieve the siege with about 30,000 men. The relief force set up a palisade wall about 3 kilometers long anchored on mountains on one side and a river on the other. This neutralized Takeda's mobility advantage, since he could not flank the relief force with his formidable cavalry. He was now caught between the uncaptured castle and the strongly positioned relief army. His best option would have been to withdraw completely and raise the siege since he had been so clearly outmaneuvered. He chose instead to attack in a direct charge against Nobunaga's line. That line, bolstered by spearmen and samurai, held against repeated charges, subjecting the Takeda cavalry to regular arquebus and bow fire. After five charges, the Takeda army shattered under the weight of casualties. It would never recover.

The Battle of Nagashino on June 28, 1575 is sometimes called Japan's first modern battle, because it supposedly witnessed the success of Western-style firearms and tactics against a traditional Japanese cavalry force. A great deal has sometimes been made of Oda Nobunaga's use of volley fire by his 3,000 arquebus men firing from behind stockades at the charging Takeda cavalry. Unfortunately, there is no reliable evidence that Nobunaga's arquebus men fired in a rolling volley and, indeed, it appears as though there were only perhaps 1,000 arquebus-armed men behind the stockades. Moreover, the Takeda cavalry was by no means a traditional-style force; it had been trained in new tactics only the previous generation. The arquebuses were quite important, but so was Nobunaga's wise placement of his troops and Takeda Katsuyori's willingness to play into his hands.

---

[11] This account follows Joeren P. Lamers, *Japonius Tyrannus: The Japanese Warlord Oda Nobunaga*, Leiden: Hotei, 2000, 112–13.

Takeda Katsuyori was willing to smash his cavalry repeatedly against a barricaded infantry army with superior numbers not simply because he was rash, or a poor general, but because he believed his smaller, elite force could break through an army primarily composed of *ashigaru* and commoners, regardless of their arquebuses. Nobunaga understood the possible weakness of his infantry in this regard, and had placed many trusted men among the infantry to bolster them physically and psychologically. This was all part of the process of learning how to command non-elite troops using weapons with severe limitations.

Cannon played almost no role in the consolidation of Japan, though why this should be so is unclear. When Nobunaga built a small group of seven iron-plated warships, each with three cannon, to defeat the Honganji fleet and take control of Osaka Bay (in order to cut off Honganji completely from outside aid), one Christian missionary remarked: "[Each ship] carries three pieces of heavy ordnance, and I have no idea where these could have come from. With the exception of a few small pieces ... we know for sure that there are no others in the whole of Japan."[12]

These cannon-armed ships proved very effective, but they were top heavy and not very sea worthy. Japanese naval practice remained oriented toward small arms fire and boarding tactics, which would cost them dearly in their invasions of Korea. Yet the Christian missionary was wrong in his understanding of Nobunaga's battleships. Ships just like them had already been in general use by the sea lords of Japan's inland sea. The cannon they carried were most likely obtained from either European or Chinese traders, and very likely manufactured in China. But the ships and cannon were designed for combat in Japanese coastal waters, and to capture, rather than destroy, opposing ships. Nobunaga's battleships were consistent with Japanese sea lord practice, rather than a new invention. It seems likely, based upon the limited number of cannon on board Japanese ships, at sieges, or in the field, that the Japanese lacked both the technical capability to manufacture them, and the interest to purchase them from either the Portuguese or the Chinese in larger numbers. This is indicative of a particular mind-set, or military culture, that readily accepted arquebuses because of the pre-existing milieu, but had greater difficulty assimilating cannon. In this sense, the gunpowder revolution was abbreviated even before the Tokugawa reversed the social changes in warfare begun during the Warring States period.

---

[12] Cited in *Japonius Tyrannus*, 155.

Sea lords[13]

The struggles for dominance during the Warring States period did not take place exclusively on land, since naval forces were necessary to extract wealth from international trade, to transport and protect the movement of armies by water, and to defend coastal populations from raiding. Rather than develop their own navies, land-based warlords hired groups possessing the necessary skills and equipment, entering into uncomfortably tenuous patronage relationships with them. These groups were often referred to as "pirates," depending upon whom they were working for and who was describing their actions, but Peter Shapinsky reasonably prefers the more neutral term "sea lords." Shapinsky's work presents these sea lords in similar terms to land-based warlords, but functioning in a different ecological niche. They played critical roles in several important battles, but remained fluid in their loyalties.

Japanese sea lords were particularly important in the importation and deployment of gunpowder weapons. This makes a great deal of sense when we consider that new military technology all came from abroad, whether from China, Korea, or Europeans trading in East Asian waters. Moreover, as I have argued in the previous chapter, early guns and gunpowder weapons were initially developed for use in siege and naval warfare. While the sea lords Shapinsky deals with were not themselves related to the *wokou* pirates assailing the Chinese and Korean coasts, the long-running conflict in Japan attracted the attention of those continental pirate/traders as a good opportunity to sell weapons, particularly guns.[14] They began to sell firearms in the 1540s; by 1550 a Japanese monk sailing from the port of Sakai recorded that the ship he was traveling on drove off some "pirates" with arquebus fire. Indeed, the crew of his ship made fun of the pirates when they fired arrows at them. Of course, the monk's ship was itself sailed by a different band of sea lords, so this was actually a skirmish between two differently armed "pirate" ships.

As war on land shifted in the middle of the sixteenth century from intraregional struggles to interregional struggles, its scale increased dramatically. Similarly, sea lord bands grew in size and resources, leading to the creation of the *atakebune*, a kind of early battleship. Sea lords had previously sailed more multi-purpose vessels that allowed them to engage in both trade and war as needed. These more flexible vessels did not provide any protection from missile fire for the crews, and relied upon boarding and

---

[13] This discussion of Japanese sea lords follows Peter Shapinsky, "Lords of the Sea: Pirates, Violence, and Exchange in Medieval Japan," Ph.D. dissertation, University of Michigan, 2005, especially 304–95.

[14] Udagawa Takehisa, *Teppoo denrai*, 10–13, cited in Shapinsky, "Lords of the Sea," 354.

hand-to-hand fighting, preceded by a barrage of missiles. The main goal of such operations was to capture an opponent's ship, not sink it.

In the late sixteenth century, sea lords had sufficient resources and ambition to construct purpose-built warships designed with the newest technology to facilitate capturing other vessels. At around 50 meters long, displacing 200–250 tons, they also served as symbolic demonstrations of sea lord power. *Atakebune* had multiple decks with wooden or iron plates to protect the crew from missile fire. They also possessed several cannon (three appears to be the maximum number mentioned) that could be used against ships or fortifications on land. They were provided with both sails and fifty to a hundred rowers. Chinese-style watertight bulkheads below decks made them less prone to sinking. Arquebuses and grenades completed their armament, making these quite formidable in Japan's inland sea, and along its coast. They proved ineffective, however, in Hideyoshi's Korean campaigns. The *atakebune* were still designed, however, with the previous goal of sea lord warfare: to capture other ships. Thus, the revolution in design was not joined to a revolution in goals or tactics.

Interregional warfare leading up to the recentralization of Japanese rule in the second half of the sixteenth century required the ability to cross bodies of water with armies. An army had to cross the straits of Shimonoseki to move from the island of Honshu to the island of Kyushu, and vice versa. Sea lords were critical in the contest between the Mori, attempting to go south into Kyushu, and the Otomo, attempting to go north into Honshu in the 1560s and 1570s. Yet both land powers were constantly frustrated by the fluidity of sea lord allegiance. The sea lords needed the patronage of land-based powers, but their naval services were of such crucial importance, and the competition between those land powers so heated, that they could always find employment.

The sea lords were not, themselves, a united group, and they could be used against each other. In 1582, the Mori dispatched several bands of sea lords against the Kurushima Murakami band, because the Kurushima Murakami had shifted their patronage to Oda Nobunaga. This attack entailed besieging two of the Kurushimas' island fortresses, Kurushima and Kashima. These were both small islands in Japan's inland sea, and besieging them brought into play the specialized skills of sea lords in maritime siege operations, amphibious operations, and blockade, as well as their specialized technology in the form of the *atakebune*. Kurushima, with a circumference of about 850 meters, was more vulnerable, and its harbor village was quickly incinerated by a barrage of fire-arrows, and its village chief beheaded. Kashima, with a circumference of about 1,700 meters and a peak elevation of 114 meters, could only be blockaded.

The *atakebune* proved more effective against ships, and their cannon and arquebuses made little impression on the defenses of Kashima. Kashima held out until Hideyoshi pacified the entire region in 1584, bringing an end to the conflict.

When peace finally came to Japan with Hideyoshi's completion of Nobunaga's project, the sea lords lost most of their autonomy and were fitted into the larger discourse of warlord service. Some may have served in Hideyoshi's subsequent invasions of Korea, but their ships and their way of fighting were ill suited to the new theatre. *Atakebune* and ships like them did poorly against Korean and Chinese ships designed to stand off and use cannon to bombard opposing ships, rather than to close with them and board. Whereas the Japanese fought to seize vessels, Koreans and Chinese, accustomed to fighting *wokou* and understanding naval warfare as a contest to destroy, not capture, an opponent, repeatedly crushed Japanese fleets. Regardless of whether the sea lords of Japan's inland sea took part in Hideyoshi's invasions in the 1590s, their earlier activities helped to advance Japanese ship design, weapon use, and naval tactics.

Korea

Although we will discuss the Japanese invasion of Korea in the following chapter, it is important to place those campaigns in the context of Japanese warfare. Even before the Japanese invaded Korea, their armies relied increasingly on arquebuses wielded by infantry. Army size had grown, as had all of the concomitant administrative and tactical structures necessary to accommodate that growth. Strategic planning, which had been so nuanced and skillful within Japan, failed utterly when power was projected outside it. Toyotomi Hideyoshi, who had seized Oda Nobunaga's mantle after the latter's assassination, completed the unification of Japan in 1591, with the defeat of the Odawara Hojo. Arquebus manufacturing continued apace as these wars were fought out, and armies deployed thousands and thousands of handguns. Even so, the Korean invasions accelerated the transition to handgun-dominant armies.

Hideyoshi had been extremely concerned about providing enough handguns for his final subjugation of Kyushu in 1590, and he was similarly concerned about the forces going to Korea. The Shimazu of Satsuma were ordered to provide 1,500 arquebusiers, 1,500 bowmen, and 300 spearmen for the invasion of Korea.[15] This gives us some idea of

---

[15] Asakawa Kanichi (ed.), *The Documents of the Iriki: Illustration of the Development of the Feudal Institutions of Japan*, New Haven: Yale University Press, 1929, 332–5, cited in Brown, "The Impact of Firearms," 240.

the initial proportions that might be requested from a provincial lord. Japanese handguns gave them a tremendous advantage over the Koreans, though the Korean army began the conflict poorly armed and led. Even so, as the campaign progressed, Japanese commanders sent requests home for still more guns: "Please arrange to send us guns and ammunition. There is absolutely no use for spears. It is vital that you arrange somehow to obtain a number of guns. Furthermore, you should certainly see to it that those persons departing [for Korea] understand this situation. The arrangements for guns should receive your closest attention."[16] And similarly: "When troops come [to Korea] from the province of Kai, have them bring as many guns as possible, for no other equipment is needed. Give strict orders that all men, even the *samurai*, carry guns."[17]

The arquebus was an infantry weapon, and its slow rate of fire left handgun-armed units vulnerable to cavalry charges. This vulnerability was diminished at the Battle of Nagashino by protecting the arquebuses with barricades, spearmen (*ashigaru*), and dismounted swordsmen. When the Japanese army reached Korea, however, it was realized that spearmen were no longer useful. Partly this was because the terrain of Korea was generally not good for cavalry, as the northern Chinese troops also discovered. Whatever Korean cavalry units there were early in the war were soon destroyed. By the time that Chinese cavalry units arrived, the Japanese were fighting from defensive positions and ambushes, which made them less vulnerable to cavalry charges. When a northern Chinese cavalry unit did manage to get to grips with Japanese soldiers, they found that they could not stand up to samurai swordsmanship. Spearmen therefore diminished the firepower of a unit, without adding significantly to its close combat strength. By increasing the percentage of shot to spear and sword, Japanese units became much more effective.

This shifting picture of weapon use is characteristic of an overall change of practice by all three sides. The Koreans and Chinese mirrored the Japanese move toward infantry. At least in the case of the Chinese, however, this was accomplished not by changing all military practice, but by including a higher percentage of southern Chinese troops in the Korean theatre. Northern Chinese troops with their cavalry-focused units were still necessary to oppose the steppe threat. Indeed, cavalry continued to be necessary in northern China until well into the nineteenth century, and even the twentieth. The Japanese army adapted to the new environment by rapidly discarding the spear that, absent the threat of cavalry charges, was of limited use. It was similarly of limited use in

[16] Quoted in Brown, "The Impact of Firearms," 240.   [17] Quoted in ibid., 241.

street fighting and ambushes. All of these factors further reinforced not only the primacy of infantry in the Japanese army, but also the value of conscript troops trained to use handguns and fight in units. The highly trained warrior class with its focus on individual martial skills, particularly horsemanship, archery, and swordsmanship, was losing its military value on the battlefield.

Southern Chinese troops arrived in Korea with the necessary infantry unit tactics to defeat skilled Japanese swordsmen. This was not to say that they did not regard Japanese swordsmen as formidable opponents, far from it, but that they understood that it required a group of men co-operating with a variety of weapons to defeat them. Qi Jiguang had developed a systematic training regime to combat Japanese fighting techniques in the course of suppressing the *wokou* pirates in southern China (see chapter 3). These methods, including the extensive use of Portuguese arquebuses and cannons, were based upon infantry formations mixing polearms and close fighting weapons. Chinese troops were thus already conscripts trained by the state; Japanese armies were moving in that direction. Korea almost saw the end of the Japanese warrior class and its dominance of Japanese military operations. That end would be averted, and the gunpowder revolution in Japan frozen or even reversed, but in the militarily fluid environment of sixteenth-century Japan the widespread adoption of handguns nearly caused a social revolution. Hideyoshi's invasion of Korea hastened those changes.

The troops that returned from Korea to fight the final stage in Japan's wars of unification had experienced other revolutionary forms of warfare. They faced massed cannon fire in the field, and in sieges, as they had never experienced in Japan. At sea, they had been defeated again and again by Korean and Chinese fleets armed with cannon, and armored against small arms fire. None of these experiences seems to have changed Japanese warfare, despite their defeats. Japan could not sustain Hideyoshi's continental campaigns, and the costs of those efforts weakened Hideyoshi's power base. After great expense in blood and treasure, the Japanese army came home to political instability and further warfare.

Sekigahara (October 21, 1600)

Toyotomi Hideyoshi's death in 1598 did not immediately cause his regime to collapse. In his declining years he had become obsessed with insuring the succession of his son to power, knowing that several ambitious men, most obviously Tokugawa Ieyasu, were keen to take over. His venture in Korea had not turned out well, but many of his domestic reforms had gone a long way toward establishing a stable system of unified rule. What Hideyoshi had been unable or unwilling to do was unify his own vassals. He may well have thought that maintaining a rivalry between his vassals protected him from being overthrown, but without his control, those rivalries tore his clan apart. Two of the top commanders of the Korean invasions, for example, ended up on opposite sides of the subsequent struggle for power.

Tokugawa Ieyasu exploited the rivalries within the Toyotomi clan to build up his own power and undercut those remaining loyal to Hideyoshi's son. The political struggles eventually broke out into open military confrontation, leading to a battle at Sekigahara between Ieyasu's army of about 88,000 men and an opposing, loyalist, Toyotomi army of about 82,000 men. In terms of weaponry, both sides were equal, with high proportions of infantry armed with arquebuses. As in so many battles of the Warring States period, it was decided not by superior generalship, but by betrayal during the fighting. Ieyasu managed to entice Kobayakawa Hideaki to change sides with his 15,000 men in the midst of the battle, along with several smaller forces. What began as an inconclusive struggle suddenly became a rout. Although Ieyasu spent several more years consolidating power, the Battle of Sekigahara was the major turning point in establishing him as Shogun.

Keeping the gun

One of the enduring myths in the West about the sixteenth-century unification of Japan and the establishment of the Tokugawa Shogunate that lasted until the mid-nineteenth century was that the Japanese "gave up the gun." Noel Perrin, a professor of English who did not read Japanese, first proposed this idea in a 1965 article in *The New Yorker* and later in his 1979 book *Giving up the Gun*, and it has remained for many a touchstone of gun control and disarmament. Unfortunately, it did not happen. Kenneth Chase pointed out, albeit in a footnote, that Japanese historians were shocked when Perrin's book was finally translated into Japanese in 1984.[18] Perrin's view was simply wrong; the Japanese did not give up guns. Conrad Totman was correct to comment that "Guns went out of style because war ended. Had it continued, the use of guns would have continued."[19] But there is still more to this issue.

Hideyoshi instituted a country-wide policy of disarming the commoner population in 1588, even while his armies were conscripting or otherwise

---

[18] Chase, *Firearms: A Global History to 1700*, 253 fn. 84.
[19] Conrad Totman, "Review of Noel Perrin's *Giving up the Gun*," *Journal of Asian Studies*, 39/3 (1980), 600.

drawing in men from outside the warrior class and training them to use arquebuses. He also ordered surveys of the land and people of the country, leading to prohibitions on travel outside of the province one lived in. All of this was done to pacify the countryside and gain greater control over the population. Commoners were being proscribed from owning weapons just as they were becoming more important on the battlefield, showing a remarkably modern sense of a state asserting its sole right to organize and administer violence. But there was a distinctly retrogressive part of this policy as well, since the hereditary warrior class, or at least those who had come to claim that status (Hideyoshi himself was not born into the warrior class), were allowed the private ownership of weapons. Indeed, they were required to carry those weapons, in this case two swords, to mark them as members of that class. Theoretically they were also supposed to be expert in the use of those swords, and to be ready to fight at a moment's notice.

Before the wars of unification were over, the political powerholders were shaping Japanese society into what they considered an acceptable form. The first requirement of that society was political stability, which necessitated a balance of power between the center and the provinces. In exchange for sufficient central power to maintain overall unity, provincial lords were given a fairly free hand within their own domains. Those lords were themselves the subject of extensive institutional controls by the shogunal authorities, most notably the requirement that their families remain in the capital under supervision as hostages. Society was clearly separated into warrior and non-warrior classes, with weapon ownership the privilege solely of the former.

The gunpowder revolution in Japan that was founded upon the changing nature of warfare in the late fifteenth and early sixteenth century was not so much halted or reversed as rendered irrelevant by peace. Social fluidity caused by evolving political and military developments allowed many men, most notably Toyotomi Hideyoshi, to advance themselves from the bottom to the top of society within a single generation. But larger armies and the consolidation of political units into more cohesive and bigger groups were well under way before *wokou* trader/pirates brought handguns into Japan in large numbers. Those handguns were seen as useful because armies now contained large numbers of untrained or poorly trained conscripts. Japanese armies had become more like continental armies: commoner forces raised, trained, and armed by some governmental authority, no matter how provincial, rather than the purely elite, warrior-class forces of the preceding centuries. By the late sixteenth century the central authorities began to separate the military necessity of conscripting commoners from the government's desire to fix social classes into a stable matrix resembling the pre-Warring States period. The government decided that the military revolution would not lead to a social or political revolution. Peace allowed the government to make that policy stick.

A similar effort by the founder of the Ming dynasty in China to fix social groups, separate out the military, and strictly limit the mobility of the population had utterly failed in the fourteenth century. The Tokugawa *bakufu* was successful not only because Japan remained at peace, and its closing of the country to the outside world limited external influence, but also because it lacked the economic, social, and political dynamism of China. This is not to say that Japan was not developing in any of these areas; it was, as the gradual impoverishment of many samurai, their salaries fixed in the late sixteenth or early seventeenth century and left unchanged into the nineteenth century, and the rise of affluent merchants attest; but this change was slower. The modernization, if one can call it that, of Japan proceeded without a military component, as the warrior class was undermined economically over two and a half centuries. When the modern world made its abrupt appearance in Japan in the nineteenth century, its society was again ready to wrestle with the problems of incorporating new technology into it. But once again, this would be due to the social, economic, and political changes that preceded the introduction of that technology, not to the technology driving those changes.

FURTHER READING

Adriana Boscaro (ed. and trans.), *101 Letters of Hideyoshi*, Tokyo: Sophia University, 1975.

Delmer Brown, "The Impact of Firearms on Japanese Warfare, 1543–98," *The Far Eastern Quarterly*, 7/3 (May 1948), 236–53.

Jonathan Clements, *Pirate King: Coxinga and the Fall of the Ming Dynasty*, Stroud: Sutton, 2004.

Thomas Conlan, *In Little Need of Divine Intervention*, Ithaca: Cornell University Press, 2002.

State of War: The Violent Order of 14th Century Japan, Ann Arbor: University of Michigan Press, 2003.

Peter Duus (ed.), *The Cambridge History of Japan*, Vol. VI, Cambridge: Cambridge University Press, 1988.

William Wayne Farris, *Heavenly Warriors: The Evolution of Japan's Military, 500–1300*, Cambridge, MA: Harvard University Press, 1992.

Karl F. Friday, *Hired Swords: The Rise of Private Warrior Power in Early Japan*, Stanford: Stanford University Press, 1992.

Samurai, Warfare and the State in Early Medieval Japan, New York and London: Routledge, 2004.

John W. Hall and Jeffrey P. Mass (eds.), *Medieval Japan*, New Haven and London: Yale University Press, 1974.

Jeroen P. Lamers *Japonius Tyrannus: The Japanese Warlord Oda Nobunaga*, Leiden: Hotei, 2000.

Helen Craig McCullough (trans.), *The Taiheki*, New York: Columbia University Press, 1959.

Jeffrey P. Mass (ed.), *The Origins of Japan's Medieval World*, Stanford: Stanford University Press, 1997.

Peter Shapinsky, "Lords of the Sea: Pirates, Violence, and Exchange in Medieval Japan," Ph.D. dissertation, University of Michigan, 2005.

Kwan-wai So, *Japanese Piracy in Ming China during the 16th Century*, East Lansing: Michigan State University Press, 1975.

H. Paul Varley, *The Onin War*, New York and London: Columbia University Press, 1967.

Kozo Yamamura (ed.), *The Cambridge History of Japan*, Vol. III: *Medieval Japan*, Cambridge: Cambridge University Press, 1990.

3   The Chinese military revolution and war in Korea

We now return to the consideration of China begun in chapter 1, and connect the advances in guns there with the Japanese adoption of Portuguese muskets through Hideyoshi's invasions of Korea in the 1590s. Although guns were widely available in the struggle for supremacy in China during the mid-fourteenth century, they became a cornerstone of the Ming army only after the Ming conquest of China. Before the end of the fourteenth century, almost 10 percent of the army's 1.2–1.8 million soldiers were armed with guns. The capital's arsenals produced 3,000 cannon and 3,000 handguns annually from 1380 to 1488. These weapons were widely deployed and initially gave Ming armies an advantage over neighboring states that were not so armed. European advances in gun technology were quickly adopted in China, and the cannon it brought into the field owed as much to the West as did the Japanese army's muskets.

Hideyoshi's invasions of Korea brought about a direct clash between three different gun-armed forces, the Japanese, Chinese, and Koreans. Japanese forces were armed with muskets and trained in volley fire; Chinese forces relied upon cannon; and Korean forces used cannon on armored warships to interdict Japanese maritime supply lines. On the strategic level, the Japanese were completely defeated, achieving none of their political or military goals at a tremendous loss of life. Tactically, the results were more mixed. Chinese armies succeeded when they brought their cannon up to the battlefield, and lost when they did not. The Korean navy defeated the Japanese navy using cannon to oppose their boarding tactics, but was ineffective when poorly commanded. Overall, the conflict demonstrated that guns, whether muskets or cannon, were now critical in East Asian warfare.

After the first Japanese campaign (1592–3) was driven back to the southern tip of Korea, the Ming attempted to improve the Korean army by training its soldiers to use firearms. The course of the war surprised all sides, revealing deep-seated weaknesses within everyone's armed forces. By campaigning outside of Japan, Hideyoshi subjected the Japanese army

Map 4 Korea

to new military problems that it struggled to overcome. The Korean and Chinese forces suffered similar difficulties in dealing with new modes of warfare. For example, the Ming army, which possessed several different kinds of troops based upon their regional origins, had to bring southern Chinese troops, who had previously fought against "Japanese" pirates, to the battlefield in order to engage the Japanese in close combat. Northern Chinese troops, who emphasized cavalry and had no experience of the Japanese, were generally regarded as ineffective.

It is impossible to draw conclusions about which mode of warfare was superior without taking into account the specific conditions and commanders of a given battle. Japanese superiority in close combat, and in medium-range missile firing through their use of muskets, was negated when Chinese cannon were present on the battlefield. At the same time, the test of combat could be rendered moot by larger strategic issues. Japanese attempts to hold and control Korean territory, combined with a desire to avoid large-scale battles with the Chinese and their cannons, induced them to disperse their troops and focus on ambushes and placing small garrisons in key locations. These tactics then exposed them to even greater risk, as Korean partisans were able to ambush small Japanese units, or harass their supply lines.

Hideyoshi's invasions, like the construction of the Great Wall, demonstrated once again the close connection between siege warfare, naval warfare, and guns. While troops in the field could maneuver to take advantage of their own strengths and avoid those of their opponents, sometimes to the extent of refusing battle entirely, siege and naval warfare quite often did not allow that possibility. Strong points had to be taken if territory was to be controlled, certain sailing routes had to be used at certain times if ships were to reach their destination. One of the greatest weaknesses of the Japanese war effort was the Japanese navy, a rather surprising circumstance given the competence of Japanese sea lords earlier in the sixteenth century, described by Peter Shapinsky in the previous chapter.

The conflict in Korea is difficult to understand without further reference to what happened in China from the thirteenth to the sixteenth centuries. This chapter will begin by discussing the limited progress in Chinese gun technology before the arrival of the West, and then turn to the creation of the Ming dynasty. The establishment of the Ming placed a self-consciously "Chinese" dynasty in control of China, both north and south. The problems of northern border security led to the beginning of the construction of what we now call the Great Wall in the fifteenth century. Also in the fifteenth century, the Ming court dispatched a series of naval expeditions under the Muslim eunuch Admiral Zheng He. Ming strategic policy thus varied greatly even within the reign of a single emperor, let alone over the course of several. Although the naval expeditions were discontinued, China remained connected to the maritime world on its coast. Guns were part of the Ming response to the *wokou* pirates in the mid-sixteenth century, and in some ways prepared at least part of the Ming army to fight the Japanese at the end of that century. Yet larger issues of morale, training, command, and supply far exceeded the importance of guns by themselves. Better guns were not decisive on their own, though Jesuit-supplied military technology would play a significant role on all sides during the invasion of Korea.

Lack of progress in Chinese guns

The earliest known specimen of a gun was excavated in July of 1970 in Acheng county, Heilongjiang province. Made of bronze, it is 34 centimeters long, weighs 3.5 kilograms and has three distinct parts to its length: a barrel, powder chamber, and socket for a handle at the rear end. It has been dated no later than 1290.[1] Other finds have provided similar kinds of guns, with even more exact dating. A 1962 find with an inscribed date of 1332 was 35.3 centimeters long and weighed 6.94 kilograms.[2] Both weapons had touchholes to allow ignition of the gunpowder from the back. The similar sizes, forms, and materials are striking, suggesting that this simple design was being manufactured to regular specifications. As we have seen, weapons in China were usually manufactured in government arsenals under bureaucratic supervision. The guns that have so far been excavated are thus not experimental weapons, but standard weapons built to agreed-upon specifications. These early examples of guns are critical in establishing that true guns were deployed on the battlefield in the thirteenth century. The textual evidence is often complicated by the evolving meaning of the terms involved, rendering many passages ambiguous. It is even possible that true guns were used in the Mongol invasion of Japan.

What is more surprising, however, given the early development of guns in China, is how little progress in design was made after the thirteenth century. Early fifteenth-century guns were virtually identical to late thirteenth-century weapons. Yet even in the midst of this slowdown in development,

[1] Wei Guozhong, "Heilongjiang, Achengxian, Banlacheng zi chutu de tong huochong," *Wenwu*, 11 (1973), cited in Liu Xu, *Zhongguo Gudai Huoyao Huoqi Shi*, Zhengzhou: Daxiang chubanshe, 2004, 50–1.

[2] Wang Cai, "Yuan-Ming huochong de zhuangzhi fuyuan," *Wenwu*, 3 (1962), cited in Xu, *Zhongguo Gudai Huoyao Huoqi Shi*, 51–2.

Chinese arsenals still produced two innovations that were ahead of their time: cast iron guns and solid metal roundshot. The *c.*1338 cast iron gun held by the Rotunda Museum in Woolwich is important only for its date, whereas the cache of hundreds of cast iron cannons found in Nanjing manufactured between 1356 and 1357 is significant both for the number of weapons and for the fact that, as Needham so perceptively pointed out, they are, indeed, cannon and not handguns. Their inscribed weight was 500 catties, or about 670 pounds. These guns had been buried at Nanjing after the defeat of Zhang Shicheng by the army of the rising regional power that would become the Ming dynasty about a decade later. Neither cast iron guns nor metal ammunition elicited much comment in the Chinese sources, and it may be that the transition, impartial in the case of cast iron guns, to the use of these innovations happened so early that there was no sense of a sudden improvement in practice.[3]

We are forced to ask that most difficult of historical questions: why didn't something happen? Why did innovation in guns slow so dramatically after the thirteenth century? The answer may lie somewhere in the curious behavior of the Ming army in burying several hundred cannons after defeating Zhang Shicheng. Where else in the world would an army have discarded functional cannons that came into its possession? It was not, apparently, even worth the effort to melt down those cannons to reuse the metal. Nor were these cannons buried at the end of a war; considerable fighting remained. It is possible that the cannons were not of a high enough quality to warrant reuse, but that does not answer the question of why they were not melted down. The only conclusion we can come to is that they were simply not worth keeping or melting down. Neither the cannons, nor their constituent iron, were useful. They were junk as far as the Ming army was concerned.

It is a commonplace in the twenty-first century to see China as one of the world's great manufacturing centers. This was also true of China in the past. The scale of Chinese gun production in the thirteenth and fourteenth centuries must have been so great, and the material resources so plentiful, that storing, hauling away, or melting down the captured iron cannon was not worth the effort. Had the weapons in question been handguns, rather than cannon, they might have been retained for further use, but actual cannon had much more limited functions. Cannon could not knock down the low, thick, packed earth walls of Chinese cities and fortifications, though they were useful in positional warfare, and they were difficult to transport. Cast iron was a cheap material, and manufacturing

---

[3] Needham, *Science and Civilization*, 295–6.

cannons and guns was not particularly expensive. The cannon were hauled back to the Ming capital and buried to prevent anyone else using them, but they were otherwise discarded.

The treatment of these cannon demonstrates the place of cannon and guns in the context of Chinese warfare in the fourteenth and fifteenth centuries. Kenneth Chase is surely correct to point to the pull that the demands of war made on gun development. Since guns did not appear to offer a solution to steppe cavalry for Chinese armies, they did not press for more development. But guns were extremely useful in siege and naval warfare, both critical modes of combat for empire builders. Guns, and particularly cannon, were less useful in the open field. Handguns might slightly improve the fortunes of an infantry army attempting to fend off a steppe cavalry force without changing the overall tactical balance of power. Of course, seen in this light, the combination of walls and guns makes a great deal of sense. Bow and arrow or crossbow and bolt were still needed for volume, speed, and reliability in the missile contests of Chinese and steppe warfare. Even naval contests were, for the most part, anti-personnel battles fought primarily with missile weapons, sometimes followed by hand-to-hand weapons.

Chinese gun development matured in the thirteenth and fourteenth centuries as warfare incorporated the new capabilities of handguns and cannon. Guns were now understood, but no one conceived of a further broadening of their possibilities. Much of the combat that established the Ming dynasty was naval, frequently combined with siege operations. Peace, however, dramatically diminished the number of battles fought by the Ming army. Knowledge of gun and gunpowder making became more restricted outside of the military, and bureaucratic controls were placed on who within the government had access to that information. What further advances there were tended to come from active duty officers campaigning on the borders. This was a much smaller group of people than during the twelfth and thirteenth centuries, and fewer people meant less innovation. Guns became a fact of warfare and military life, leading to an acceptance of what they were and what they could do. This weapon was now so familiar that it seemed as though there was nowhere else for it to develop.

The creation of the Ming dynasty

By 1279, the very last remnants of the Song dynasty had been completely destroyed. The Mongols were now the unquestioned rulers of China under the rubric of the Yuan dynasty, a Chinese-style regime created by Khubilai Khan in 1272 in order to diminish Chinese resistance to foreign control. Khubilai exploited Chinese resources in his struggle with his brother in the steppe, as well as in his desultory adventure against the Japanese discussed in the previous chapter. When he died in 1294, the Yuan state was an odd patchwork of conflicting institutions and ideologies. Although nominally a Chinese imperial structure, in reality its resources were haphazardly distributed among the Mongol aristocracy and the imperial clan without regard for the subject population or the realities of finance. Khubilai's grandson and successor, Temür, succeeded in having himself declared Khaghan over all the Mongol khanates in Eurasia in 1304 as the result of a decisive victory in September of 1301. This was probably the highest point of Mongol unity, notional as it was, since the reign of Chinghis.

When Temür died in 1307, Mongol rule began a long slide into chaos. Temür had designated a successor in the hope of avoiding the usual bloodshed that accompanied the death of a Mongol leader, but his son predeceased him and he died before designating another. Given the violent struggles for the throne that marked the remaining decades of Mongol rule, it is unlikely that Temür's attempts to manage his succession would have worked even if his son had outlived him. Local Chinese society was mostly left alone under the Yuan dynasty as long as it remained peaceful. The trend toward local leadership and activity that had developed so strongly during the Song dynasty as a result of the oversupply of qualified men to serve in government supported this implicit pact with the Mongol government. Relatively few Chinese served in the upper reaches of the Yuan government, and loyalty to the imperial institutions was limited. When religious and regional rebellions began to erupt in the mid-fourteenth century, and court politics hobbled the ability of the few effective generals to suppress them, the dynasty broke apart.

Zhu Yuanzhang (1328–98), the man who eventually emerged victorious from the enormous struggles for power in China and founded the Ming dynasty (1368–1644), began his life in abject poverty. While his background and personality were certainly unique among Chinese founding emperors, the fact that the dynasty he established began its path to conquest in southern China is even more peculiar. Unlike any other great dynasty in Chinese history, Ming power was forged in an extended series of naval battles and sieges up and down the Yangzi River. This was the logical return to the military environment of the twelfth and thirteenth centuries, and the struggles between the Jurchen Jin, Song, and Mongols. Khubilai had been forced to build a navy to defeat the Song, but it was a strange branch of the military for the Mongols, and it crumbled after he died.

While the Yuan dynasty was struggling politically and militarily in north China and the steppe, Chinese strongmen struggled for power in the south. Three regimes consolidated their rule on the Yangzi River in the 1350s and 1360s: Chen Youliang in the upper reaches, Zhu Yuanzhang in the middle, and Zhang Shicheng, whose cache of iron cannons we discussed above, on the lower reaches. Siege and naval warfare became combined, as the walls of many cities abutted the Yangzi and other waterways. It even became possible for the castles of a ship to overtop the walls, allowing the attacker to fire down on to a city's defenders. City walls were soon moved back from the water's edge to prevent this sort of attack. Cannon and handguns continued in their previous roles as anti-personnel weapons, though they were still incapable of breaking through city walls or sinking ships.

Once again, warfare in China demonstrated all of the aspects of early modern warfare in Europe. Heavily fortified cities were almost impossible to capture without long sieges, though these sorts of operations were difficult to carry out while fending off the other armies of one's opponent. The various regimes could field armies of a hundred thousand men without exhausting all of their troops. Multiple forces maneuvered over extensive territory fighting pitched battles that often achieved very little territorial gain. The regimes themselves were resilient, possessing enough resources in men and material, and enough political and institutional strength, to withstand serious setbacks. This was important because casualties could be appallingly high, as when Zhu Yuanzhang ambushed Chen Youliang's army near Nanjing in 1360, killing 20,000 men, and capturing a hundred large warships, and several hundred smaller ships along with their crews. Yet Chen returned to the struggle the following year, and even after another naval defeat, was able to rebuild his fleet in 1362.

The turning point in Ming fortunes was Zhu Yuanzhang's decisive victory over Chen Youliang at Lake Poyang in 1363. Chen's newly rebuilt fleet sailed downstream, entered Lake Poyang, and laid siege to the city of Nanchang. His fleet was centered around massive three-decker ships with armored castles, each holding 2,000 to 3,000 men. These vessels were clearly designed to function as moving fortifications capable of dominating any other ship. His entire force was reportedly 300,000 men; while this was likely an exaggeration, even including the men on the smaller ships, it probably numbered more than 200,000 men. Even this enormous force could not rapidly overwhelm Nanchang, and with both sides making great use of firearms the siege ground on and on. After eighty-five days, Chen had already suffered a strategic defeat, and was anxious for a way out of the situation. He had presumably begun the campaign planning to capture Nanchang and, by so doing, lure Zhu Yuanzhang into a direct confrontation with his superior fleet. If Zhu showed up before the city fell, Chen might still have expected to defeat Zhu's fleet, and thus force the city to capitulate. Unfortunately for Chen, the city held out, and Zhu was preoccupied with internal matters. So, when the defenders offered a truce with a set surrender date, Chen accepted, even though he suspected that it was a play for time.

Zhu finally arrived at the lake on August 28 with a reported 1,000 ships and 100,000 men. Once he had placed forts at the mouth of the lake to contain Chen's fleet, he sailed into a four-day naval battle that commenced the following day. With handguns, bows, and crossbows, the two fleets fired away at each other to little effect on the first day. The second day Zhu took advantage of a favorable wind and used gunpowder-packed fire ships to burn a proportion of Chen's close-packed ships. Several hundred warships were destroyed and 60,000 casualties inflicted, but Chen's fleet was still not broken. Meanwhile, a land force Zhu had dispatched earlier relieved the siege of Nanchang. Zhu could still not make much of an inroad against Chen's fleet, and he fell back to blockading positions on September 2. Had Chen immediately broken out of the lake, he might have recovered the initiative and at least dealt Zhu a serious naval defeat. As it was, it took Chen until October 3 before he broke out. Zhu managed to get upstream from Chen and send down fire ships before the two fleets closed and clumped into ship-to-ship combat. While this inconclusive fight continued, Chen was struck and killed by an arrow, handing Zhu an unexpectedly decisive victory.

Chen's bad luck still did not prevent some of his fleet from returning home, and it took Zhu Yuanzhang until 1365, after a great deal of campaigning, to take control of Chen's former territories. It was finally Zhang Shicheng's turn in late December of 1366. Although the city of Hangzhou fell quickly before Zhu's 200,000-strong army, Zhang's capital at Suzhou would prove a different matter. Despite relatively weak fortifications, Suzhou held out for ten months. Zhu's army completely enclosed the city in a circumvallation, and pounded it with artillery. Ten months of firing resulted in that rare occurrence in Chinese city fortifications, a wall breach. Zhang was soon captured and the city, and the regime, fell.

It would take another five years to drive the Mongols back to the steppe, after which Zhu Yuanzhang settled down to run his new empire. But the remnants of the Yuan dynasty were not destroyed, having dealt the Ming army two serious defeats in 1372. The Mongols would remain a looming threat to the Ming, if sometimes only in the imperial court's imagination, until the end of the dynasty in 1644. Guns had played a key role in the battles that established the Ming, and were a regular part of the army's equipment, but they could not yet solve the military problem of steppe cavalry.

Gunpowder and the Great Wall

Building of what we now know as the Great Wall began in the middle of the fifteenth century in response to Mongol raiding, though earlier dynasties had constructed similar fortifications from time to time.[4] Sections of wall were initially constructed as local responses to that raiding, and only gradually linked into a continuous defense line. This was not a xenophobic response to non-Chinese, or an attempt to divide what was China from the steppe, but rather an ad hoc measure to mitigate a particular military problem. It took some time for the imperial court to sanction wall building as a policy, and to provide extra funds to support it. These long walls had an ancient pedigree in Chinese history, but they were not the walls of the first emperor of China, as they are so often described. Indeed, their construction was not so much a policy, as the failure of policy. Unable to decide either to advance or to withdraw the Ming army to more defensible positions, the court chose to adopt a temporary measure that effectively became permanent.

The Great Wall was not a total failure in as much as it did make raiding more difficult for small bands of steppe cavalry. This is hard to quantify, since we are only informed when a raid succeeded in getting through, but the Great Wall considerably raised the stakes for a would-be steppe raider. A force not only had to get through the wall on the way in, it also had to get back through it on the way out, possibly while laden with booty and being pursued. Larger armies were more able to break through, though this was still time consuming, and the wall may have tended to increase the difficulty of raiding so much that only a very serious enemy was willing to make the attempt. The invading Manchu army in the seventeenth century was able to penetrate the Great Wall line seemingly at will, for example, but large armies like those of the Manchus preferred to use the main roads that had strong fortifications blocking strategic passes. Well-garrisoned positions were still extremely difficult to overcome.

Guns were placed along the Great Wall to enhance its defensive strength. Both cannon and handguns were issued to the garrisons, which improved their ability to fend off raids without creating a completely impermeable barrier. Placing guns on a fortification made perfect sense, as we have seen, as a way of increasing the range and killing power of infantrymen

---

[4] Arthur Waldron, *The Great Wall of China: From History to Myth*, Cambridge: Cambridge University Press, 1990.

while protecting them from the mobility of cavalrymen. The best situation for infantry armed with early handguns was to wait for attack behind a defensive wall. Ming strategy on the northern border was defensive, at least as much for financial reasons as any other, and the construction of the Great Wall was a means to avoid facing steppe cavalry in the open field. Since guns by themselves did not provide a sufficient margin of superiority over steppe armies, fortifications were necessary.

The Great Wall should not be seen in terms of the repair or revival of a simple and ineffective ancient barrier against the steppe threat. It was neither ancient nor simple nor ineffective. Rather, the Ming dynasty's Great Wall must be seen in the context of warfare increasingly marked by cannon and handgun. Earlier dynasties also built long walls for defense against steppe, and even other Chinese, armies with mixed results. The Ming Great Wall was created not so much because similar fortifications had been built in the past, but because guns and walls together made for a potent combination. Chinese infantrymen had become comfortable using guns from fortifications or ships; walls allowed them to use these slow-firing weapons against steppe raiders. Initially the walls merely redirected steppe raiders, but as the line of walls was completed, it was necessary actually to defend them.

Zheng He

While the Ming army was pulling back from the steppe and establishing the Great Wall as its northern border, the Yongle emperor was dispatching a series of naval expeditions to the south and west. Under the command of the Muslim eunuch Admiral Zheng He, these events were practically insignificant at the time and only received much attention in the twentieth century, after the European voyages of discovery had become a symbol of Western technological prowess and outward expansion. Strictly speaking, Zheng's fleet was not exploring, in the sense of going where no one had gone before; they followed the paths of pre-existing trade routes. His seven voyages between 1405 and 1433 projected Ming power to South and Southeast Asia. They were military and diplomatic expeditions, well armed and provided with soldiers, and intended by the Ming court to make its power known.[5]

Chinese trading in South and Southeast Asia began before Zheng He's voyages and continued after the court ended them. These gun-armed fleets could be massive, with the 1405 expedition comprising 255 ships

---

[5] Edward L. Dreyer, *Zheng He: China and the Oceans in the Early Ming, 1405–1433*, New York: Longman, 2006, 3.

and 27,800 men, and were not intended as economically viable trading ventures.[6] The largest ships were 115 to 135 meters long and 48 to 55 meters wide, demonstrating that the Chinese possessed impressive ocean-going as well as riverine ships.[7] Keeping in mind Chen Youliang's massive three-decker warships with armored castles, Zheng He's fleet stems directly from an impressive naval tradition. Moreover, even after European ships discovered and hooked into the pre-existing Asian trading network, large Chinese merchant vessels still carried the bulk of all goods in the area.

Merchants from southern China engaged in extensive trade with South and Southeast Asia, and merchants from all over Asia traveled to China for trade. The Ming court initially seemed to support this activity, or at least did not object to it, but later became quite hostile. Many of the Ming court's difficulties with maritime trade were tied up with the problem of the *wokou*, or "Japanese" (lit. "dwarf") pirates, discussed below. With respect to Zheng He, we can see a desire on the part of the Ming court, at least temporarily, to make its presence officially known in the surrounding region by means of court-sponsored expeditions. But the Chinese government had no need to promote trade where it already existed, or to work hard to attract merchants to its shores. Guns of foreign design from Turkey as well as Europe did, however, reach China through these channels. Indeed, by 1644 the Chinese recognized the superiority of foreign firearms, ranking Ottoman muskets as the most effective, followed by European muskets.[8]

Even had the Chinese government maintained its official naval activities in maritime Asia, its ships would still not have been able to stand up to European vessels in the eighteenth century. By the late sixteenth century, the superiority of southern Chinese and Korean ships over Japanese vessels prompted Hideyoshi to try to obtain European ships from the Portuguese. While the Chinese and Japanese eagerly sought the latest guns and handguns from the Europeans, their warship designs languished. Despite the fact that every Chinese dynasty had to cross multiple rivers to create an empire controlling north and south China, and therefore every successful dynasty was forced to create a riverine navy at least temporarily, no Chinese dynasty ever required a sea-going navy.

---

[6] Ibid., 122–6.

[7] The size of the vessels has been a matter of debate, but modern archaeology has resolved the problem in favor of the extremely large figures contained in Chinese sources. See ibid., 99–113.

[8] Zhao Shizhen, *Shengqi Pu*, Changluo Zhengshi, 1941, 2/3a–b, and repeated in Qian Zhan, *Chengshou Choulie*, 5/18a–b in *Zhongguo Bingshu Jicheng*, Vol. XVIII, Beijing: Jiefangjun Chubanshe, 1994. Cited and translated in Chase, *Firearms: A Global History to 1700*, 2.

Blue-ocean navies were often useful, as we will see during the discussion of the Japanese invasion of Korea, but not vital. Zheng He's voyages highlight the trade that existed, not a missed opportunity for China to have become a center of world trade.

Wokou

Before the Ming dynasty was even established, the Korean king sent an envoy to Zhu Yuanzhang to obtain help against Japanese pirates. What he asked for and received were guns, though they were only of limited help against the pirates. *Wokou* raids continued through the fourteenth and fifteenth centuries, ranging all the way from Southeast Asia to Korea. From the Chinese perspective, they only became a particularly serious problem in the mid-sixteenth century. Unlike the position of the sea lords discussed by Peter Shapinsky, who were sometimes called pirates and sometimes called loyal servants, the *wokou* fit the description of pirate quite closely. It is true that many of them were probably, like European and other merchants throughout history, pirates when an opportunity arose and peaceful traders when trade was more advantageous. But the Ming state was concerned to manage trade as it saw fit, and to suppress anyone who raided the coast.

It is unclear what percentage of the *wokou* were actually Japanese, and it seems likely that the percentage changed over time, with a higher number in the earlier period and a lower number later on. The most damaging raids were conducted with a great deal of local Chinese assistance. We should not, of course, hold too closely to strict categories of modern nationality. *Wokou* raids increased in frequency when there was political turmoil in Japan and the central authorities could not control provincial lords. These Japanese raiders or merchants were connected to the East and Southeast Asian maritime world, which included a mobile population of sailors and their families. Sailors from one place might take up residence in another and marry locally. Their offspring might be considered transcultural, or multicultural, from the false perspective that each locality was part of a monolithic national culture that coincided with a unified polity. More realistically, the sailors and their families were part of a maritime culture that also had ties to various lands.

This floating population and culture was fundamentally at odds with the ideology and control methods of agricultural land-based political power. Land powers like the various governments, local and central, of China or Japan, expected their subject populations to remain in fairly fixed locations where they could be taxed and controlled. The maritime population moved when it wanted to, and often lived in places inaccessible to land powers, like islands. It was therefore very difficult to control the actions of these people. The Japanese central government was sometimes unable and sometimes unwilling to control the *wokou*, something that complicated relations between China and Japan.

The Japanese central government was in no position to control the *wokou* during the reign of Zhu Yuanzhang, and in any case refused to establish diplomatic relations with the Ming court. The Ming emperor built forts up and down the coast to improve defenses against the *wokou*, and ordered the navy to patrol the coast, but raiding continued. This changed with a return to political stability in Japan, and regular relations were established during the reign of the Yongle emperor, with Japanese tribute missions permitted every ten years on two ships with two hundred men. Tribute missions to China, whether by land or sea, were extremely profitable ventures for those involved, as a considerable amount of private trading was allowed, and the imperial government always gave more valuable gifts than it received. For the Chinese court, these missions affirmed Chinese suzerainty over the world; for the foreign participants they were a chance to make a good profit.

The size of the Japanese mission was increased to three ships and three hundred men in 1433. For the next century, Japanese tribute missions continued under these terms, as did occasional *wokou* raids. The Japanese government did occasionally capture and extradite *wokou* to China, but it also occasionally threatened the Ming court with *wokou* raids. After the Onin War (1467–77) in Japan (see chapter 2), political disunity led to competing Japanese missions to China. In 1523 the Ouchi and Hosokawa families each sent missions to Ningbo, which ended up fighting each other. Despite this, several more missions reached China before relations broke down entirely in 1549, probably because of political turmoil in Japan.

The 1523 incident persuaded the court to ban all foreign trade in southern China. This prevented foreign merchants from collecting debts owed them by Chinese merchants, and stimulated raiding and smuggling. As long as the ban was not too strenuously enforced, raiding was light and smuggling made up for much of the legal trade. Unfortunately, this made criminals out of traders, and brought more hardened criminals into the process of trading. The court was then caught between strict enforcement, which alienated locals, including some powerful families, but which did not stop *wokou* raids, and lax enforcement, which allowed raiding and smuggling to increase. What the court did not understand was that there was an explosion of international trade during the sixteenth century, in part because of the arrival of European traders (the Portuguese first arrived in Chinese waters in 1516), which was fueling enormous demand for goods in the maritime world.

As *wokou* raids increased not just in frequency, but also in seriousness, with market towns burned and garrison posts captured, the court increased its military presence around the Yangzi delta. Increasingly facing imperial troops armed with guns, the *wokou* also began to use more guns. Indeed, guns and gunpowder were two of the contraband goods that the government had tried to prevent Chinese merchants/smugglers from selling abroad from early on. These merchants were also guilty of building ships that exceeded the government's size limitations. Many Chinese officials were quite clear that the majority of *wokou* were, in fact, Chinese pirates, often connected to important families on the coast. They noted with some surprise when a few Japanese were actually found in the midst of the *wokou*. Of course, "*wokou*" had originally referred to Japanese pirates specifically, and later became a general category for pirates. By the mid-sixteenth century, not only had Chinese taken over the majority of the *wokou* operations, vastly improving the quality of their ships, but trade in firearms was widespread. People from Fujian were particularly observed to have been selling firearms to the Japanese.

Although the Portuguese sold cannon and arquebuses to all the powers in East Asia, and sometimes gave them as gifts, the numbers in use can only be explained by local copying of these weapons. Portuguese artillerymen were brought in to teach cannon founding where possible, and their base at Macao (established 1557) would become a regular source of weapons and skills, but the technical demands of reproducing arquebuses were well within the capability of East Asian blacksmiths. Even cannon were not beyond the ability of Chinese craftsmen, many of whom would have already possessed a good working knowledge of Chinese cannon manufacturing. Here it is important to stress not only that Chinese artisans had already been making guns and handguns for centuries, but also that China in the sixteenth century was the most developed industrial power in the world. Arquebuses were easy to reproduce and likely, as in Europe and South Asia, cheaper than bows or crossbows.

Perhaps the greatest problem underlying the government's difficulties in combating the *wokou* was the dilapidated state of the military establishment in the area. On paper, there appeared to be sufficient patrol boats and soldiers to keep order, but the reality was very different. Less than half the stated number of soldiers was actually available, and they had been paid only intermittently; there were very few horses; often less than a fifth of the indicated ships even existed, of which most were in disrepair. Once the government began to address these problems by placing competent military and civilian leaders in charge, the *wokou* problem diminished markedly. It was mostly over by the 1560s.

Qi Jiguang is the general most closely associated with the successful suppression of the *wokou*, though several other men were equally important. Qi recorded his training and deployment system, making it clear how much Western handguns and cannon had become central to southern Chinese military methods. These weapons were used in conjunction with ships, adding mobility to their deployment as well as hitting power. Of five squads of ten men and one officer each, two squads used Portuguese arquebuses, two manned two cannon, several flame-throwers, and some rockets, and the fifth squad used other types of firearms. Infantry squads were less firearm-dependent, in part for reasons of money, but they were trained to operate as units combining a variety of weapons.

The southern Chinese troops trained to fight the *wokou* made extensive use of Portuguese guns and cannon; on land they fought as infantrymen, and on ships they used firearms rather than boarding tactics. Their infantry squads used spears and close fighting weapons, stressing cooperation to overcome the strength of Japanese swordsmanship and individual prowess. These troops were also accustomed to their enemies using arquebuses, both foreign and locally copied. Unit cohesion was critical. Archery was no longer stressed, but overall skills in martial arts and high morale were. Fortifications also played an important role in blunting the effects of raiding. In other words, the military revolution of the twelfth and thirteenth centuries, which had advanced in the fourteenth century and deepened in the fifteenth, took a further step forward in the sixteenth century with the improvement in small unit tactics and the adoption of Western guns.

Korea

The army that Toyotomi Hideyoshi dispatched to Korea in May of 1592 was the product of the preceding decades of warfare in Japan, in which arquebuses and infantry warfare had become increasingly important. This shift from earlier practice continued during the campaigns against first the Koreans, and then the Ming Chinese forces that came to their aid. Over the course of the invasions the Japanese increased the number of arquebuses fielded by the army, together with the number of cannon employed by the navy. It availed them very little, because Hideyoshi's basic strategy was so deeply flawed. His grand plans to conquer China were entirely unrealistic, let alone his even more far-fetched idea of going on to conquer India. On the operational level, Hideyoshi on the one hand failed to secure control of the sea between Japan and Korea and, on the other, failed to plan for a lengthy stay in Korea (beyond promising the lands that would be conquered to his troops). Hideyoshi seems to have believed that the Japanese army would be so tactically superior that battlefield victories would overcome any other problems. Not only did the Japanese army not win every battle, its initial successes exacerbated, rather than ameliorated, Hideyoshi's fundamental operational and strategic mistakes.

In 1586, Hideyoshi sent envoys to the Korea court to ask them to help him in his plan to conquer Ming China. The Koreans rejected this idea, and Japanese envoys continued to attempt to persuade the Korean king for the next few years, without success. The king and his court were concerned about a Japanese invasion, but they were uncertain whether Hideyoshi was really intending to invade or just posturing. On several occasions, Japanese envoys presented the Koreans with Portuguese-style arquebuses, perhaps to demonstrate the sort of high tech weapons they possessed. A Korean embassy to Japan, in turn, presented the Japanese with Portuguese cannons. Neither side was entirely clear on the other's intentions. The Korean court was divided by factions with vastly different assessments of the likelihood of invasion, and both main factions corresponded with the Japanese. The Koreans also understood that Hideyoshi's plan to conquer China was impossible. Hideyoshi, for his part, could not accept the Koreans' unwillingness to assist him, or to recognize his greatness. He was confident that the Chinese would simply flee at the sight of his army. By 1591, Hideyoshi resolved to punish the Koreans on his way to conquering the Ming.

Hideyoshi claimed he would raise an army of a million men, which would include some 300,000 arquebuses. The actual invasion force was about 160,000 men, with another 140,000-man reserve mobilized for a possible second wave. A large part of this army was composed of veteran warriors and experienced generals, but there was also a significant component of non-samurai, who were in many cases the men armed with arquebuses. This distinction is reflected in some of the letters sent home by Japanese leaders, demanding that more arquebuses be sent and that even samurai should be so armed. The influence of the West is also apparent in that Konishi Yukinaga, one of the three overall commanders, was a Christian convert.

When the Japanese invasion began in 1592, the Koreans were woefully unprepared for it. The army was poorly trained, led, and equipped, with only the navy armed with some cannon. It proved impossible to oppose arquebuses with bows, because of the guns' greater range. Despite a few brave stands, the Korean forces were quickly defeated and driven off the field and out of the cities. They fared somewhat better at sea, inflicting a good number of casualties on the Japanese with their cannon, but with the navy poorly led, the Japanese rapidly defeated it. Indeed, much of the initial failure of the Korean navy was self-inflicted with the commanders of both of the Kyongsang fleets ordering their own ships scuttled. Some Korean generals believed that Japanese arquebuses were too inaccurate and slow to be a threat, and paid a terrible price for that evaluation. A favorite Japanese tactic familiar to us from the previous chapter was to establish dug-in lines of arquebus men and induce the Koreans to charge them.

Korean resistance soon collapsed, and the major question for the Japanese commanders was whether to consolidate their initial gains in preparation for a more systematic advance and a possible defense against Ming troops if they intervened, or to try and seize the entire kingdom as quickly as possible. They chose the latter course, though Hideyoshi soon dispatched more troops to support them and admonished them to consolidate their positions. Korean guerrilla forces were already forcing the Japanese to travel in large groups, however, and the occupation was not proving as easy as the quick battlefield victories. The Japanese were also helped by the Ming army's preoccupation with a revolt in Ningxia, which prevented the best Chinese generals and troops from immediately going to aid Korea. By the middle of the year, the Korean king had fled all the way to his northern border with China.

The tide began to turn with a Korean naval victory on June 16, when a fleet of eighty-five ships cobbled together under the command of Yi Sun-sin destroyed twenty-six Japanese ships at Okpo off the southeast coast. Admiral Yi began a string of naval victories using the superior seamanship and cannons originally developed to deal with the *wokou*. A new Korean warship, the turtle boat, saw its first use in these battles, and proved devastating. The turtle boat was an oared ship about 34 meters long, with thick wooden planks and metal spikes covering the deck, armed with one or two large guns, and forty or more smaller guns.[9] Japanese ships depended upon their arquebus fire and boarding tactics, leaving them almost helpless before an enemy who stayed at cannon range. When the Koreans did close with the Japanese, they made extensive use of bombs and other fire weapons. In short order, Admiral Yi crushed the Japanese navy, annihilating fleet after fleet with his superior tactics and weaponry.

Korean guerrilla activity was taking its toll on the Japanese even as Ming troops were beginning to trickle across the border. Just as Hideyoshi

[9] Samuel Hawley, *The Imjin War: Japan's Sixteenth-Century Invasion of Korea and Attempt to Conquer China*, Berkeley: The Royal Asiatic Society and The Institute of East Asian Studies, University of California, Berkeley, 2005, 195–8, disputes the notion that the turtle boats were covered with metal plates.

underestimated the Chinese, the Chinese underestimated the Japanese. Neither Japanese nor Chinese thought much of the Koreans, who were caught in the middle. Hideyoshi thought his army would be able to supply itself by light taxation on the Koreans at a level that would not instigate rebellion, but this generally failed. Japanese reprisals against Korean resistance were brutal, hardening Korean attitudes. In all of this, firearms were continually emphasized in the assistance the Ming court provided the Koreans, the warnings the Koreans gave the Chinese about the number of arquebuses possessed by the Japanese, and the tens of thousands of guns the Chinese commanders expected would be required to repulse the Japanese.[10]

The Battle of Pyongyang on February 8, 1593 saw a head-to-head clash between the Ming-Korean army and the Japanese defenders of the city. The city was captured in a brutal assault backed by cannons, fire-arrows, and smoke bombs. Fierce hand-to-hand street fighting dislodged the Japanese, who lost 6,000–7,000 men in the city, another 6,000 who drowned while fleeing, and several hundred more to planned ambushes. Ming dead numbered about 800. The Japanese army had never before faced the sort of firepower brought to bear on them in Pyongyang.[11] This was in many ways the decisive battle of the war, and all subsequent campaigns. The Japanese saw that they could not face Ming cannon, and that as long as the Ming supported the Koreans, they could not conquer Korea. After the Battle of Pyongyang they avoided direct clashes with Ming forces armed with cannon, preferring ambushes and hit-and-run tactics. The Japanese were also required to defend a number of fortified positions.

This was not to say that the war was over; Japanese troops continued to acquit themselves well, fighting an essentially defensive war. Northern Chinese troops not only found Korea unsuitable for cavalry tactics, they found their armaments left them at a severe disadvantage in fighting the Japanese. Horses, bows, and short swords could not contend with muskets and Japanese long swords. Southern Chinese troops, in contrast, were extremely effective, fighting on foot and using polearms to counter

---

[10] For the particular importance of military technology in this war see Kenneth M. Swope, "Crouching Tigers, Secret Weapons: Military Technology Employed during the Sino-Japanese-Korean War, 1592–1598," *The Journal of Military History*, 69 (Jan. 2005), 11–42.

[11] See Kenneth Swope, "The Three Great Campaigns of the Wanli Emperor, 1592–1600: Court, Military and Society in Late Sixteenth-Century China," Ph.D. dissertation, University of Michigan, 2001, 243–8 for the Battle of Pyongyang, and his footnote 341 on page 248 concerning the Japanese casualty figures. Swope's casualty figures, used here, seem to be supported by both Chinese and Japanese scholars.

Japanese swords. The Japanese abandoned Seoul on May 18, 1593, leaving a brutalized population and, surprisingly, significant amounts of supplies. Shortly after the Japanese captured the city of Chinju on July 27, after fierce fighting, and slaughtered perhaps 60,000 inhabitants, peace talks began between the Ming and Japanese. The majority of Ming troops withdrew from Korea as a gesture of good will, leaving behind a small force to train the Korean army, particularly in firearms, and the Japanese fell back to positions on the southeast coast.

The years of farcical diplomacy that followed need not concern us here, but it seems clear from most accounts that not only did the negotiators repeatedly deceive their own masters, but Hideyoshi also did not really understand the military situation in Korea. The Japanese leader seems not to have grasped that his armies had been, in fact, badly beaten on several occasions, and that his grand design was entirely in ruins. Hideyoshi ordered a second invasion of Korea, this time to punish the Koreans, who he felt had slighted him, and to vent his fury at the Ming's unwillingness to acknowledge his greatness. It was a pointless and tragic military adventure, even more filled with Japanese atrocities against the Koreans.

When the second invasion began in 1597, the Japanese had learned enough about the strength of the likely Ming response to proceed cautiously. They had also increased the number of ships transporting troops to Korea, though without really adapting to the Korean and Chinese navies' superior naval technology. Neither the Koreans nor the Chinese, however, had increased naval strength in the interim in order to patrol the crossing points in strength. Indeed, a strong Korean or Chinese navy could have stopped the second invasion before it even really started. Japanese forces were entirely dependent upon food transported from Japan this time, because they had so badly destroyed Korea in the first invasion. Some of the Korean naval unpreparedness was likely due to Yi Sun-sin's dismissal, after he fell foul of factional politics.

The Ming response was quicker the second time around, with somewhat more stress on ship-building, southern Chinese fighting techniques, and firearms. Even before the Chinese fully mobilized, the Japanese offensive collapsed short of reaching Seoul. This was due in part to a defeat at the Battle of Chiksan on October 16, 1597, when a Chinese ambush set up with many cannon crushed the advance guard of the Japanese forces advancing on Seoul, and in part to the arrival of the Chinese and Korean navy, with Yi Sun-sin back in command. On November 2, 1597, at the Battle of Myongyang, or the Miracle at Myongyang as some Koreans would have it, Admiral Yi annihilated a fleet of 133 Japanese ships. Once again, Korean ships armed with cannon, bombs, and smaller caliber firearms, and properly led, decisively defeated Japanese ships dependent upon arquebuses and boarding tactics. With the arrival of the Chinese navy in December, the supply lines to Japan were extremely tenuous.

Ming troops and material poured into Korea to push the Japanese out. By late December 1597, about 40,000 Ming troops, along with 1,000 cannon, 118,000 fire-arrows, almost 93,000 pounds of gunpowder, and more than 2 million pounds of bullets of all sizes were poised to attack Japanese positions.[12] The initial push did not go well, and the war continued into the following year. By then it was clear even to Hideyoshi that the Japanese position was untenable. Even before he died in August, the Japanese began to withdraw. On December 14, at the Battle of Noryang Straits, a Chinese–Korean fleet destroyed more than two hundred Japanese ships with cannon fire. Admiral Yi was killed in this battle, but it was made clear at the end of it all, that Chinese and Korean naval tactics developed to fight the *wokou* were superior to Japanese boarding tactics.

The clash between differently armed gunpowder armies in Korea makes it clear how critical cannon, handguns, and bombs were in East Asian warfare in the late sixteenth century. Guns became more important over the course of the conflict, though each side tended to emphasize its manner of gun use, rather than adopt the methods of its opponents. This was not necessarily the paralyzing effect of a given group's military culture; all sides could point to victories won using their particular methods. Neither side felt compelled to revise its technology, only its tactics. Here again, the results of the battlefield reinforced preconceived notions of warfare. People learned the lessons they were inclined to learn, and even those were strongly affected by their political implications.

FURTHER READING

Albert Chan, *The Glory and Fall of the Ming Dynasty*, Norman, OK: University of Oklahoma Press, 1982.

Jonathan Clements, *Pirate King: Coxinga and the Fall of the Ming Dynasty*, Stroud: Sutton, 2004.

Edward L. Dreyer, *Early Ming China*, Stanford: Stanford University Press, 1982. *Zheng He: China and the Oceans in the Early Ming, 1405–1433*, New York: Longman, 2006.

Peter Lorge, *War, Politics and Society in Early Modern China, 900–1795*, London and New York: Routledge, 2005.

[12] Swope, "The Three Great Campaigns," 346–7.

Joseph Needham, *Science and Civilization in China*, Vol. V, part 7: *Military Technology: The Gunpowder Epic*, Cambridge: Cambridge University Press, 1986.

Henry Serruys, *The Mongols and Ming China: Customs and History*, London: Variorum Reprints, 1987.

Kwan-wai So, *Japanese Piracy in Ming China during the 16th Century*, East Lansing: Michigan State University Press, 1975.

Kenneth Swope, "The Three Great Campaigns of the Wanli Emperor, 1592–1600: Court, Military and Society in Late Sixteenth-Century China," Ph.D. dissertation, University of Michigan, 2001.

Arthur Waldron, *The Great Wall of China: From History to Myth*, Cambridge: Cambridge University Press, 1990.

Kozo Yamamura, (ed.), *The Cambridge History of Japan*, Vol. III: *Medieval Japan*, Cambridge: Cambridge University Press, 1990.

4　Southeast Asia

The military revolution in China gave the Ming army an initial advantage in its wars in Southeast Asia, but that advantage was quickly lost as guns spread to its neighbors in that region. Ming armies conquered and controlled Đại Việt from 1407 to 1427, and Đại Việt absorbed much of the Ming's military technology. Once they were sufficiently capable with guns, they were able to defeat the Ming forces and drive them out of their country. Đại Việt then expanded its own territory using left-over Ming guns, and their own reproductions of them. The Maw Shans and Lan Na benefited similarly from contact with the Ming, through either conflict or trade, and extensively adopted guns. The northern part of Southeast Asia was thus familiar with guns more than a century before European contact became regular and sustained. Indeed, some early European travelers were favorably impressed with several Southeast Asian troops' facility with muskets, particularly those of Đại Việt.

Maritime Southeast Asia was also acquainted with guns, but they were not widely used. It is unclear why this was the case, but their contact with the Ming was much more limited in scale than that of the mainland Southeast Asian kingdoms, and their limited access to the necessary resources may well have handicapped them. As in all the other Asian polities, Southeast Asians were quite familiar with guns long before Europeans arrived, and exploited their military potential to the extent that they could. That potential was quite limited, even after the introduction of better European weapons, and it is not surprising that they initially played a very limited role in actual fighting.

Southeast Asian rulers eagerly sought better gunpowder weapons, but even when they were available, they were incorporated into existing military practice instead of revolutionizing it.[1] Before the eighteenth

---

[1] This discussion follows Leonard Y. Andaya, "Interactions with the Outside World and Adaptation in Southeast Asian Society, 1500–1800," in Nicholas Tarling (ed.), *The Cambridge History of Southeast Asia*, Vol. I, Cambridge: Cambridge University Press, 1992, 385–7.

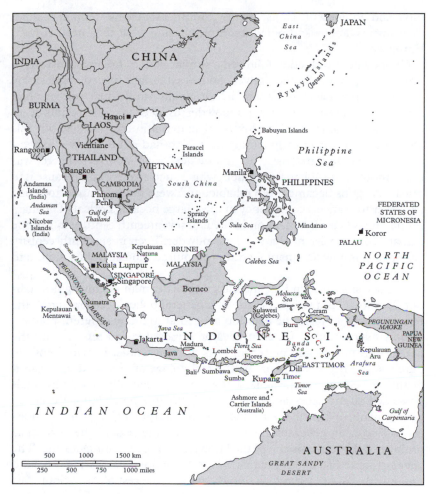

Map 5 Southeast Asia

century, both guns and gunpowder were manufactured in Southeast Asia, and many of the weapons produced were of high quality. Metallurgical skills in weapon making and the casting of religious artifacts transferred well into cannon founding and handgun manufacture. In the eighteenth century, however, European firearms became increasingly complex and technologically advanced, as well as more effective. A sword and dagger maker could no longer reproduce a European handgun, nor, for that matter, could a captured European soldier. Cannon and handgun manufacture became a highly technical, specialized skill, requiring advanced tools and equipment. Consequently, Southeast Asians stopped making their own weapons and relied upon purchasing what they needed from Europeans.

Gunpowder production followed a similar path to firearms. Instead of producing gunpowder themselves, Southeast Asians turned increasingly to foreign purchases to obtain it. Originally, individual soldiers had actually produced their own gunpowder as needed. The results were quite uneven, often leaving clumps of material in the powder, but this could be tolerated in early handguns, which had a much lower expectation of reliability. Inconsistent gunpowder, or an incorrect charge, was much more of a problem for cannon, where such an error could cause it to burst.[2] As guns became more reliable, and were manufactured to much narrower tolerances, consistency in the charge became critical. The mass production of cast iron cannon in the late seventeenth century in Europe demanded a consistent charge of gunpowder. Even in sixteenth-century Europe, gunpowder manufacturing required considerable skill and knowledge.

The decision to abandon gun and gunpowder manufacturing throughout Southeast Asia was not made as a general policy decision across the region; it was a pragmatic decision arrived at in many different political centers over decades. When it became impossible to keep up with the newest technology and better imports were available, it made sense to purchase the better weapons. As the technology of guns and gun manufacturing became so specialized that only a relatively few individuals possessed all the necessary knowledge, it became possible for European governments to control the technology. Not surprisingly, given the interest of European governments in dominating the region, they expressly prohibited the transmission of the knowledge of gun manufacturing. The effect of these two developments was to leave Southeast Asia far behind not only the West in gun technology, but also the rest of Asia. Southeast Asian rulers made themselves completely dependent upon Europe just as the Europeans were restricting the spread of the best weapons. Outdated and antiquated weapons continued in use, and Europeans occasionally dumped stocks of old weapons on the market, but Southeast Asian technological progress in firearms slowed nearly to a halt.

While Southeast Asia was shifting to reliance on Europe for its guns, it was also undergoing what would prove to be the final stages of large-scale political consolidations. Since these political developments culminated

---

[2] Handguns were less susceptible to bursting because the pressures involved were much smaller, and the barrels of the handguns were proportionately much thicker, than in cannon.

after the arrival of European influence in the region, it seems circumstantially possible that the changes came as a result of that contact. If that were the case, then a secondary question would be whether the European military revolution caused or contributed to this effect. Unfortunately, there is no simple cause and effect relationship discernible across the entire region. It seems likely that European influence was significant in some places, such as Aceh in the early sixteenth century (though Turkish influence was even more important), but not in others, like Java, where a more coherent territory and ethnic identity contributed to the formation of a larger polity. Generally speaking, European influence in the form of conquest or coercion was quite important in archipelagic Southeast Asia, and only marginally important on the mainland.[3] On the other hand, European weaponry was just as significant on the mainland as in the archipelago. European commercial and mercenary activities were influential from the sixteenth century, with the First Toungoo dynasty of the sixteenth century more dependent upon Portuguese firearms than anywhere in the archipelago.

It is critical to understand that the political and social diversity in Southeast Asia that existed before the introduction of guns did not disappear after their arrival. Even the advent of European influence could not wholly stamp out that diversity despite frequently brutal attempts to configure local society to European colonial interests. Guns did not unify the forms of Southeast Asian states, even though they were important in the developing polities and in the interstate struggles. It is therefore difficult to observe the diverse reactions to guns in Southeast Asia because it was diverse before and after the new weapons began to be used. Rather than in diverse reactions to a single military practice, our proof of varied reactions lies in the continued political, social, and cultural variety throughout the region until the present.

The modern political boundaries of Southeast Asia obfuscate the often-fragmented socio-political landscape of the region in pre-modern and even early modern times. Modern nationalist agendas have created "natural" and "historical" polities to support whatever current regime controls a particular territory, or asserted that the contemporary state apparatus has some objective reason to rule over obviously disparate groups. Contemporary states are, in a sense, tightly linked by their very nature to a Western understanding of political organization.

A comprehensive account of the variety of military, political, and social responses to both the Chinese and European introductions of guns into

---

[3] Barbara Watson Andaya, "Political Development between the Sixteenth and Eighteenth Centuries," in Tarling, *Cambridge History of Southeast Asia*, Vol. I, 417.

Southeast Asia would be both cumbersome and quite beyond the available scholarship. Moreover, a very serious issue arises with respect to defining the political units of analysis. It may well be that any reasonable theoretical definition of the ideal political, social, economic, or military unit for study would have no practical value owing to a lack of corresponding historical sources. We are therefore left with the usual historical problem of going where the documents are, even while acknowledging that this favors literate societies and more complex governments. The secondary literature on the better-documented societies is, consequently, more developed, further prejudicing our selection. It is also often the case that there are descriptions of non-literate societies by literate outsiders, be they Asian or European, which must be used with great care. Fortunately, these limitations are not a concern for our present comparison because it is possible to choose several well-studied polities that followed different historical trajectories with respect to their reactions to gunpowder weapons.

My choice of the places and times to use as examples is opportunistic; I have followed the line of least resistance and used some of the most recent scholarship in English. Much of this work is highly comparative and accepts, even emphasizes, the utility of Southeast Asia as a unit of analysis. As a direct consequence of this, after a brief discussion of the general geography and culture of Southeast Asia, I will discuss Southeast Asian warfare as a whole rather than attempt to render individual military histories of states or cultures. Following this general discussion, as well as an overview of political developments, I will present brief military histories of Burma (Myanmar), Siam (Thailand), Vietnam, and archipelagic Southeast Asia. Several other polities, contemporary and early modern, are left out of these larger groupings, but will be included where their histories bear on our discussion. This chapter will stop short of the period of European colonialism, leaving that to be taken up in chapter 7.

Geography and culture

The category "Southeast Asia" as a unit for historical study only emerged in the 1950s.[4] Before that time, scholars studying the various cultures and states confined their researches to their area of specialty. Certainly

---

[4] J. D. Legge attributes the first use of the term in a major history to D. G. E. Hall's *A History of South-East Asia*, which appeared in 1955, even though Brian Harrison's *South-East Asia: A Short History* was published the previous year, because Harrison's work was not directed at specialist readers. J. D. Legge, "The Writing of Southeast Asian History," in Tarling, *Cambridge History of Southeast Asia*, Vol. I, 1, fn 1.

Southeast Asian scholars did not previously conceive of the area around their respective modern countries as part of a distinct region. Western scholars have, with some reservations, come to accept the category, and even to discuss the interconnectedness and commonalities that do make it a coherent unit of study. The term's taint of colonialism, as a region constructed by European imperialism, is somewhat obfuscated by its contemporary political reification in organizations like the Association of Southeast Asian Nations. These caveats aside, we must define the territory indicated by the term "Southeast Asia" and discuss its cultural background before exploring the histories of several of the modern states with respect to gunpowder and guns.

There are currently eleven nations comprising Southeast Asia: Brunei, Cambodia, East Timor, Indonesia, Laos, Malaysia, Myanmar (Burma), Philippines, Singapore, Thailand (Siam), and Vietnam. They are divided between the mainland (Cambodia, Laos, Thailand, Vietnam, Myanmar, and parts of Malaysia), and the Malay archipelago to the east and southeast (Brunei, East Timor, Indonesia, Malaysia, Philippines, and Singapore). These groupings are also sometimes called Indochina (or Further India) and maritime Southeast Asia, respectively. Southeast Asia is geographically fragmented both on the mainland and in the archipelago, through a combination of dense jungle, mountainous terrain, extensive river networks, and widely distributed islands. At the same time, the population is relatively small compared with the span of territory. Taken together, then, the earliest political units tended to be fairly small, sometimes no more than a village, with very little real connection to a larger polity. Even when more complex or larger political centers developed, their control over outlying areas was usually weak. Water routes, whether by river or via the sea, were much more important than roads, which were frequently no more than paths. Much of the later political consolidation therefore struggled against not only cultural, but also geographic factors.

Three main polities, Burma, Siam, and Vietnam, developed into large, stable kingdoms running north–south on mainland Southeast Asia between 800 and 1800. Victor Lieberman has presented a convincing argument for mostly indigenous factors in that development, while acknowledging the important contributions of exogenous factors like maritime trade.[5] We shall return to the issue of political consolidation shortly, but with respect to geography, it is important to recognize that these kingdoms spread along the paths of geographic least resistance, and were divided by mountains and jungle. Rather than expending great effort

---

[5] Victor Lieberman, *Strange Parallels: Southeast Asia in Global Context, c.800–1830*, Cambridge: Cambridge University Press, 2003.

to create and maintain east–west transport links to span these physical obstacles, the respective governments concentrated their efforts on developing the agricultural potential of their river valleys and spreading their authority over the populations dispersed in their adjacent highlands. Perhaps, given time, someone would have attempted to create a larger empire that embraced the entire Southeast Asian mainland, but this did not happen before European intervention overtook Burma and Vietnam.

Archipelagic Southeast Asia was not headed toward the same kind of consolidation into larger political units before the arrival of Europeans. The island of Java was a natural center of power given its concentration of land and people, but in the region as a whole, there were simply too many islands and the population was too mobile for any ruler to maintain a high level of exaction from his subjects. A ruler was measured by the number of people he controlled, rather than the amount of land. Trade was much more important in enriching a ruler, but he had to make his port attractive to merchants and ships if he was to gain any revenues from that source. Once again, as with people, trade was highly mobile, and could seek more amenable ports at will. Europeans penetrated the archipelago much earlier and more seriously than mainland Southeast Asia, since they sought spices and transit trade with places like China, and were much more effective in controlling the many small, scattered polities. The geographic dispersion of the archipelago cut both ways, however, as European trading companies also found it difficult to make a profit with their own high administrative overhead costs. Even today, modern states like Indonesia find it difficult to administer their territory.

The culture of Southeast Asia is not, however, simply a mixture of Chinese and South Asian, or Indic, culture, with a later admixture of Islamic influence. While all of those old civilizations exerted great influence on the region, there was also a variety of pre-existing cultures that then absorbed varying amounts of external stimuli. Consequently, both linguistically and culturally, Southeast Asia is not just more populous than Europe, but far more varied. The cultural variety placed similar brakes on political integration, which even the introduction of more universal ideologies like Islam and Theravada Buddhism could only partially ameliorate. Warfare was more effective over time in persuading people to choose sides and identify with a particular political center, but considerable cultural indoctrination was also necessary to make the resulting territorial authority stable or effective. Pockets of culturally distinct groups who did not accept the authority of a distant government, or identify themselves culturally or even racially with the rulers of that government, always existed, particularly in the hills and mountains, or on outlying islands, persisting even into the twenty-first century.

Southeast Asian warfare

Anthony Reid characterized Southeast Asian warfare as virtually the polar opposite of Western warfare, with low casualty rates, few pitched battles, and a general willingness to abandon positions in the face of hostile forces. This was due to the relatively low population density, and greater focus on controlling people rather than territory, which caused leaders to regard the men in their army as a scarce resource.[6] The point of war was a net gain of people, not winning at all costs. H. G. Quaritch Wales' work[7] reinforces this characterization by emphasizing the more ritualized aspects of Southeast Asian warfare, the desire to take captives rather than massacre people, and the willingness of men to flee into the jungle rather than stand and fight. Quaritch Wales' work, however, is predicated on using a mid-twentieth-century model of headhunting societies to extrapolate backwards and describe pre-European warfare. It has value as a description of a very specific kind of ritualized combat found in the hills on the mainland, which, however, must be understood as a very different kind of fighting from the state warfare focused on here.

Reid's and Quaritch Wales' description of Southeast Asian warfare was well accepted until recently, when Michael Charney and Felice Noelle Rodriguez, among others, have stressed the bloodiness of many conflicts where the point was to capture enemy heads. Charney specifically challenges the Reid–Quaritch Wales position, pointing out that their description is "difficult to reconcile with a wider range of indigenous and foreign sources. As they indicate, face-to-face battles were common in Southeast Asia and according to indigenous sources, extremely bloody."[8] He also draws attention to the recent work of Gerrit Knaap, who found extremely high casualty rates in Ambon in the middle of the seventeenth century.[9] Knaap suggests that the introduction of firearms may have increased the casualty rate, and that more aggressive Dutch expansion, as compared with that of the Portuguese, led to a greater scale and intensity of destruction.[10] Commenting on the conflicting descriptions of Southeast Asian warfare, Victor Lieberman has pointed out that the very different methods often reflected the extremely variable access of Southeast Asian polities to foreign trade and weaponry. Warfare was extremely important

---

[6] Anthony Reid, *Southeast Asia in the Age of Commerce*, Vol. I, New Haven: Yale University Press, 124.

[7] H. G. Quaritch Wales, *Ancient South-East Asian Warfare*, London: Bernard Quaritch, 1952.

[8] Michael W. Charney, *Southeast Asian Warfare, 1300–1900*, Leiden: E. J. Brill, 2004, 20.

[9] Gerrit Knaap, "Headhunting, Carnage and Armed Peace in Amboina, 1500–1700," *Journal of the Economic and Social History of the Orient*, 46/2 (2003), 190.

[10] Ibid., 190.

in state formation, particularly as an instrument of more universal ideologies and expanded political concepts of rulership and the nation.[11] War, not firearms, created states and consolidated polities. Demand for firearms was created by the interest of many leaders in waging war.

The distinction between war and peace as states of political or social being may not have been very clear for the less complex groups in Southeast Asia; among headhunting societies warfare was mainly a personal activity that demonstrated leadership, rather than being a tool of the state. This understanding of warfare, which stressed beheading opponents and even eating their flesh to obtain their "soul stuff," underlay later developments in Southeast Asian warfare. Nevertheless, outside of those small headhunting societies, most warfare in Southeast Asia was waged for all of the usual reasons states waged war. Even as some groups changed the way they thought about war, the earlier cultural perspective still informed their thinking and, in some cases, biased the records of war. It may also be the case that smaller-scale warfare could yield extremely high casualty rates, even to the complete annihilation of the losing side, without causing large overall numbers of dead. Larger battles, which almost by definition required a higher order of political organization, may have produced the same number of dead as a smaller battle, but with a much lower casualty rate.

The possibility of the complete annihilation of a group or village, whether through beheading or enslavement, may explain the reluctance of Southeast Asian forces to stand and face a numerically superior army. Weak fortifications would be an obstacle to small war parties, but not large ones, and while village fortifications could be weak, town fortifications could be quite strong. Firearms did not initially change this reality until they were available in large enough quantities and calibers to kill at longer ranges, before one side could judge the opposing force too powerful to face. European forces demonstrated this when their naval gunnery along the coasts and rivers proved impossible to withstand. Resistance then withdrew into the interior where it was very difficult to eliminate. Southeast Asian forces still frequently stood and fought, falling back only in the face of overwhelming power. Europeans frequently misunderstood the rational decision to avoid a losing battle as indicative of a "native" way of war developed before the introduction of firearms.

The increasing availability of firearms to those groups with access to foreign trade, and the wealth that accompanied that trade, gave them an advantage over their less well-armed opponents. This process had been apparent with even the earliest introduction of Chinese firearms. Wealth

---

[11] Victor Lieberman, "Some Comparative Thoughts on Premodern Southeast Asian Warfare," *Journal of the Economic and Social History of the Orient*, 46/2 (2003), 215–25.

and firearms, often backed by European technical assistance, allowed some archipelagic Southeast Asian rulers to build and sustain armies of conquest. Several of these polities were puppets to a greater or lesser extent of European powers, or indirect beneficiaries of their presence. Europeans exploited the pre-existing rivalries in Southeast Asia to tip the balance of power in favor of their clients (although sometimes they were manipulated by one side or another in a conflict). It is, therefore, difficult to parse the effects of the introduction of better and more firearms from the actual political programs of the Europeans.

In the final analysis, it is difficult to generalize about the nature of Southeast Asian warfare across the entire region and over many centuries. Southeast Asian warfare could be very bloody, or not, depending upon the time and place. Before the rise of large states major set-piece battles were infrequent, as were extended sieges, but when they did happen they could be temporarily decisive in political contests, particularly if the ruler of one side or the other were killed or captured in the contest. As polities developed and created stable governments, the importance of a particular ruler to the continued existence of that polity diminished. Extended sieges became increasingly frequent in the early modern period, marking both political consolidation and the increased use of firearms that accompanied it. More stable polities emerged on the mainland exclusive of the introduction of firearms or European military methods; Europeans and their weapons were more directly important in archipelagic polity formation. All this is to say that firearms were welcomed in Southeast Asia, and were certainly used in the pursuit of conquest, but they did not create larger states by their technical requirements. Firearms by themselves were politically important when only one side of a conflict had access to large numbers of weapons.

The political evolution of Southeast Asia

There are currently two competing theories of Southeast Asian development over the long sweep of early modern history.[12] The first, proposed by Anthony Reid, is the Age of Commerce thesis. Reid argues that there was an economic crisis in the seventeenth century that reversed the trend toward greater prosperity begun in the early fifteenth century through engagement with external trade. Maritime trade led to more powerful governments because the various rulers were able to exploit increased

---

[12] I have limited my discussion to the most recent theories, and avoided an extended historiographical discussion of the earlier ones. For the earlier theories, see Lieberman, *Strange Parallels*, 6–15.

revenues to improve their military, and thus also political, power by buying and using foreign firearms and ships. When this trajectory faltered and then terminated in the late seventeenth century, the earlier consolidations fragmented.

The second thesis, proposed by Victor Lieberman, posits a mostly internally driven, long-term integration of Southeast Asian polities over the period *c*.800 to 1830. Lieberman rejects the idea that indigenous peoples and polities were passive bystanders as foreigners brought Southeast Asia into the modern age, as well as the notion that Southeast Asian culture and society did not change before the arrival of outsiders. But the importance of internal factors does not, in Lieberman's schema, argue for isolated development. Rather, he believes that Southeast Asia developed in ways similar to the rest of the world as the result of complex and multiple factors including ecological, economic, military, political, institutional, educational, and religious forces. At root, Lieberman proposes that Southeast Asia was very much like the rest of the world in its development, and was therefore subject to, and proceeded along similar paths to other Eurasian polities like France or Russia.

Lieberman may well be correct in what he proposes, at least for Southeast Asia, but he includes so many factors in his analysis that the depth and breadth of his data is often quite overwhelming. For our purposes here, however, we need not engage all of his data in all of their complexity to establish that it was not the adoption either of European military technology or of European military methods that created the early modern Southeast Asian states. Mainland Southeast Asia was well on its way toward political consolidation before the arrival of the Europeans. Archipelagic Southeast Asia, for its part, was consolidated by the Europeans themselves (excepting Melaka in the early sixteenth century and Aceh, Mataram, and a few other kingdoms before the seventeenth-century crisis reversed this trend) rather than by the introduction of European military technology.[13]

The sources of the differences between Reid's thesis and Lieberman's are their respective focuses on maritime Southeast Asia and mainland Southeast Asia, and the time frames they choose to consider. Archipelagic Southeast Asia was clearly not headed toward political consolidation into larger states when Europeans arrived to trade in the sixteenth century. Geography by itself limited aggregations of territory into viable large

---

[13] The distinction between the technology and the European powers is quite important. As I will argue more extensively in chapter 7, while technology gave Europeans a military advantage, their ultimate dominance over much of the region was owing to their broader goals, their organizations, and their willingness to spend blood and treasure in what were, on balance, unprofitable ventures all in the interest of glory.

politico-economic units, and made most of the land accessible to European incursions. Spices drew Europeans to the islands, where they used their organizational and military advantages to reorder local government ruthlessly. European exploitation was breathtaking in its brutality. Where previously local rulers were hard pressed to establish lasting dominion over populations and lands, the financial benefits the Europeans obtained from the trade in spices supported the military means necessary for a higher-order political structure.

The indigenous political structures in the archipelago did not support the kind of military organization necessary to prevent European incursions, despite pre-existing familiarity with firearms. In 1511, for example, the Portuguese found Chinese bombards dated 1421 in Melaka.[14] European muskets were quickly adopted, when possible, with the percentage of Javanese troops so armed rising from 2 percent in 1515 to 10–13 percent by the mid-seventeenth century, Mataram supporting 4,000 musketeers in 1624, and Banten 10,000 by 1673.[15] Turkish influence in the form of the large cannons they favored was also widespread in the Malay Sultanates, part of the Turkish desire to support Islamic states and counter European influence. Yet maritime Southeast Asia was simply too geographically and politically vulnerable to European incursions, regardless of its knowledge of firearms and openness to useful military technology, to prevent colonization.

Mainland Southeast Asia, by contrast, had a long history of large-scale political identification, if not exactly sovereign control, over broad swathes of land well before the arrival of Europeans. The difference in historical experience of political organization on the mainland is directly connected with Lieberman's stress on a much longer time frame, 800–1800, in considering the political consolidation of Southeast Asia. Without reference to the history of even mainland Southeast Asia before 1500, it is easy to imagine that the large polities of Burma, Siam, and Vietnam were stimulated to consolidate by the arrival of Europeans. This consolidation is much less sudden, and more obviously a native development, when the earlier history of the area is taken into account.

The introduction and effects of guns in Southeast Asia highlight, once again, the inherent weakness of the modern history approach to Asia. By emphasizing the rising power of the European nation-states after 1500, particularly the economic, technological, and political developments that led in a neat Hegelian progression to our present perceived Western-dominated world, the actual histories of these non-Western

---

[14] Charney, *Southeast Asian Warfare*, 46.   [15] Ibid., 67.

polities are relegated to the realm of antiquarian interest. Guns were integrated into Southeast Asian warfare without causing a "modernizing" rupture, or even dramatically reconfiguring the political map. Michael Charney has pointed out that "Firearms entered Southeast Asia ... and were integrated into an already mature local system of warfare. The ability to choose technology based on local necessity and to adapt it according to indigenous perceptions of warfare meant that foreigners found Southeast Asian warfare to be both familiar and somehow different."[16] As we turn now to capsule histories of Burma (Myanmar), Thailand (Siam), Vietnam, and parts of archipelagic Southeast Asia, the longer-term political and cultural progressions of those polities is more apparent, and the effects of guns seen as more limited. It was only with the increasingly aggressive European political and economic incursions in the nineteenth century that Burma and Vietnam were colonized.

Burma (Myanmar)

The Burmans created a powerful kingdom ruled from the city of Pagan. Pagan unified Myanmar in 1057, when it captured the Mon city at Thaton, though it would take another century to consolidate its rule. At its height in the twelfth century, Pagan divided rule over most of mainland Southeast Asia with the Khmer empire, but the power of Buddhist monasteries gradually undermined the political center. Pagan was dealt a severe setback when it confronted the Mongols in the thirteenth century. A Burmese army sent into Yunnan was crushed by the Mongols at the Battle of Ngasaunggyan in 1277, followed by defeats at the Battle of Bhamo in 1283 and the Battle of Pagan in 1287, when the Mongols invaded. The last-named battle effectively ended the Pagan empire, though the state itself lasted into the fourteenth century, eventually collapsing as a result of internal factors.

Myanmar was now divided into a northern, Burman, kingdom centered at Ava (with a number of competing centers between Pagan and Ava), which continued Pagan culture, and a Mon kingdom in the south (Pegu), which was commercially developed as well as being a center of Theravada Buddhism. Ava was destroyed by the Shan in 1527, but a new kingdom was reconstituted by remnants of Ava at Toungoo in 1531. Toungoo soon reunited Myanmar, while Thai power grew in neighboring Ayutthaya (Siam). The new players in Southeast Asian politics were the European traders who both increased the value of maritime trade and

---

[16] Ibid., xv.

seized territory. The former factor led to the shift of the First Toungoo dynasty's capital south to the port of Pegu; the latter would later constrain southern expansion after the Portuguese captured Malacca.

The First Toungoo dynasty's reach soon exceeded its grasp, however, as successful campaigns against Manipur (1560) and Ayutthaya (1569) provided only temporary territorial gain. Both states quickly regained their independence, and the tremendous military effort left First Toungoo internally weakened. Different political centers in the south, at Ava, the town of Toungoo from which the dynasty now based at Pegu stemmed, and others, broke away from First Toungoo's rulers. The First Toungoo dynasty was finally defeated in a siege of Pegu by forces from Arakan and Toungoo. Portuguese mercenaries at Syriam, close to Pegu, rebelled against their Arakanese employers and created their own pirate enclave. In the north, Ava expanded its control over other breakaway centers. The Portuguese could not withstand the power of a renewed Ava, and were permanently driven out, and Myanmar was reunited, in 1613. Ava fell to a Mon rebellion in 1752, the result of long-term internal factors, like bad rulers and the growth of ministerial power that limited the throne's control of manpower. The cultural and territorial integrity of at least the core of Myanmar nevertheless continued to contribute to an impressive resilience with respect to political coherence, and a new dynasty arose to replace Ava.

Pegu, which had rebelled and even invaded the north, was driven out in 1753, and conquered by 1759. The process of Burman conquest of the south was particularly brutal this time, taking on a distinctly genocidal air with respect to the Mon. By the time Pegu fell in 1759, there were very few Mon left. This new Konbaung dynasty was based in the north, and soon took control of Manipur. Its forays against Tenasserim and Ayutthaya initially stalled for a variety of reasons, but Ayutthaya was conquered in 1767 (though later lost) and Tenasserim annexed in 1793.

Konbaung expansion brought it into contact with larger powers, first Qing China and then British India. The subjugation of chieftains on the Qing–Burma border in 1765 inadvertently brought about clashes with Qing troops and then war with the Qing empire. Fortunately for the Burmese, despite the Qianlong emperor's determination to punish them, Qing armies were repeatedly decimated by disease and every incursion failed. Large-scale operations ended in 1769, after a truce negotiated by the opposing generals and rejected by their respective courts established a lasting peace.[17] This was, perhaps, one of the few instances in history

[17] Peter Lorge, *War, Politics and Society in Early Modern China, 900–1795*, London and New York: Routledge, 2005, 166–7.

when military reality successfully resisted political reconstruction. Although neither court accepted the truce politically, they were unwilling or unable to overturn the reality on the ground militarily. Peace won out over the obdurate civil leadership. The conquest of Assam in 1824, however, not only put Myanmar in direct contact with British India, but also threatened British interests.

For all of the Qing dynasty's displeasure with Myanmar, Konbaung expansion was not a real threat, and so could be safely ignored after military action accomplished nothing. This was not true for the British, who faced an unstable border with Myanmar and likely French intrigues to gain further power in Southeast Asia. Growing British ambition in the region and desire for expansion clashed directly with Kongbaung ambition and desire for expansion. In the course of the First (1824–6), Second (1852) and Third (1885) Anglo-Burmese Wars, the British reduced Myanmar to colonial status (see chapter 7).

Thailand

Thailand is the only Southeast Asian state to have avoided European colonial rule, though it was overrun by Burma on several occasions, as we have seen above. While the discussion of how Thailand managed to retain its independence will be taken up in chapter 7, it is worth pointing out here that its history before the nineteenth century was quite similar to that of Burma and even Vietnam in as much as internal political, cultural, and military developments gradually led to a more coherent and cohesive polity. Also like Burma and Vietnam, Thailand's relations with India and China remained more important than those with the European powers until well into the early modern period. Often threatened by its western and eastern neighbors, Britain's takeover of Burma and France's takeover of Vietnam did not really change Thailand's fundamental geo-political situation so much as add in two new actors.

The territory of what is now Thailand was populated for several thousand years before the arrival of Thais in the first millennium of the Common Era. In that sense, our use of the word "Thailand" to refer to the history of the territory of modern Thailand is both teleological and anachronistic (a problem we have run into throughout this chapter and book). The origin of the Thai nation is usually assigned to the declaration of the independence of the city of Sukhotai from Khmer control in 1238. Sukhotai established Theravada Buddhism as its religion, created a Thai alphabet, and extended its nominal control beyond the limits of modern Thailand. Sukhotai's power began to unravel in the fourteenth century, and Ayutthaya reduced it to vassalage in 1378, and finally to provincial status in 1438.

Ayutthaya intensified the Thai commitment to Theravada Buddhism and compiled a legal code that continued to be used into the late nineteenth century. The Thai commitment to Buddhism, particularly Theravada Buddhism, was an important element in the solidification of the Thai polity. Political development was tied very strongly to the cultural coherence that a literate, universal religion provided. This was particularly true in the multicultural environment of Southeast Asia, where religion was often connected to other concepts of ethnicity. Ayutthaya's control extended into the Malay peninsula, where Islam was the dominant religion. Thai Buddhism therefore bounded the world of internal Thai politics, while not restricting the reach of the state. Similarly, the law code provided a stable core social and political framework that reinforced the ideological legitimacy of a Thai state, regardless of its actual use in practice.

Both Theravada Buddhism and the law code survived Ayutthaya's conquest by Burma in 1767, amply demonstrating the resilience of the Thai polity. After a few years of instability, a new Thai dynasty, the Chakri, established itself at Bangkok in 1782. The new dynasty proved itself in the 1790s by driving the Burmese out. Thai strength and Burma's increasing problems with the British in the nineteenth century relieved pressure from the west, allowing the Thai polity, now called Siam, to develop further. The Thai court was wise enough to recognize the threat that the British posed, and to see that a power that could defeat Burma and advance so strongly into Southeast Asia after having taken control of South Asia threatened it as well. It accordingly signed the Treaty of Amity and Commerce with Britain in 1826, not long after the British had defeated Burma in several encounters.

Vietnam

The name "Vietnam" has been around for only about two centuries, since the Qing court in China granted it to the then ruler of Annam, Gia Long, in 1804. Before that it was known, in reverse chronological order, as Đại Việt, Đại Cồ Việt, Jiaozhi (or Jiaozhou or Annan [Annam], when it was part of China), Nan Yue (Nam Viet), Au Lac, and, the earliest, Van Lang.[18] The

---

[18] The reader will have noticed that the pronunciations of several names shift between the Chinese and the Vietnamese. "Nan," south in modern Mandarin Chinese pronunciation, is pronounced "Nam" in Vietnamese. Similarly, "Yue" in Chinese is pronounced "Viet" in Vietnamese. "Annan" (Chinese) or "Annam" (Vietnamese) meant Peaceful or Pacified South. For the most part, I will maintain the Vietnamese pronunciation of words in this section; in the two periods where I have used the Chinese pronunciation, Jiaozhi (or Jiaozhou or Annan [Annam]), and Nan Yue (Nam Viet), the Chinese controlled the territory.

last name brings us back to the Hong Bang dynasty (2879–258 BCE) and a period of less certain dating. Most of early Vietnamese history is derived from Chinese accounts of the lands to their south, and it is unclear who those people really were, or what land they actually controlled. Even during the period of direct Chinese control, from 111 BCE to 939 CE, there were strict boundaries only where Annan abutted other Chinese administrative units.

The end of Chinese control in 939 inaugurated a new era of dynastic kings, though after centuries of rule, Chinese cultural influence, particularly over the elites, was fairly strong. Vietnam was the most culturally Chinese of all the kingdoms in Southeast Asia, as well as the one most subject to Chinese incursions. Most Vietnamese like to point out, however, that during the period of Chinese control the populace frequently rebelled against their Chinese overlords. In this, the Vietnamese were no different than many Chinese, who also rebelled against the central Chinese government with some regularity. These rebellions have been retrospectively constructed into early indications of a coherent Vietnamese identity, but that developed more clearly after direct Chinese control receded.

The subsequent series of Vietnamese dynastic houses struggled to expand to the south, and to fend off repeated Chinese incursions. From the Chinese perspective, their difficulties in defeating the Vietnamese stemmed from disease and supply problems, with some armies completely disintegrating independent of hostile actions. Vietnamese accounts tend to emphasize their resolute resistance to often numerically greater armies armed with superior weaponry. The echoes of France and then America's disastrous attempts to control Vietnam play into this narrative. The Lý dynasty, which called the country Đại Việt and placed its capital at what is now Hanoi, fell to the Trần dynasty in 1225.

The Trần successfully resisted three Mongol incursions, in the process formulating a quasi-nationalist ideology to support its military efforts. Trần efforts at southern expansion were less impressive, with Champa responding to these attacks by capturing the Trần capital in 1372 and again in 1377. In 1400, Hồ Quý Ly overthrew the Trần dynasty that he had previously served, and established the short-lived Hồ dynasty. It was under Hồ Quý Ly that government documents began to be written in the native Chữ Nôm characters, rather than in Classical Chinese. This step away from Chinese culture and toward a more distinct Vietnamese culture was a significant break with the past. Hồ Quý Ly has been blamed for creating the political chaos that allowed troops from China's Ming dynasty to seize control of the country in 1407, but while his actions may have created the pretext for Ming intervention, the Trần dynasty was clearly not in good shape when he seized power. Both Hồ Quý Ly and his

Map 6 Vietnam

son, Hồ Hán Thương, to whom he had ceded the throne in 1401, were captured by the Ming.

A man by the name of Lê Lợi emerged to wage a successful protracted guerrilla campaign against Ming control, leading to the creation of the (Hậu or "Later") Lê dynasty in 1428. Contact with the Ming brought firearms into the regular Vietnamese arsenal, and the Lê dynasty continued the basic Vietnamese policy of expanding south at the expense of Champa, only now with guns. Whether or not guns hastened the long process of Champa decline and Vietnamese rise is unclear, particularly as it was not until 1471 that a Vietnamese army was able to capture the Champa capital. By that time, guns were used on both sides, so, in the sense that firearms were now not only regular, but also required, weapons for armies, a military revolution had already occurred. It does seem, circumstantially at least, that firearms had been incorporated into the developing Vietnamese polity, and it was this coincidence with political development that allowed them to be used effectively in war. Or perhaps, to echo Geoffrey Parker's theory, the requirements of using firearms in warfare instigated or accelerated political development. Despite the massacre of the capital's inhabitants, Cham resistance continued, as it would until the nineteenth century. The kingdom of Champa, however, was permanently destroyed. The Chams were fierce fighters, and their declining fortunes appear to have been due to a failure to develop politically and institutionally, as the Vietnamese had, into a more unified polity.

The former territory of Champa was now open for colonization by the Vietnamese, a process that continued through a succession of subsequent dynasties. In 1527 the Lê dynasty was overthrown by the Mac, but a Lê official, Nguyễn Kim, resisted this and replaced the Lê emperor the Mac had killed with another Lê prince. The Mac were defeated in 1592,[19] by which time real control over the Lê emperor had fallen to the Trịnh family. One of Nguyễn Kim's sons, in turn, resisted the Trịnh usurpation of Nguyễn power, starting a century and a half of civil war. Even this civil war did not stop the Vietnamese push to the south, and it may well have fueled it. The Nguyễn needed to expand their territory and resources to fight the Trịnh, so they conquered the Mekong delta region then occupied by Khmer.

War fueled war in this case, as well as political and military consolidation. Ironically, unification of the Trịnh–Nguyễn split state was effected by a third group, the Tây Sơn. The Tây Sơn rebellion began in 1771 in

---

[19] Remnants of Mac rule persisted until 1677 in the mountains of Cao Bằng province.

Nguyễn territory, and by 1777 had completely overthrown the Nguyễn.[20] A subsequent Nguyễn invasion supported by Siam was decisively defeated. The Tây Sơn then marched north and, in 1788, crushed the Trịnh and unified the country. At this point, the now deposed Lê emperor, who had been absolutely powerless under the Trịnh, escaped to China, where he persuaded the Qianlong emperor to restore him to his throne. A three-pronged invasion force quickly seized control of Hanoi and duly restored the Lê emperor, but a month later, during the lunar new year celebration, the Tây Sơn attacked the Qing army and drove it out. The Qianlong emperor then accepted the change in government.[21]

The first Tây Sơn emperor died in 1792, and his dynasty did not long survive him. Nguyễn Phúc Ánh, a Nguyễn prince, took advantage of the instability in the new state and, with French help, conquered it in 1802. Nguyễn Phúc Ánh took the name Gia Long when he became emperor, establishing the Nguyễn dynasty, which continued until 1945. He petitioned the Qing emperor for a name for his state, receiving the name Vietnam in 1804. This placed a Chinese imprimatur on the new state, concealing the fact that it would soon become a French colony.

Archipelagic Southeast Asia

While mainland Southeast Asia underwent consistent, if intermittent, consolidation into larger polities independent of European influence, the kingdoms and statelets in archipelagic Southeast Asia followed a different course. Most of them were smaller and able to command fewer resources in manpower and money from their subject populations. They were also more dependent upon maritime trade, particularly the flow of goods between China and South Asia. The arrival of the Europeans did not initially upset this situation, since their main interest was in connecting to the pre-existing trade. As the European presence increased and their interference in local politics escalated, the course of development veered sharply from its previous trajectory. Not only were the archipelagic polities more geographically exposed to European influence, they also possessed much smaller populations, and were consequently easier to conquer with limited military means.

The particular path of archipelagic Southeast Asia is amply demonstrated by the examples of Melaka and Java. In both cases, Europe had much more significant influence much sooner than on the mainland.

---

[20] Confusingly, the rebellion was led by three Nguyễn brothers unrelated to the ruling Nguyễn lords.

[21] Lorge, *War, Politics and Society in Early Modern China*, 169.

In Melaka it began about 1400, and it was conquered by the Portuguese in 1511.[22] Melaka's roots were in the Malay kingdom of Srivijaya, which controlled both sides of the Melaka Straits and the many islands approaching that waterway starting some time in the seventh century CE. Located in the Palembang region of southeast Sumatra, it was a transit port for goods traveling between China and South Asia, as well as a collection and distribution center for local jungle products. By the thirteenth century, however, Srivijaya's missions to the Chinese court stopped. Other cities collected considerable wealth in the Malay world, but few records of them remain because they did not contact the Chinese court. Indeed, even the better records for Srivijaya are quite fragmentary, and scholarly debate over the origin, extent, and power of the kingdom remains active.

Over time, Srivijaya's control slipped and the centrifugal tendencies of the widely dispersed vassal domains dissolved the kingdom's central authority. Continuing war with the increasingly powerful kingdoms in Java from at least the eleventh century, as well as conflict with Chola India, and a change in Chinese trading practice that diminished the value of Srivijaya's official connections to the Chinese court, allowed other trade centers to develop economic and political independence. Not only did Javanese forces attack Srivijaya's capital in 1275, but the Javanese state of Majapahit also asserted supremacy over southeast Sumatra from the thirteenth century on. By the middle of the fourteenth century, the rising power of Ayutthaya was also pressing down on Srivijaya from the north. The kingdom collapsed entirely in the 1390s after a Majapahit invasion.

Srivijaya's control over the island of Java had been undermined by an incursion from Chola India in the late eleventh century, but it was not until the 1290s that the Singhasari kingdom drove it out completely. This led directly to the rise of the Majapahit state, founded in 1293, which would soon control Java and much of the Malay peninsula. It was also in the thirteenth century that Islam spread throughout archipelagic Southeast Asia, adding a new influence to the pre-existing Hindu–Javanese culture of the area. Although it was a Majapahit invasion that destroyed Srivijaya, Melaka, the kingdom founded by a Srivijayan prince, in turn whittled away Majapahit's influence. Soon after Melaka's founding around 1400, its ruler converted to Islam, turning it into a Sultanate. In 1511, however, the Portuguese conquered Melaka. Parts of Java fell under European colonialism soon after, as did much of archipelagic Southeast Asia.

---

[22] This account of Melaka is drawn from Barbara Watson Andaya and Leonard Y. Andaya, *A History of Malaysia*, London and Basingstoke: Macmillan, 1982.

Conclusion

European influence and the introduction of firearms into Southeast Asia produced neither a marked consolidation of military or political systems toward a single model, nor a common cause and effect or diffusion model response to these new technologies. This variety of responses to firearms and even European military practice in Southeast Asia lends itself to two possible explanations. The first, for those who believe that European influence in general, and the full panoply of early modern European military technology in particular, must cause a single response, that is, the move toward a European style of warfare and government, would argue that Southeast Asia's failure to respond in this way was simply the result of the partial and imperfect introduction of influence or technology, and local resistance to that influence. That is to say, had the complete European model been fully introduced into and accepted by the pre-existing culture, the new, European, model would have subsumed the old system and transformed it into something recognizably European. The second explanation is that there is no inherent single response to encountering either European culture or technology.

European military methods as practiced in Europe were only partially used in Southeast Asia. Similarly, the European political institutions demonstrated in Southeast Asia were not typical of the institutions in place in Europe itself. We cannot, therefore, assert that Southeast Asians rejected or proved incapable of taking up the European model for war or politics. They did adopt European military technology and incorporate it into their own armies, as Java did in the sixteenth and seventeenth centuries, Mataram did in 1624, and Banten did in 1673. But since the early modern and modern European military system demanded not only certain qualitative kinds of military technology, political and financial institutions, and social structures, including particular practices such as military training and discipline, but also a growing manufacturing base to provide a quantitative as well as qualitative suite of weapons, this argument cannot be proved. Local resistance to European rule, but not to its commerce or technology, by contrast, was not a rejection of European culture; it was simply a power struggle. Europeans were simply new players among many old ones in the wars for control and wealth. Gunpowder weapons had already affected Southeast Asian warfare before the arrival of the Europeans, and new European arms in greater quantities contributed to the gradual revolution in warfare that made Southeast Asian warfare as gunpowder dependent as that in much of the rest of the world.

Unlike the great civilizations of China and South Asia, however, Europeans gradually became more and more directly engaged in Southeast

Asian politics. Some Chinese or Indian rulers had, on occasion, briefly interceded in some parts of Southeast Asia. These adventures might even last for a few decades before the difficulties and the expense persuaded them to withdraw. This was not the case with the Europeans, despite the fact that they also found that while trade by itself might be profitable for the merchants involved, actual political control of an area was not. National resources in money and troops subsidized the trade in spices and coffee, something neither Chinese nor South Asian rulers were willing to countenance. European dominance was thus much more to do with European willingness to maintain a much deeper and more costly relationship with Southeast Asia, than with superior military technology or methods. Superior technology certainly made that dominance possible, but so did greater wealth and the fundamental strategic advantage of great distance from the battlefield.

Great distance is usually seen as an obstacle to the projection of military power, as it was for the European colonial powers, but it can also be an advantage when it keeps one side out of range of any retaliation from the other. Europeans could organize and arm all sorts of military adventures in Southeast Asia far from the reach of Southeast Asian rulers. It was usually possible to exploit the fragmented Southeast Asian political milieu and obtain local allies for any European military effort. This was not always possible – the Portuguese presence in Ternate in the sixteenth century was insecure long before it was dislodged – but over the long term the Spanish and Dutch were a greater threat to the continued Portuguese presence in Southeast Asia than any local ruler. Any mistake by a local ruler could be mortal; a European failure was merely a temporary setback. The military and political contest was therefore generally one sided because the Europeans always retained the strategic initiative. Europeans could decide how much effort to gamble on an objective and strike without warning. Southeast Asian rulers could only react to what were often existential threats.

When Europeans first reached Southeast Asia, they found a politically and geographically fragmented region already familiar with gunpowder and international trade. European weapons and trade accelerated the pre-existing military and political developments; it seems unlikely that they altered the trajectory of those developments very much. Where Europeans initially made a difference was not in causing political consolidation or introducing gunpowder, but in focusing their attention, and thus arms and wealth, on particular places in Southeast Asia. Real European dominance, that is to say colonialism, grew out of gradually improving weaponry, but also a desire and willingness to take control of polities that had become coherent enough to be grasped. That phase of Asia's history will be taken up in chapter 7.

FURTHER READING

Barbara Watson Andaya, "Political Development between the Sixteenth and Eighteenth Centuries," in Nicholas Tarling (ed.), *The Cambridge History of Southeast Asia*, Vol. I, Cambridge: Cambridge University Press, 1992, 402–55.

Barbara Watson Andaya and Leonard Y. Andaya, *A History of Malaysia*, London and Basingstoke: Macmillan, 1982.

Leonard Y. Andaya, "Interactions with the Outside World and Adaptation in Southeast Asian Society, 1500–1800," in Nicholas Tarling (ed.), *The Cambridge History of Southeast Asia*, Vol. I, Cambridge: Cambridge University Press, 1992, 345–95.

Oscar Chapuis, *A History of Vietnam*, Westport, CT and London: Greenwood Press, 1995.

Michael W. Charney, *Southeast Asian Warfare, 1300–1900*, Leiden: E. J. Brill, 2004.

G. E. Harvey, *History of Burma*, New York: Octagon Books, 1983.

Charles F. Keyes, *Thailand: Buddhist Kingdom as Modern Nation-State*, Boulder and London: Westview Press, 1987.

J. D. Legge, "The Writing of Southeast Asian History," in Nicholas Tarling (ed.), *Cambridge History of Southeast Asia*, Vol. I, Cambridge: Cambridge University Press, 1992, 1–50.

Victor Lieberman, *Strange Parallels: Southeast Asia in Global Context, c. 800–1830*, Cambridge: Cambridge University Press, 2003.

Michael Smithies, *A Resounding Failure: Martin and the French in Siam, 1672–1693*, Chiang Mai: Silkworm Books, 1998.

D. J. M. Tate, *The Making of Modern South-East Asia*, Vol. I (rev. edn), Kuala Lumpur: Oxford University Press, 1977.

5   South Asia to 1750

There were three periods of change in South Asian warfare immediately prior to the introduction of European military practice from 1750 to 1850: the eleventh- and twelfth-century rise to dominance of cavalry, primarily horse-archers; the advance of siege techniques in the thirteenth and fourteenth centuries; and the "false dawn" of the gunpowder age from 1400 to 1750.[1] This chapter will survey these three periods to adumbrate the military developments that underlay the political and social structure before the post-1750 South Asian military revolution. This groundwork will allow a later comparison with the other polities, particularly China, and show how earlier military technologies were adopted and incorporated into South Asian warfare.

In the first period, Central Eurasian tribes in northern India and warrior tribes in south India rose to political prominence through horse-archer based military power. This established a cavalry-focused military elite, whose values continued up to and even after the introduction of more effective guns in the eighteenth and nineteenth centuries. In the second period, gunpowder weapons reached South Asia through the advancing Mongols, and counterpoise trebuchets arrived from the Middle East. Together these two new technologies overwhelmed existing fortifications and caused significant changes in military architecture. Some of these changes presaged the kind of alterations that true cannon would later require, putting fortifications somewhat ahead of siege artillery. Of particular importance was siting installations in inaccessible locations. The third period was therefore somewhat anti-climactic, since the introduction of true cannon and handguns failed to overturn the existing military or political order.

Cannon and handguns were critical in the establishment of the Mughal empire (1526–1857), but only in combination with other modes of

---

[1] This breakdown follows Jos Gommans and Dirk Kolff (eds.), *Warfare and Weaponry in South Asia, 1000–1800*, New Delhi: Oxford University Press. 2001, 32–41; and Jos Gommans, *Mughal Warfare*, London and New York: Routledge, 2002, 134–6.

112

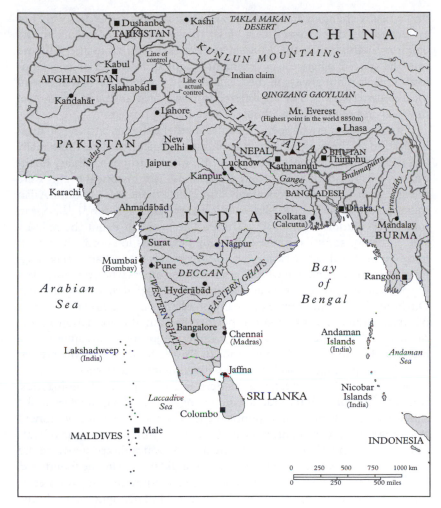

Map 7 South Asia

warfare, particularly the Central Eurasian horse-archer. Yet it is also undeniable that the first use of cannon and handguns on the battlefield at Panipat in 1526 was the opening act of a process that would unify South Asia for the first time since the Mauryans (322–184 BCE) or the Gupta (320–550 CE). A political revolution of immense importance did take place in the early sixteenth century coincident with the introduction of guns on to the battlefield. Even so, the new superstructure of Mughal government was added to the existing military and political order without dramatically changing it. Local and even regional powerholders were not systematically dispossessed as a class; they were incorporated into the empire. In this sense the Mughal system was similar to the Chinese imperial system, where the government accepted the power of local land-lords in fact, if not always in theory, and tacitly ceded a certain degree of local control to them. The big difference, however, was that in South Asia the local and regional powerholders were heavily armed.

If it is indeed mere happenstance that battlefield guns and the political unification of the South Asian subcontinent coincided, then there really was no revolution to speak of before 1750, when European military meth-ods arrived. But if, as seems more likely, these two historical events were related, then one could reasonably argue that there was a South Asian military revolution in the sixteenth century, and a second, European military revolution from 1750 to 1850. The problem is not the military side of the equation – because employing field guns in coordination with horse-archers and heavy cavalry was clearly a new tactical and technolog-ical development, one that would be adopted by others when possible – but the political side. Were the Mughal empire and Mughal rule revolutionary? Om Prakash has summarized the many problems this question raises, most of which concern contemporary perspectives on the formation of the modern Indian state.[2] As an Islamic imperial government ruling over a primarily Hindu population just prior to British colonial rule, the evalua-tion of Mughal South Asia is fraught with contemporary issues.

Setting aside the perspective of modern India, the picture is ambiguous. A new system of military practice did change South Asian warfare in the sixteenth century, and a new political entity, a true imperial government spanning the subcontinent, appeared, helped by that new mode of war-fare. But the underlying social, political, and even military structure did not change. The Mughal central government did not create the foundation of the modern Indian state, or move the subcontinent toward an early modern political system. Gunpowder, cannon, and handguns contributed to changes that were momentous, and even revolutionary in the realms of war and politics, without effecting a larger transformation. More damn-ing for those who look to gunpowder to usher in the modern world, is that before the arrival of European military practice the changes inaugurated by the new technology did not create a continuous momentum for further change. The new weapons were eagerly acquired and used, and adapted to South Asian conditions, but they did not, by themselves, begin a cycle of increasing improvement and transformation.

---

[2] Om Prakash, *Downfall of the Mughal Empire*, New Delhi: Anmol, 2002.

Geography

The Indian subcontinent is climatically divided between the moist east and dry west.[3] The west coast and parts of the east coast are also wet, leaving the center dry. Crop yields in the east are better, with rice as the staple, while wheat and millet prevail in the west. This wheat/millet zone is a famine area, where farmers are forced to supplement their unreliable, low-yield, and relatively lower-labor crops with other occupations including military service. At the same time, however, parts of the arid zone, those well watered by rivers (thus allowing irrigation), contained the ancient centers of civilization. Dry grasslands also allow the raising and mainte-nance of horses, a critical component of cavalry-based political power. Elephants, the other vital war animal, by contrast, had to be captured in the moist eastern forests of southern Bengal and Orissa. Warfare on the subcontinent thus allowed, even demanded if one was to be successful, the combination of a wide variety of men, animals, and modes of fighting.

This variety of climatic areas was joined by a system of major roads running north–south from Kabul in Afghanistan to the southeast coast, along with several east–west routes intersecting it and connecting the other "nuclear zones of power." The major roads ran through the arid center, providing a channel for trade and war. Large armies with tens of thousands of animals had to follow along an ecologically liminal area, close enough to the moist, productive agriculture regions to provide food, and close enough to the arid zone to provide space and fodder for the animals. Powerful political centers arose in these liminal areas, connected by the main roads to other centers of politics and culture. The roads marked the geographically optimal routes of trade and war, but also spanned and directed routes of connection between political centers. Overall, the subcontinent's geography and road system neither favored nor undermined unification under a single government. Unity was a political and military problem.

Arms and military organization before gunpowder

In order to understand the effects of the introduction of gunpowder on South Asian warfare and society, we must first describe conditions before the arrival of that new technology.[4] Very little is known about the military

---

[3] This discussion of South Asian climate and geography follows Gommans, *Mughal Warfare*, 7–15.

[4] Dietmar Rothermund, "From Chariot to Atom Bomb: Armament and Military Organization in South Asian History," in Jos Gommans and Om Prakash (eds.), *Circumambulations in South Asian History*, Leiden: E. J. Brill, 2003, 325–40.

aspect of the Indus Valley civilization before 1500 BCE, except that the main cities were heavily fortified. Around 1500 BCE the Aryans arrived on the subcontinent with fully developed chariots. Chariot warfare brought with it horses and an aristocratic elite who used them. But chariots were extremely inflexible instruments of war, requiring flat, open ground, and, consequently, a well-developed and adhered-to code of behavior to make them relevant. The early South Asian states were small, and chariot warfare adapted itself to this political structure.

Chariot warfare came to an end when elephants were tamed for use in battle, though chariots did persist on the battlefield for a little while as a remnant of the older system. Rather than the single, aristocratic archer carried by a chariot, the war elephant provided a platform for perhaps ten non-aristocratic archers. A chariot simply could not, therefore, compete in terms of sheer firepower. Similar to chariots, elephants were expensive to acquire and maintain, and an effective force required hundreds of animals. More significantly, the shift to elephants dramatically shifted political power and government structure.

The financial requirements of an effective elephant corps meant that only more powerful rulers could afford them. This tilted the balance of military and political power toward centralization. As minor lords lost the ability to compete on equal footing with more powerful lords, the chariot-based aristocracy disappeared. Royal or imperial officials appointed by the ruler replaced the noble warriors. The men who rode on elephants were not high born; the Mauryas who would create the first great empire on the subcontinent were low caste. In a single stroke then, the introduction of a new tool of war, the elephant, overturned the pre-existing political and social order, and created a vast empire. Even after the Mauryan empire broke up, local rulers often depended upon elephants to maintain their power.

The next major innovation in warfare was the introduction of cavalry. Elephants were not, however, completely driven from the battlefield by Islamic cavalry in the eleventh century, though this marked the arrival of some new social and political forms. Cavalry came to the subcontinent with a distinct Islamic slave society in which the soldiers were specialized slaves trained from childhood in that particular military art. Although an individual warhorse was less expensive than an elephant, the enormous expense of purchasing and maintaining thousands or tens of thousands of animals on the subcontinent, where most of the environment was unsuitable for horse raising, once again favored the greater rulers over the lesser. Even so, the smaller unit cost of a warhorse allowed local strongmen to develop small cavalry forces adequate for local conflict. Moreover, the more dispersed supply of horses prevented any higher-order government from monopolizing ownership. No local strongman could match an important ruler in cavalry, but many horses were distributed among local strongmen.

Suitable warhorses had to be imported in large numbers on a regular basis from Central Asian semi-nomadic groups through Afghanistan or from the Persian Gulf by sea. There were roughly half a million horses on the subcontinent at any given time from the thirteenth to the eighteenth century, requiring the importation of 30,000–40,000 replacements every year.[5] The men who brought these horses south could easily shift from trade to war when the opportunity presented itself. Possessing one of the principal tools of war, some of these men took political power as well. The Afghan Lodi sultans of Delhi reportedly began their careers as horse-traders.[6]

The Delhi Sultanate based its power on the military slave system and an ample supply of warhorses, usually in the range of 100,000 animals. Southern rulers were forced to develop their own cavalry forces to fend off northern incursions, though they did not create a slave system to supply cavalrymen. Instead, they established a kind of feudalism whereby the cavalry commander based at a town or garrison also controlled all civil affairs in his district. North and south soon shared a similar local political structure based upon rule by the local cavalry commander. In the north he was a military slave and in the south a free man, but in both cases the need to support a strong cavalry force produced the same political effect. Local government was transformed by the introduction of cavalry.

We come now to the introduction of gunpowder, guns, and rockets into the subcontinent, that diffuse transit of technologies from different places over several hundred years which changed the South Asian mode of warfare without shifting the underlying local organization of political power. Guns would ultimately enhance the power of horse-archers, forming an extremely effective system of combined arms. In South Asia, as in Europe, the greater lords (often kings in Europe) could afford to buy siege guns that allowed them to destroy the forts of local strongmen. But as in China, guns did not drive the horse-archers from the battlefield.

Early gunpowder weapons

Gunpowder was first introduced into South Asia from China, probably during the Mongol invasions of the late thirteenth and early fourteenth

---

[5] Jos Gommans, *The Rise of the Indo-Afghan Empire, c. 1710–1780*, Delhi: Oxford University Press, 1999, 89.

[6] Gommans, *Mughal Warfare*, 116.

century. The sources at this early stage are somewhat problematic, particularly since new technologies with foreign names are hard to decode in cryptic battle accounts. It seems possible that deserters from the Mongol army who were knowledgeable about gunpowder weapons were present within the fortress of Ranthambor when it was besieged by 'Ala al-Din Khalji in 1300.[7] These deserters used bows, likely larger multi-bowed artillery pieces, or counterpoise trebuchets, to throw gunpowder-enhanced flaming missiles at the besiegers. Also in the same period, at least one ruler was advised to alter the forts subject to Mongol attack, and other villages and towns were rebuilt in general. Moats were added to keep besiegers from getting close to the walls, suggesting to some scholars that the Mongols used gunpowder charges to destroy walls after mining under them.[8] In the south and Bengal, gunpowder and gunpowder weapons were probably brought in from China by sea, and to Assam by land via Burma.

Even in these early notices of gunpowder it is important to acknowledge the interest of all parties in using and learning to defend against new military technology. The most practical way to acquire immediate access to these devices was by obtaining men skilled in their use. Knowledgeable men could reproduce technology in short order if backed by a wealthy enough ruler. But intelligent men could also formulate responses to those weapons by taking advantage of pre-existing technologies. Gunpowder in the hands of the Mongol invaders was not overwhelming by itself, even when it provided a temporary advantage, and their opponents soon acquired those weapons for themselves.

Although more developed weapons replaced most early gunpowder weapons, the *ban*, or rocket arrow, which also came into use during this period, remained in use into the late eighteenth century. The *ban* was a narrow iron cylinder, about a foot long, filled with gunpowder and attached to a ten- or twelve-foot-long stick (usually bamboo). The gunpowder in the cylinder, once ignited, drove the *ban* about a thousand yards. Since the rocket was also invented and used for war in China, the *ban* may have come directly from there as well. The use of an iron tube was a South Asian improvement, and the easy availability of construction materials and flexibility of use perhaps explain its continued presence in South Asian warfare even after more effective firearms became available.

---

[7] These deserters may not have been Mongols, as Iqtidar Alam Khan indicates, but siege experts from one of the many other groups incorporated into the Mongol army. There were very few ethnic Mongols expert in siege warfare. Iqtidar Alam Khan, *Gunpowder and Firearms*, Oxford: Oxford University Press, 2004.

[8] Ibid., 22.

By the late sixteenth century, thousands of *bans* were provided for even a small Mughal force.[9]

The idiosyncratic prominence of the *ban* in South Asia is matched by the similarly delayed practice of using gunpowder in mining operations against fortifications. Despite the early Mongol use of this technique, it was first used by a South Asian power in 1472 at the siege of Belgaum. Yet even after its successful use at Belgaum, mining was not commonly used in South Asia until the sixteenth century, and even in the seventeenth century Europeans criticized South Asian mining practice. Just as with the attachment to the *ban*, there is as yet no good explanation for the South Asian reticence in this regard.

It is, of course, cannon and handguns that should have persuaded South Asians to abandon the *ban*, though their introduction did change other aspects of warfare. A writer who lived at Jaunpur from 1457 to 1464 mentions cannon, and a clear description of the trial of a brass or bronze piece that threw a 1,200 kilogram projectile in 1443–4 at Herat puts very early cannon credibly within reach of South Asian rulers in the fifteenth century.[10] These early devices could have reached Central Asia, Iran, and South Asia from either Europe or China. Rulers were concerned with effectiveness and price, not culture or country of origin. Firearms also reached South Asia by sea from China and Mamluk Egypt, the latter adopting European technology.

The market for cannon and handguns was global, or at least pan-Eurasian by the fifteenth century, and South Asia was in the middle of that trade. Early cannon were made of brass or bronze, and South Asian rulers would preserve an idiosyncratic preference for pieces made of these metals long after cheaper iron pieces became available. As was so often the case, the earliest weapons were initially used only in siege operations. Mortars were set up in fixed, protected firing positions to lob heavy rounds into a fortress or city. The defenders used smaller pieces from the walls to fend off the attackers. Gunpowder artillery exceeded both the range and destructive power of the pre-existing mechanical siege artillery. After several forts in the fifteenth century were captured or forced to

---

[9] The *ban* was useful for harassing large bodies of men, since it could hit such large targets and inflict casualties at great range, but was ineffective against British units arrayed in lines. See ibid., 39 fn. 46.

[10] For the Jaunpur writer see ibid., 41, citing *Sharafnama-I Ahmad Munairi*, under the title *Farhang-I Ibrahami*, under *Kashakanjir*, and for the Herat trial, see ibid., 42, citing Mir Khwand, *Rauzat al-safa*, Vol. VI, p. 242. Khan argues quite persuasively that indications of artillery in the Bahmani kingdom in the fourteenth century cannot be supported by a careful reading of the *Tarikh-i Firishta* (ibid., 205–9). Similarly, Khan convincingly demolishes Akram Makhdoomee and Abu Zafar Nadvi's claims for artillery in the thirteenth and fourteenth centuries in north India (ibid., 210–17).

capitulate after being bombarded, other forts had to be redesigned. By extending the outer curtain wall to encompass a larger area, the keep itself would be beyond the range of the mortars.

Brass and bronze pieces were extremely expensive to produce, confining the ownership of such weapons to the wealthier rulers. Lesser local rulers were now no longer able to defy their more powerful overlords because their forts could not resist the new artillery. Internal consolidation quickly followed the adoption of heavy mortars in the Lodi empire, Malwa, the Bahmani kingdom, and Gujarat. In Gujarat, for example, mortars were instrumental in destroying the fortifications of Champanir, one of three great chiefs who had hitherto resisted the Sultan of Gujarat's authority.

Zahiruddin Muhammad (1483–1530), usually referred to as Babur,[11] described the casting of a large mortar on October 22, 1526 by his Iranian gun maker Master Ali Qulii:

Around the place where it was to be cast he had constructed eight smelting furnaces and had already melted the metal. From the bottom of each furnace he had made a channel straight to the mortar mold. Just as we got there he was opening the holes in the furnaces. The molten metal was pouring like water into the mold, but after a while, before the mold was filled, one by one the streams of molten metal coming from the furnaces stopped. There was some flaw either in the furnaces or in the metal. Master Ali Qulii went into a strange depression and was about to throw himself into the mold of molten bronze, but I soothed him, gave him a robe of honor, and got him out of his black mood. A day or two later, when the mold had cooled, they opened it, and Master Ali Qulii sent someone to announce with glee that the shaft was flawless. It was then easy to attach the powder chamber. He took out the shaft and assigned some men to fix it, and got to work connecting the chamber.[12]

Babur had ordered the casting of the mortar in question for use against several fortresses he intended to capture.

This entry demonstrates several of the distinct aspects of South, really Central, Asian (via Ottoman and other parts of the Islamic world) cannon founding, at least in the north. Most obviously, the process of gun founding was an imperfect art, subject to unexpected outcomes. The metal used was bronze, whereas in Europe wrought iron was mainly used, and multiple furnaces were used to liquefy the metal. This was a serious problem because the metal was not consistent throughout the

---

[11] "Babur" was a nickname derived from the Indo-European word for beaver, not the Persian word for tiger (*babr*). See Wheeler M. Thackston (trans.), *The Baburnama*, New York and Oxford: Oxford University Press, 1996, 9, fn. 1 for a discussion of the derivation of "Babur."

[12] Ibid., 363.

cannon, but Islamic and South Asian gun makers as yet lacked bellows strong enough to construct a single large furnace with adequate capacity for the task. The solution in the Islamic world, as Babur also indicated, of casting the powder chamber separately from the stone chamber, actually exacerbated the problem of inconsistent metal in the construction.[13]

Portuguese experts were beginning to found European-style cannon in the south by at least 1506, and to train local craftsmen in their manufacture. Local craftsmen were not skilled at creating the moulds for larger pieces, something the Portuguese presence may have corrected. As the quote from Babur above shows, however, the European practice of using a single furnace to found a one-piece cannon had not reached the north by 1526. Mamluk and Ottoman men and artillery also went to Gujarat to help that kingdom defend itself against Portuguese incursions. Very little of this armament, particularly the lighter pieces and matchlocks, was available in north India.

Babur invaded the Delhi Sultanate in 1526 equipped with several kinds of guns, ranging from very large mortars for reducing fortifications, to matchlock muskets. The large mortars were two-piece cannon hauled by two or three elephants or 400–500 men. This weapon was already known on the subcontinent by the sixteenth century, but the lighter field guns that Babur brought were not. Babur had two kinds of field guns, the *firingi* (Frankish culverin) and the *zarb-zan*. Iqtidar Alam Khan argues for a Chinese rather than European origin for the former weapon,[14] and an Ottoman or Egyptian origin for the latter, though the *zarb-zan* may well have been modeled on European field guns. Khan does not believe that Babur acquired either model of light field gun from the Portuguese in the south. In the case of the *zarb-zan*, it is clear that Babur only acquired them after 1519, about the same time he obtained the services of Mustafa Rumi, an Ottoman artilleryman.

The heavy mortars were mounted on four-wheeled carts for transport and firing, while the field guns were mounted on two-wheeled carriages with an unwheeled leg projecting behind. In both cases most of the barrel was supported by the undercarriage. The field guns would continue to improve in mobility and number during the sixteenth century as their utility in open battle was repeatedly proved. Portuguese influence resulted in an increasing number of shorter, wrought iron barrels, and metal projectiles for field guns. Siege artillery remained resolutely bronze

[13] Khan, *Gunpowder and Firearms*, 61–2.
[14] Of course, Khan points out that the Chinese weapon, the *folangji*, was itself modeled on European breech-loading naval guns carried by the Portuguese when they reached China some time before 1511.

or brass, along with many of the lighter pieces including field guns. Babur's field guns were designed as small mortars, but this changed by the mid-sixteenth century into narrow cylindrical-barreled pieces slightly more than four feet long with a 1½ inch diameter bore.[15] These smaller guns were cheaper in terms of metal used and the amount of gunpowder they consumed, particularly as they shifted over to metal, rather than stone, balls. Metal balls also improved hitting power.

Wrought iron and bronze or brass field guns were not, however, the product of entirely different technicians, and thus cultural influences, in South Asian arms manufacturing. Sher Shah's Ottoman artillery experts manufactured both bronze and wrought iron field guns of about the same size in 1542–3. These threw a brass shot weighing about 2.8 pounds. Sher Shah is reported to have had 4,000 field guns of about 150 pounds each in 1545. Islam Shah (r.1545–52), who succeeded Sher Shah, focused his attention on manufacturing massive mortars considerably larger than anything Babur had owned. These proved worthless in his campaign against the Mughals, who captured the entire artillery park before the Second Battle of Panipat in 1556.

Sher Shah

Sher Shah,[16] an Afghan of undistinguished pedigree who managed to raise himself up through military and administrative accomplishment, would overthrow the second Mughal emperor, Humayun. Where Sultan Mahmud, a son of Ibrahim Lodi, rebelled unsuccessfully against the Mughals in 1537, Sher Shah succeeded in temporarily re-establishing Afghan rule over Hindustan. He changed the previous Afghan system of tribal and clan rulers that had undermined the Delhi Sultanate by paying his Afghan troops and requiring adherence to strict military discipline. Sher Shah himself actually served both Ibrahim Lodi and Babur in succession, but departed Mughal service in 1529 because his non-aristocratic background left him no real prospect for advancement there.

---

[15] These smaller pieces were also slightly higher quality in terms of casting because fewer furnaces were required to feed metal into the mould. Khan, *Gunpowder and Firearms*, 74.

[16] For simplicity's sake, I use Sher Shah throughout this discussion, even though that was his title only from 1540, when he became Sultan of Hindustan. His given name was Farid, and he received the title Khan around 1526, when he was referred to as Sher Khan. See Dirk H. A. Kolff, *Naukar, Rajputard Sepoy*, Cambridge: Cambridge University Press, 1990, 33, fn. 6.

Men armed with handguns protected Babur's field guns and artillery at Panipat. Although handguns were first invented in China, the handguns that appeared in Central and South Asia appear to have been transmitted from Europe through the medium of the Ottomans and possibly Mamluks. Early mentions of the term that later came to mean handgun, *tufang*, may have meant "crossbow," obfuscating an already blurry picture, but it is possible that handguns reached parts of the subcontinent by the mid-fifteenth century. Given their widespread use in China during the Jurchen–Mongol and Song–Mongol wars, it seems strange that they did not reach South Asia earlier through Mongol transmission. Certainly by 1498 Vasco da Gama reports the presence of a musket at Calicut. Handguns were thus available, if not widespread or militarily significant, at the beginning of the sixteenth century.

That situation soon changed as the number and quality of handguns increased, and as new tactics in their deployment developed. Babur brought 1,200 handgunners with him when he invaded the Delhi Sultanate, and this number increased dramatically over the sixteenth century. Sher Shah had 25,000 handgunners in his army, though spread among various important garrisons. The handguns used were probably matchlocks of Turkish design, though by the middle of the sixteenth century the original brass-barreled Turkish models had been replaced with wrought iron barrels. Interestingly, whereas Babur had come from Central Asia with more advanced weapons in 1526, in a few decades it was Central Asian rulers who sought the more advanced iron-barreled matchlocks. Nevertheless, Portuguese matchlocks were far superior to the matchlocks in widespread use on the subcontinent. Portuguese weapons fired a one ounce shot more than 400 yards; the locally produced weapon fired a round half the weight for half the distance.[17]

Just as important as the new technology was the new way of using it. Gunpowder enhanced siege artillery and, owing to its expense, tilted the balance of power toward central rather than regional authorities. But the signal event that had so much military and political impact on the subcontinent was the use of artillery, field guns, and handguns in the field at the First Battle of Panipat. This first use of guns in the field in South Asia heralded the beginning of a series of campaigns that would unite South Asia under the Mughal empire. The idea of empire that no one had been able to achieve for centuries was realized through the use of guns and Ottoman tactics. This was a revolution in both war and politics.

---

[17] Khan, *Gunpowder and Firearms*, 129–35.

The First Battle of Panipat (April 21, 1526)

The First Battle of Panipat marked the first effective use of firearms in the field in South Asia.[18] But the battle was noteworthy for more than this technological advance; it also marked the beginning of the Mughal empire and the end of the Delhi Sultanate. At its height in the late seventeenth century the Mughal empire extended beyond the bounds of even twentieth-century British India, and included Afghanistan within its borders.[19] Panipat was therefore a key political event in South Asian history, and the importance of firearms in the Mughal victory would be repeated in many subsequent battles, and indeed was a key component of Mughal rule.

Babur took the throne of Samarkand when he was twelve, and was driven out of his patrimony soon afterward. A descendant of Chinghis Khan and Amir Temür (1336–1405, sometimes referred to as "Tamerlane"), he initially concentrated his energies on maintaining his territory and capturing his former capital at Samarkand. Unsuccessful in both endeavors, he shifted his efforts toward Afghanistan, where he captured Kabul in 1504. He failed to capture Samarkand again in 1512, and turned south to raid Hindustan (India). The governor of the Punjab invited him to overthrow the Afghan Sultan of Delhi, Ibrahim Lodi, in 1525. Babur invaded the following year, marching south with a force of about 18,000 cavalry, 2,000 infantry, and 5,000 gunners. Although not numerically overwhelming, the Mughal army was a standing force of veteran professionals whose striking power was further enhanced by Babur's ability to combine their different modes of warfare into a coordinated whole.

Ibrahim Lodi responded to Babur's invasion by turning to the military labor market in Delhi. He recruited farmers looking for military service to round out their annual incomes, eventually assembling a force of about 30,000 infantry. Ibrahim's main strength, however, was his force of a hundred elephants. None of this added up to a very effective force, particularly since its indiscipline and slowness not only ceded the strategic and tactical initiative to the Mughals, but also failed to block the invaders from moving through the narrow mountain passes and into the Punjab plain. This flat, open land was ideal territory for cavalry.

Babur appears to have copied the tactics used by the Ottomans against the Persians at Tabriz on August 23, 1514. The 5,000 gunners were

---

[18] Ibid., 132.
[19] Kaushik Roy, *From Hydaspes to Kargil: A History of Warfare in India from 326 BC to AD 1999*, New Delhi: Manohar, 2004, 85–6.

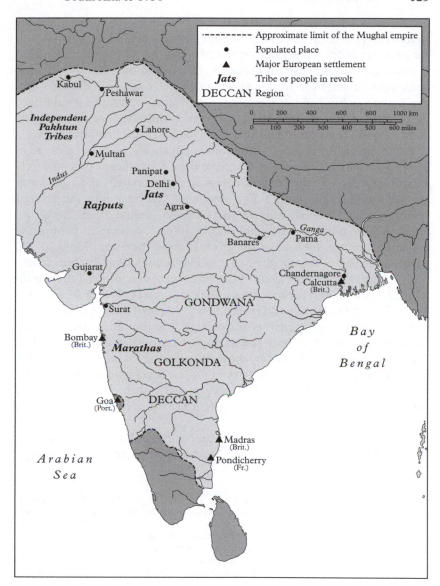

Map 8 The Mughal empire

placed at the center, surrounded by wagons. In between the larger pieces firing five and a quarter pound balls and twenty-one larger pieces firing 52 pound balls, were men armed with matchlocks. There was a vanguard force of 5,000 cavalry with swords, two wings of horse-archers with

12,000 men between them, and a reserve.[20] Ibrahim placed his elephants in front and the entire mass of his 30,000 infantry behind. His plan was to make a simple frontal assault on the Mughal position, a tactic perhaps dictated by the composition of his force, but also one that clearly misunderstood the nature of the Mughal army.[21] Even had Ibrahim succeeded in reaching and overrunning the Mughal center, he would have been completely incapable of coming to grips with the Mughal cavalry.[22] Babur's guns, however, denied the Delhi Sultan even that possibility.

Babur's guns opened fire on Ibrahim's advancing troops at a range of about 400 yards. While there may have been a significant psychological effect to the barrage, the impact of the actual cannon balls and bullets was probably more important.[23] The elephants fled back into the massed infantry, while Babur's horse-archers closed around them from two sides. At that point, the Mughal reserve force rode around behind the Sultanate army and the vanguard drove in from the front. Some 20,000 men were killed in the slaughter that followed, including Ibrahim Lodi.

Although the political effects of the battle were unequivocal, the significance of cannon and firearms was initially less clear. They had certainly been effective in blunting and reversing the charge of the elephant corps, a noteworthy accomplishment in and of itself, but Ibrahim's internal political problems may have been just as important in his defeat. The Afghan leader was not very well liked by the tribal chiefs he led into battle, and the large infantry force he brought to the field was a very limited instrument. Ibrahim acquitted himself well, however, dying at the front of his army among piles of enemy dead. Babur for his part went on to take over Agra and Delhi a few weeks later.

In retrospect, the First Battle of Panipat marked a dramatic shift in warfare. The real power of Babur and Mughal firearms came in combination

---

[20] The reserve does not appear to have figured in the 18,000 cavalry listed for Babur's force. I cannot explain the discrepancy, except to assume that the reserve force was not more than a few hundred men.

[21] One of Babur's subordinates, Darwesh Muhammad Sarban, actually wondered whether Ibrahim Lodi would in fact attack such a well-prepared position: "With so much precaution what possibility is there that he will come?" *Baburnama*, 324. Babur reassured him that Ibrahim was too ignorant of battle tactics to realize the strength of the Mughal position.

[22] As indeed happened at the Second Battle of Panipat. Although the Mughals did not, in that case, have a line of artillery at their center, they were subject to an elephant charge directed at their center. The Mughal center fell back behind a ravine while their mounted archers fired into the Afghan army from the flanks.

[23] Kaushik Roy places some emphasis on the surprise effect of the sound of the cannon, since "Ibrahim's soldiers and elephants had never seen such brass monsters before, and the sound of 'hell fire' unnerved them" (93). I suspect that a 52 pound cannon ball tearing through elephants and men was reason enough to panic, particularly given that the cannon were some distance away when they opened fire.

with the excellent horse-archers of Central Asia. Operating together, guns and horse-archers effectively ended the era of elephant dominance on the South Asian battlefield.[24] Neither arm was new, but the near monopoly the Mughals exercised over the best horsemen, and their new tactics, learned from the Ottomans, brought unprecedented results. There was a revolution in military practice that led to a political revolution. South Asia would soon be united under the Mughal empire.

Modern historians have evaluated the significance of Mughal rule in light of contemporary ideas of nationalism, imperialism, or world history.[25] The former two paradigms do not directly concern us here, but we must engage the last, world history, with respect to the idea of "gunpowder empires" put forward by V. V. Bartol'd, Marshall G. S. Hodgson, and William H. McNeill.[26] The gunpowder empire thesis proposes that increasingly expensive and powerful artillery led to the creation of larger and more centralized empires, because only central governments could afford to field the most effective cannon. These new cannon could destroy any local military power, thus conclusively establishing the central government as more than first among equals. In Asia, this also led to a stagnation of military technology since the central governments that effectively held a monopoly on cannon production were not interested in further weapon development.

Heavy mortars certainly increased the power of regional rulers over their local subordinates as long as those subordinates relied upon their fortifications to defy their overlords. This did not lead to further conquest and integration, however, because the regional rulers had no real technological or economic advantage over each other. Moreover, the limited mobility of mortars made it extremely difficult to bring them into play in remote or difficult terrain. Forts regained some of their pre-gunpowder strength by placement in locations that cannons could reach only with the greatest efforts.[27] Military practice was revolutionized not by mortars but

---

[24] Simon Digby, *War Horse and Elephant in the Delhi Sultarate*, Karachi: Oxford University Press, 1971.

[25] For an overview of these positions see Douglas E. Streusand, *The Formation of the Mughal Empire*, Delhi: Oxford University Press, 1989, 2–13.

[26] Vasilii Vladimirovitch Bartol'd, *Mussulman Culture*, trans. by Shahib Suhrawardy, Philadelphia: Porcupine, 1977, 99–102; Marshall G. S. Hodgson, *The Venture of Islam*, 3 vols., Chicago: University of Chicago Press, 1974, III:17–18; William H. McNeill, *The Pursuit of Power*, Chicago: University of Chicago Press, 1982.

[27] This particular fortification practice was only available to lesser strongmen, or for the retreats of greater lords, because an important urban center could not exist without convenient access. Any location well situated to collect large amounts of taxes from agriculture or trade was by definition within easy reach of cannon.

by field guns and handguns combined with horse-archers. And while field guns could be expensive, particularly when produced in large numbers out of bronze or brass, handguns became relatively cheap when their barrels were made of wrought iron. The major shift in power was not with respect to fortresses, but with respect to the battlefield.

Yet guns by themselves without horse-archers did not provide an overwhelming military advantage. The Mughals would win with guns on an unprecedented scale, even lacking a monopoly over their use or manufacture. Mughal armies won a series of battles, proving to be almost invincible in the field. They created a South Asian empire not because they were the only force able to afford sufficient siege artillery. Their opponents, like Islam Shah in 1556, sometimes possessed heavier weapons and considerable wealth. Mughal success required superior horse-archers and light field guns. Their strength lay also in the correct combination of those arms. This included siege artillery where it was useful, but relied upon lighter weapons in the field.

Seen in light of early Mughal success, it is hard to substantiate the particulars of the gunpowder empires thesis. Babur was not the only ruler with sufficient funds to purchase effective guns, nor was his use of heavy artillery anything new. Cannon had already had something of an effect in increasing the power of regional rulers, but this had been limited. South Asia was perhaps too wealthy for economic access to cannon to be limited to a single rich king. Moreover, the shift to cavalry warfare, and the political organization that accompanied it, dispersed considerable military and political power back to the local level. What South Asia most resembled before the sixteenth century was Europe, where contending regional powers fought with similar technology, and no single power was able to conquer the rest.

The final issue, that the monopoly of the central government over cannon production stagnated innovation, may be true but is hard to prove. There was very little in the way of native innovation, but then almost the entire range of gunpowder weapons had been developed elsewhere. The rise of the Mughals did not end the constant flow of foreign gun technology into South Asia, mostly in the form of experts brought in to manufacture weapons. Here it might be useful to recall Kenneth Chase's argument that Europeans developed better guns because they were much more effective in the European military milieu. There were, however, further developments in the South Asian arsenal that reflected their particular modes of warfare.

Light swivel cannons mounted on camels, *shaturnal* (camel barrel), came into use in sixteenth-century Mamluk Egypt. This weapon reached South Asia by 1614 at the latest, and thereafter became part of the regular

Mughal artillery.[28] With either a wrought iron, bronze, or brass barrel, its overall length was about a yard, and it fired a two-inch diameter ball weighing between three and four ounces.[29] The *shaturnal* was fired from a kneeling camel and sometimes from atop an elephant, but not while in motion. This appears to have been an adaptation to the demands of cavalry warfare, providing an extremely mobile field artillery with good hitting power. *Shaturnal* were used in increasing numbers up to the middle of the eighteenth century, and they formed a significant part of the Mughal "artillery of the stirrup," the artillery park that traveled with the emperor as he traversed his empire. Hundreds and even thousands of *shaturnal* were used in battle into the late eighteenth century, playing a role similar to Babur's field guns.

Obviously, *shaturnal* were not used to destroy fortifications, a function fulfilled by the extremely heavy cannon that also accompanied the Mughal emperor. A modified light cannon using the swivel of the *shaturnal*, the *jaza'il*, was originally mounted on fortification walls, before further evolving into a sort of sniper rifle usable anywhere its barrel rest could be temporarily fixed. Firing a one- or two-ounce ball out of a heavy barrel solidly supported on its rest, the *jaza'il* was extremely accurate at long range. This was of great value in defensive positions to keep besiegers at bay, or in ambushes in rough country. But it was by no means a weapon of the open battlefield.

Metal shot further enhanced the effectiveness of guns as it came into general use in the seventeenth century, though brass-like shot was used in the mid-sixteenth century. The expense of metal shot often led to the use of hollow balls, and this facilitated the creation of fused explosive rounds. The English East India Company sold metal shot to the Mughals in 1649, which was only one example of the importation of foreign weaponry. Although brass was too expensive for widespread use, wrought iron brought the price down into a more reasonable range. Iron shot was so much more effective that stone balls were no longer much valued. It also became increasingly important to produce guns of a consistent caliber. The seventeenth century thus saw a marked improvement in South Asian guns and projectiles.

It was all too late for the Mughal empire, at least if guns were to have any effect in saving the centralized state. Jos Gommans has argued that the Mughal imperial army maintained its superiority over provincial forces through better mounts for its horse-archers and heavy cavalry,

---

[28] Khan, *Gunpowder and Firearms*, 107.

[29] This is a composite description based upon several sources cited in ibid., 107–9, provided for comparison purposes. Individual weapons varied in size and caliber.

and better artillery and infantry.[30] This was usually, at least in the early and middle part of the Mughal empire, more than sufficient to defeat any local strongman. But the social and political structure of the empire was not based upon the central government's monopoly over the legitimate use of force. Military, and thus social and political, power was dispersed across the empire through *mansabdārs zamīndārs* (landlords), and the large numbers (estimated at almost 350,000 cavalry and more than 4 million infantry in the 1590s[31]) of armed men. The problem for the Mughal ruler was not how to disarm this vast sea of fighters and military leaders, since such a task seemed impossible, but how to manage them.

Mughal rulers placed themselves on top of the "military labor market," to use Dirk Kolff's term,[32] and used that organic system to manipulate the means of violence in South Asia. By taking certain leaders into his employ, or offering that possibility, the emperor not only temporarily strengthened his own capabilities but also denied them to a potential rebel. The emperor thus possessed a relatively small core of the best equipment and troops, as well as the financial and intelligence capability to influence the remaining men and horsepower. Whereas before the Mughal unification these means of war were in separate polities of varying sizes (or could be summoned from Central Asia) and were used against each other, once the Mughal government superstructure was in place the military problem became a much more distinctly internal political problem. Superior firearms, or even fortress-reducing cannon, could not change this political dynamic. It was not that the central government stifled innovation: new weapons were always welcome – but they were beside the point.

Functional handguns were available throughout South Asia, and could even be produced by local blacksmiths. A handgun was actually cheaper to make than a good Central Asian composite bow. Composite bows took about a year to make, and could be destroyed by the rainy and humid climate of much of South Asia.[33] Over the course of Mughal rule, hand-guns made even small villages much better able to resist the power of the central government. As vast as the numbers of available fighters noted above seem, they represented only those men in the market for military work at some level. They may have constituted 10 percent of the total male

---

[30] Gommans, *Mughal Warfare*, 99–130, 135.

[31] Abul Fazl, *Ā'īn*, cited in Kolff, *Naukar, Rajput and Sepoy*, 3. The exact number for the census of available military men in the twelve *subahs* of the empire is 342,696 cavalrymen and 4,039,097 infantry.

[32] Kolff, *Naukar, Rajput and Sepoy*, 2 and passim.

[33] See Babur's complaint on this subject: Wheeler M. Thackston (trans.), *The Baburnama*, New York and Oxford: Oxford University Press, 1996, 351.

population, but they did not include armed men who remained in their town or village outside of the military labor market.[34] Handguns therefore acted as a decentralizing influence in an already unstable system.

The working of the military labor market is central to understanding the social and political effects of the Mughal military system. This chapter will thus conclude with an example of how that market functioned: Sher Shah's temporary overthrow of Mughal rule in 1540. In the following chapter I will take up the development of the Maratha polity and its undermining of Mughal rule, and then continue the discussion of the military labor market with the changes wrought by the British East India Company, and the move to the "true" military revolution as understood in Europe.

Between 1529 and 1539, Sher Shah developed his power as a servant of the ruling family of the Sultanate of Bihar. His power came not only from his high position at court, but also from his acquisition of large amounts of treasure. The key to the military labor market was the wealth necessary to obtain and maintain soldiers. In the political arena, wealth helped make alliances or allowed one, as in Sher Shah's case, to recruit troops without relying upon uncertain allies. Sher Shah was both lucky and canny in his pursuit of wealth; even more impressive was his ability to switch from a wartime financial system that relied upon booty and plunder to a peacetime system that relied upon regular agricultural taxation. Wealth did not mean, however, exclusive access to superior cannon. As significant as Babur's use of guns was in inaugurating Mughal rule, neither cannon nor handguns were restricted to any one group. South Asian state formation was founded on the wealth necessary to purchase the services of armed men.

Cannon played an important role in warfare, of course, as Sher Shah's six-month siege of Raisen in 1543 demonstrated. All the copper available was commandeered to make the cannon that then wrought considerable damage upon the fortifications. Puran Mal, at whom the campaign had been directed, came out and began negotiations with Sher Shah. Hostilities were resolved through the usual military labor market practice of taking Puran Mal and his men into the imperial army.

FURTHER READING

Vasilii Vladimirovitch Bartol'd, *Mussulman Culture*, trans. by Shahib Suhrawardy, Philadelphia: Porcupine, 1977.

Simon Digby, *War Horse and Elephant in the Delhi Sultanate*, Karachi: Oxford University Press, 1971.

---

[34] Kolff, *Naukar, Rajput and Sepoy*, 6–9.

Jos Gommans, *Mughal Warfare*, London and New York: Routledge, 2002.

Jos Gommans and Dirk H. A. Kolff (eds.), *Warfare and Weaponry in South Asia, 1000–1800*, New Delhi: Oxford University Press, 2001.

Jos Gommans and Om Prakash (eds.), *Circumambulations in South Asian History*, Leiden: E. J. Brill, 2003.

Marshall G. S. Hodgson, *The Venture of Islam*, 3 vols., Chicago: University of Chicago Press, 1974.

Iqtidar Alam Khan, *Gunpowder and Firearms*, Oxford: Oxford University Press, 2004.

Om Prakash, *Downfall of the Mughal Empire*, New Delhi: Anmol, 2002.

Dietmar Rothermund, "From Chariot to Atom Bomb: Armament and Military Organization in South Asian History," in Jos Gommans and Om Prakash (eds.), *Circumambulations in South Asian History*, Leiden: E. J. Brill, 2003, 325–40.

Kaushik Roy, *From Hydaspes to Kargil: A History of Warfare in India from 326 BC to AD 1999*, New Delhi: Manohar, 2004.

Douglas E. Streusand, *The Formation of the Mughal Empire*, Delhi: Oxford University Press, 1989.

Wheeler M. Thackston (trans.), *The Baburnama*, New York and Oxford: Oxford University Press, 1996.

6 The military revolution in South Asia, 1750–1850

The introduction of European firearms and training after 1750 brought the European military revolution to South Asia. European mercenary officers taught local infantry European tactics, and employed improved artillery to greater effect both in the field and in sieges. Improved flint-locks with socket bayonets, coupled with European training, shifted the balance of power on the battlefield from the cavalry to the infantry, though this really accelerated a pre-existing native trend in this direction. Cavalry remained on the battlefield, just as in Europe, for both practical and traditional reasons. The aristocracy was still wedded to the horse as its particular military accoutrement, but heavy cavalry soon disappeared. These technological and tactical changes in warfare hastened the decline of the existing social and political order at the local and provincial levels, but arrived too late to have much effect upon the senescent Mughal court. By 1750 the Mughal government was a spent force, leaving the subcontinent politically vulnerable to outside, in this case European, interference.

South Asian military practice shadowed European practice for the next century, and, it has been argued, even contributed to Western military practice through the Asian command experiences of men like the Duke of Wellington. It would still require a century for the increasing effectiveness of the infantry almost completely to undermine the battlefield use of South Asian cavalry. Moreover, the strength of infantry and artillery induced profound political shifts that laid the foundation of the modern Indian state. This was not at all clear in the mid-eighteenth century, however, and it would take at least a century of often very un-European-style fighting before the results of the military revolution were in evidence. British colonial rule accepted Mughal governing practice at the local level, but not its divided political system at the regional level, and strove for a more European system of government that knit together the subcontinent much more deeply. Political integration was made possible by the use of European military methods by the British East India Company (EIC).

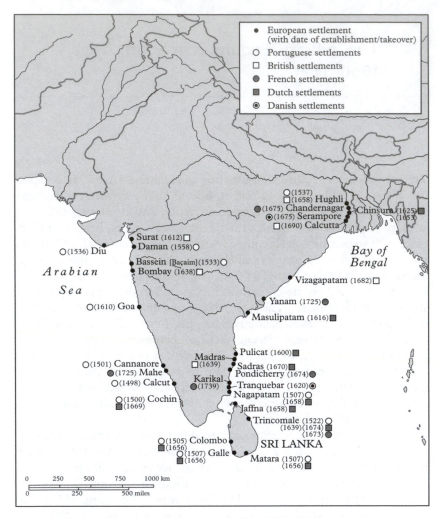

Map 9 European settlement in India, 1501–1739

The British colonial foundation of modern India and Pakistan does not sit comfortably with contemporary nationalism. At the most basic level, however, it is important to keep in mind that the British did not conquer the subcontinent with a vast influx of British soldiers employing weaponry far in advance of anything available to the natives. The EIC developed the bulk of its armed forces by training native recruits drawn from the military labor market, and arming them with slightly better handguns and cannon. Just as importantly, the bureaucracy that supported those military and political efforts was far more efficient, relentless, and ruthless than any of the native noble courts. The EIC fought for profit and power, not honor, and could maintain its long-term strategy beyond the life of a single general or governor. Relatively small numbers of British troops and trainers were able to transmit the fruits of the European military revolution to a standing army controlled by the EIC, and commanded by British officers.

Neither European military practice nor weaponry was unknown before the EIC, of course, since European mercenaries had long been employed by many rulers to improve their armies. Using European military experts, particularly artillery experts, was entirely consistent with standing native practice. Foreign experts provided technical skills from the very beginning of gunpowder use in South Asia, in both producing arms and using them in the field. Rulers expected to select particular groups or individuals for military service from the available pool of labor based upon their skills in a specific mode of warfare. One did not buy arms and marry them to one's soldiers; one bought men who used certain weapons. Part of the attraction of employing European mercenaries was that they did not fit into the existing political and social structure. It was often hoped that they would be able to improve military practice without challenging the political order. This was only partially successful because European practice required a very different kind of soldier than most native rulers were willing to support. The higher standards of infantry training necessary for European tactics to be effective required not only a standing army, but also enough of those European-trained infantry to carry them out. Raising an army when required by selecting men from the available labor market was far cheaper.

It is important, however, to emphasize that Europe was not the only factor influencing South Asian military development. The rise of the Marathas as a cohesive polity in the seventeenth century would lead to the effective destruction of the Mughal government as a real power. Before they could do this, of course, they had to find a way to defeat the Mughal military system. This they achieved by evading the Mughal army, dispersing their forces, and launching hit-and-run raids. The Mughal army depended upon winning the field, or at least being so dominant in the field that no one would actually oppose it, and then conducting political/ diplomatic negotiations simultaneous with a siege. The Marathas denied the Mughals this familiar process, overturning the existing system without the need for new technology. At the same time, events in the northwest would see the capture of Kandahar and Afghanistan by other powers, thus limiting access to the superior Central Asian cavalry which were instrumental in Mughal tactics.

Gunpowder remained an important military tool in all these conflicts, but there were no dramatic new developments in weapons, no technological breakthroughs, to alter the military environment significantly. The Mughal military system continued to rely upon the same tactical combination of arms, and the same political and strategic vision of empire. There was no reason to change the system since it continued to work until the beginning of the eighteenth century. But without reforming the fundamental social and political structure of the empire at the local level, a task that was not seriously considered, the central government remained in a continual military struggle with the *zamīndārs* and even its own *mansabdārs*. This instability, which had allowed Sher Shah temporarily to displace the Mughals in the sixteenth century, was never resolved, it was accepted. A series of good rulers had managed to maintain the regime, and even expand its territory, until the eighteenth century.

The Mughal empire went into decline long before any European power became a serious threat to it. It is important to separate clearly the collapse of the Mughals' nominally unified subcontinent from the arrival of European military methods or political goals. Nor did the Europeans, whether Portuguese, Dutch, French, or British, bring guns or violence to a peaceful society unfamiliar with firearms. European mercenaries served in South Asian armies, and Europeans sold cannon, handguns, and all manner of military supplies to native combatants. But it was the Maratha shift to light cavalry armed with swords and shields, making fast-moving raids and avoiding the main Mughal armies, that mostly negated the Mughal advantage in cannon. Maratha power would in turn fragment after the Third Battle of Panipat in 1761, leaving the subcontinent politically divided just as the British were emerging as the main European power in the area.

British administration at the local level borrowed from the pre-existing offices established by the Marathas, who had, in turn, mostly followed Mughal practice. In areas that had not been under Maratha control the British also followed the pre-existing practice. This led to a patchwork of different systems at the local and regional level, united only in the administration of the EIC and then the British colonial government. There was thus no sharp break with earlier practice at least at the theoretical level, since Mughal administration had been similarly flexible. The major British innovation on the subcontinent was not technological, administrative, political, or tactical, though there were significant changes in all these areas, but in monopolizing the military labor market and disarming the countryside.

Unlike previous rulers of the subcontinent, the British expected the central government to establish a monopoly over the legitimate use of force. The European military revolution provided British-led armies a narrow margin of superiority over native forces, but this was not always enough to ensure success. European military technology and methods were adopted in whole or in part by many regional powers, and in some cases, like that of Haider Ali of Mysore, civil and military administration reformed as well. Haider Ali was able to confront the power of the British directly and impose a peace upon them in 1769. Ultimate British success should not obfuscate how uncertain their fortunes were; in several instances the deaths of significant regional rulers ended serious threats to the British position. It would be wrong, then, to conclude that because the British did control India for many years, their technological and military prowess gave them an irresistible advantage over local rulers.

The subcontinent as a whole, if it can or even should be analyzed that way, was vulnerable to European intervention because its regional rulers did not unite to fight against the Western threat. Haider Ali was the exception who believed the British to be a different and more dangerous threat than the other, local, powers he had to contend with. Even one of Haider's local opponents, the Maratha *peshwa* Madhav Rao, could see that the British were squeezing the subcontinent from all sides, but he would not join forces to defeat the external threat. Madhav Rao's only response to this threat, after he had consolidated his own position, was to enhance Maratha power. Every ruler could only strive for his own, personal power, allowing the British to play one off against the other. Indeed, it was the success of the EIC in uniting the subcontinent under a strong central administration that suggests the possibility to modern historians that local powerholders could have, or should have, acted together to resist the British. Local rulers could scarcely conceive of an "Indian" response to the European threat because the Mughal empire had not created the overriding consciousness of such a domestic polity. The mature Mughal military system maintained the Great Mughal's relationship to his subjects in a constant struggle between obedience to the center and regional and local independence. By the time the British themselves became a significant local power, the Mughal court had been losing its struggle against the local and regional powerholders, the *zamīndār*-ization of the subcontinent, for many years.

The mature Mughal military system

The Mughal army under Aurangzeb (1658–1707) differed considerably from that of Babur, though the change may be traced to the reign of Akbar

(1556–1605).[1] Unlike the agile, fast-moving Central Asian army that established the Mughal regime, the mature imperial army was a moving city that marched no more than ten miles a day, usually much less, and rested at least two days a week. The artillery was cumbersome and slow, requiring hundreds of oxen to draw it. A considerable, but necessary, group of camp followers accompanied this mass, providing it with provisions, equipment, and even entertainment. Smaller Mughal detachments were not so encumbered, but also did not possess the siege artillery necessary for capturing forts. Often just as importantly, a main Mughal army carried a large store of money and treasure with it. Although it would seem that a ponderous main army was the very antithesis of an effective campaign instrument, it could be extremely effective in maintaining and restoring order within the empire. During the middle years of the Mughal empire, the goal of most imperial campaigns was to maintain the internal balance of center and periphery, not to annihilate external threats to the throne.

Many Mughal rulers kept in motion with their army annually, touring their empire in a continual cycle of intimidation and negotiation. When the emperor passed through, local strongmen and imperial officials had either to demonstrate their loyalty by visiting the court or to go into open defiance and risk destruction by the army. But the choice was often not quite as stark as that, with some *zamīndārs* first making a show of resistance to improve their bargaining position before submitting and being accepted back into the court's good graces. Military means were the basic political capital for negotiating rights, ranks, and privileges. The Great Mughal commanded the strongest army, giving him a political advantage in real terms over and above his institutional power to legitimize any adjustment in local military power. The Great Mughal had to be able to enforce his decisions in adjudicating local conflicts.

Although the mature Mughal army was quite ponderous, it was also extremely effective in destroying any number of opponents. It remained nearly irresistible in the open field and was capable of conducting successful sieges, even in very difficult circumstances. At the same time, however, it was extremely expensive to set in motion. A Mughal army with the full panoply of military means at its disposal bore an immense logistical burden. This would be the weak point that the Marathas would consistently exploit to great effect. Neither the Mughal court nor its

---

[1] Jadunath Sarkar, *Military History of India*, Bombay: Orient Longman, 1970, 148, locates the change in the Mughal army in Akbar's reign, and the full expression of those alterations in the end of Shah Jahan's reign in 1657. My discussion of what I have termed the "mature" Mughal system follows ibid., 146–54.

generals were able to formulate a response to these tactics. What is curious is not that the Marathas could so easily undercut the Mughal military machine, but that it took so long for someone on the subcontinent to figure out how to do it.[2] Perhaps the reason for this was precisely that the Mughal army was capable, as the Marathas for the most part were not, of capturing forts. Taking and holding forts was key in controlling the surrounding lands and their revenues. If the point of a campaign was to control territory, then only a Mughal-like army made sense.

The enduring value of the Mughal military system in some circumstances was demonstrated even in the early eighteenth century by Nizam-ul-Mulk. Nizam was a Mughal governor who ended up on the wrong side of court politics. After defeating two armies sent to destroy him, he briefly rose to become prime minister, before once again falling prey to politics. Nizam retreated to his former administrative position, where he maintained himself in nominal loyalty to the Mughal throne while acting as an independent power. But he was similarly unable to overcome Maratha tactics, despite his competent execution of the Mughal military system. The great Maratha *peshwa* Baji Rao was repeatedly able to draw Nizam-ul-Mulk's slow-moving, heavily encumbered armies into untenable positions and cut him off. A Mughal army simply could not overcome a faster opponent who would not offer or accept battle.

In some senses, Mughal campaigns were almost paradigmatic demonstrations of the Clausewitzian connection between war and policy, but with particular emphasis on the financial basis of power. Money was not just the sinews of war, it was the sinews of politics as well. The center of the main Mughal army was a large treasury that disbursed funds to buy the services of fighting men. Money and cannon together could overcome any political problem by either undermining or destroying an opponent. Yet ultimately it was the army and the cannon that traveled with the Great Mughal that gave him a near-monopoly on political legitimacy. Money was a convenient instrument of political exchange and store of political capital only against the backdrop of military power.

Only a credible threat of force maintained the empire, though the knowledge that the Mughal army was not only unstoppable in the field but also expensive to operate gave Mughal opponents some counter-leverage in negotiations. The Great Mughal's army was more powerful than anyone

---

[2] The success of Central Asian cavalry in wearing down invading Mughal armies in the mid-seventeenth century should have demonstrated the particular weaknesses of Mughal practice to any interested party. Uzbek raiding undermined Mughal logistics and frustrated efforts to subdue areas. Mughal armies might capture cities like Balkh by their irresistible military and diplomatic means, but control of broader territory always remained tenuous outside of the very short reach of the army.

else's, but it was not more powerful than everyone else together. Moreover, that army could not be everywhere at once, or even in widely dispersed places in rapid succession. Committing a major army to one problem made it difficult, if not impossible, simultaneously to marshal similar resources for another. The strategic challenge for the Mughal court was to evaluate correctly the relative importance of disparate military and political problems with respect to time, space, and available military resources. Clearly, the Mughal court consistently misunderstood the nature and significance of the Maratha threat in its early stages, and then failed to adjust its tactics to compensate for Maratha tactics in the later stages.

The clash between Mughal and Maratha strategy was one of a war of annihilation versus a war of attrition, respectively.[3] Considerations of both cost and prestige required Mughal armies quickly, if often only temporarily, to force the complete political submission of opponents. An opponent might therefore offer political submission safe in the knowledge that the military exigencies of a particular time, unrest in other parts of the empire, for example, would allow him to renege on virtually all of his commitments to the throne. At the very least, the Mughal army rarely if ever moved to destroy the forces of someone who surrendered. Political surrender was an effective way to preserve one's army to await a more opportune moment. The Mughal army could plausibly threaten to annihilate any army that chose to face it in the field, or any fort that chose to resist it; political submission without resort to arms was preferable. Among the local and regional leaders willing to play the Mughal game, the rules were clear. But the Marathas did not offer or accept battle in the field, and retook forts after they surrendered or were captured without difficulty. Such actions were an obvious rejection of the Mughal imperial system, at least in the openly confrontational defiance of the throne. The Marathas effectively defined themselves as a polity, and often as an ethnic group as well, through rejection of integration into the imperial system after defeat. Shivaji's adoption of Hindu kingship made this explicit. This political and cultural shift, in turn, enabled the Maratha leadership to outmaneuver the Mughal court politically as well as militarily.

Although cannon and firearms made the Mughal army nearly irresistible in sieges and on the battlefield, it did not follow that the Mughal army always retained the strategic or tactical initiative. The Marathas were successful because they avoided annihilation, gained the strategic initiative, and made the conflict attritional. But on the other side, the

---

[3] For Kaushik Roy's comments on Maratha strategy, see his *From Hydaspes to Kargil*, 105–7.

Mughal court made serious strategic and political blunders that, more than any other factor, led to the decline of Mughal power. It was not technology or tactics that destroyed Mughal power; the Marathas soon copied the Mughals as they themselves became conquerors. Conquest and control of the empire followed a clear path, one the EIC would also follow. What undermined the Mughal court was a novel political and military system that it could not respond to effectively.

The Marathas

Since the Marathas were instrumental in undermining the Mughal regime in the eighteenth century, it is worth describing their rise to power as a polity, and how they dealt with the Mughal military system. It is also important to demonstrate the significant continuities in military practice that they and, later, the EIC followed. In this latter sense, the Marathas were a bridge between Mughal warfare and the warfare of the European military revolution. They shifted from guerrilla tactics, to Mughal tactics, to a nearly European tactical system that used handgun-armed infantry and field guns in addition to their cavalry. The European military revolution was therefore less shocking and more of an incremental improvement in certain technologies and tactics. EIC victories were neither guaranteed, nor an indication of overwhelming military superiority, though Europeans have tended to see things that way.

The Marathas emerged from a social network established in the western Deccan between the fifteenth and eighteenth centuries.[4] Several important families achieved dominance over the area as rural coloniza-tion advanced during the sixteenth and seventeenth centuries. This col-onization was internal, led by warlike groups in concert with pioneering farmers. Social mobility among the leadership allowed farmers and free-lance military entrepreneurs to advance themselves and to range through-out the area, leading to a complex and flexible organization of individuals, families, and clans. Most importantly, these internal ties were uncon-nected to the Mughal social and political network. Maratha leaders emphasized unity within the group, rather than caste, economic class, or the role of Brahmins.

The Mughal court officially took a neutral position with respect to Deccan politics in the seventeenth century. Mostly this was due to the realization that Mughal military strength was not up to direct involvement. Various Maratha leaders were given imperial ranks, *mansabs*, or military

---

[4] This discussion of early Maratha history follows Andrea Hintze, *The Mughal Empire and its Decline*, Aldershot: Ashgate, 1997, 218–43.

employment, but, as a whole, the Marathas were not brought into the imperial system. The Deccan was left to the devices of the two sultanates of Golconda and Bijapur by treaty in 1636. The Marathas were able to develop politically and militarily while these two courts struggled for power. Although in retrospect it might seem that the Mughal court was unwise to neglect the Marathas, in the mid-seventeenth century there was really no reason to imagine that a loosely organized group of *zamīndārs* in the south would one day evolve into a mortal threat to the empire.

Shivaji Bhonsle (1627–80) laid the foundation of the centrally directed Maratha polity. His father, Shahji, had served the Sultans of Ahmadnagar and Bijapur, and even received a Mughal *mansab* in 1630. The Bhonsle family switched its allegiance back and forth as circumstances changed, just like many other Hindu *zamīndārs* in the Deccan. Shahji's base was the city of Pune, though he was banished from it after the 1636 treaty that left the Deccan to Golconda and Bijapur (Ahmadnagar having been eliminated).

Shivaji grew up in Pune, and pursued his father's goal of an independent Maratha position. Golconda and Bijapur cooperated in military ventures aimed at the southeast, leaving the northwestern coast to the Marathas. Shivaji expanded both outward and inward, attacking his local rivals and his neighbors. As he gained control over territory, he built forts on the tops of mountains to solidify his power and to serve as bases for further raids. Bijapur finally sent an expedition to bring him into line in 1659. Shivaji was besieged in a fort, only managing to resolve the situation by assassinating the commanding general during negotiations.

Shivaji overreached himself in 1664 when he sacked the Mughal port of Surat. A full-scale Mughal expedition soon forced him to surrender. He could not resist an army capable of reducing his forts with cannon. Shivaji surrendered twenty of thirty-five forts in 1665 and was made a Mughal *mansabdār* with commensurate military obligations to the throne. Notwithstanding this agreement that brought the recalcitrant Maratha leader into the Mughal system, he was soon brought to Delhi and placed under house arrest while the court debated what to do with him. That the Great Mughal did not immediately order his execution is indicative of both the underestimation of the Maratha threat and the prevailing political ideology that accepted the notion of *zamīndārs* rebelling and then being reintegrated into the system. Running out of money to bribe courtiers, Shivaji contrived a successful escape from Delhi.

Over the next few years, Shivaji regained most of his earlier territory, and even sacked Surat again in 1670. The Mughal court was otherwise occupied with the Afghans, giving him an important breathing space. In 1674, Shivaji had himself crowned king in a recreated Hindu ceremony.

The problems of his family's obvious low birth were overcome by the ritual sleight of hand of a few willing Brahmins. Despite the flaws in Shivaji's claims, his military and political successes had allowed low- and middle-ranking Maratha *zamīndārs* to overthrow the power of the older, higher-ranking elites. A new kind of legitimacy was created outside of the Muslim system that had dominated the subcontinent for so long. But it did not last very long.

Shivaji's death in 1680 ultimately shifted power to the Maratha prime minister, or *peshwa*. This shift was the result of succession disputes that continued into the 1720s, complicated by much more direct Mughal intervention. The Great Mughal Aurangzeb invaded the Deccan himself in 1681–2, overthrowing Bijapur in 1686[5] and forcing Golconda to surrender in 1687. Shambaji, Shivaji's son, was captured and killed in 1689, clear recognition, in contrast to the treatment of his father, of the threat of Maratha power. With Bijapur and Golconda now Mughal provinces, called Bijapur, Bijapur Carnatic, Hyderabad, and Hyderabad Carnatic, the Deccan was theoretically under direct Mughal administration. But Mughal governors and officials were still unable to counter Maratha raiding bands by force, leaving them to make local alliances with Maratha *zamīndārs*. This engagement in turn convinced the Mughal court to allow governors more extended tenures in office in order to keep the peace. Maratha leaders and some Mughal governors were able to enhance their own power further in this relaxed system.

The Mughal court's attempts to control the Marathas by fitting them into the imperial system backfired. Rather than solidify the Maratha polity into an easily manageable unit, subject to political and military sanction, and even useful as a military resource, Mughal recognition of the Maratha king merely reified the institutions created by Shivaji, enhancing Maratha power without making it more tractable. By 1690, Aurangzeb decided to concentrate fully on settling the Deccan, and moved his capital first to Galgala, and then, from 1695 to 1699, to Islampuri. He attempted to destroy the Marathas by personally capturing each one of their hilltop forts, but this proved futile. His considerable military means, the full complement of cannon, firearms, cavalry, and infantry, could not overcome the diffuse Maratha forces, or persuade the Maratha *zamīndārs* to submit more than temporarily. Given that Aurangzeb's empire encompassed the largest territory of any Mughal ruler, this was profoundly frustrating. The strengths and weaknesses of the Mughal–Maratha

---

[5] Gommans, *Mughal Warfare*, 187, has the year as 1685.

conflict are perhaps best exemplified by the eight-year Mughal siege of Gingee.[6]

After Shambaji was executed, it fell to his younger brother Rajaram to become Maratha king. The new king was scarcely crowned before he was fleeing to the south, where he took refuge in the fortress complex of Gingee. Gingee was a set of three hill forts linked by a curtain wall, a kilometer long on each side of the triangle. The surrounding mountains limited the approaches to the fortress, and prevented it from ever being completely invested during the eight-year siege. From the Maratha point of view, it had the immense advantage of overstretching Mughal supply lines deep into the south. The fortress itself was well supplied with water and equipped with large granaries. It had also been updated since the introduction of firearms, its earlier machiolated battlements renovated to form musket loops. The steepness of the hills and solidity of its granite walls made it difficult for cannon to make much of an impression.

Zulfiquar Khan brought 26,000 soldiers with him when he initially besieged Gingee in 1690, a figure that included 10,000 Mughal cavalry and 8,000 musketeers. In addition to 1,000 *shaturnal*, he also had eight heavy cannon and seventy one- to four-pounders. Some of his powder and iron shot was supplied by the English at Madras, and a hundred European gunners were employed. In sum, Zulfiquar Khan was well equipped with the best weapons and personnel available to conduct the siege. But such a considerable army in difficult terrain required a commensurate supply system. When the army arrived beneath Gingee in October of 1690, it was served by 100 elephants, 2,000–4,000 dromedaries, and about 200,000 cattle. As was usually the case, the army itself was further swelled by camp followers and merchants. A further 10,000–12,000 draught animals then became necessary to maintain a steady flow of goods to the camp. In such difficult terrain, at the end of the Mughal logistic trail, supply itself became the main concern in what almost immediately became a war of attrition.

The siege of Gingee was a grand strategic blunder for the Mughals. Aurangzeb seems to have felt that he could concentrate and destroy the Maratha threat at Gingee, pitting Mughal strength directly against Maratha strength. This contest of strength degenerated into a contest of will that the Great Mughal refused to see as pointless. He had been lured into an exhausting fight to capture a position that would have been important only if it were the last redoubt of Maratha power. It was not, and while Mughal attention was focused on Gingee, Maratha power

---

[6] This account of the siege of Gingee follows ibid., 189–99.

elsewhere in the Deccan continued to flourish. In the end, Gingee was captured by escalade, not firearms, as had been proposed at the very beginning of the siege. Zulfiquar Khan's motivations are open to question; many of the players on both sides were waiting for the aged Aurangzeb to die, but his strategic and tactical failures are undeniable. Gingee's capture was a pyrrhic victory, accomplishing nothing and, along with the broader effort to subjugate the Deccan that had preceded and followed the siege, distracting the Great Mughal's attentions from the rest of his empire for fifteen years. Aurangzeb lived until 1707, but he left the Mughal empire overextended and enervated.

Although the Marathas initially raised armies, mostly raiding bands, by calling up farmers during the off-season, this system became untenable as growing political requirements necessitated more regular campaigning and a standing army. As the army became more professional, no longer farming during the monsoon season, it became much more expensive to maintain. The Maratha polity could not be established or expanded without the army, but the expense of a standing army encouraged its use. Having gone to so much trouble to develop an effective military and political instrument, the Maratha leadership wanted to reap the benefits of that effort. Conversely, desiring to reap political benefits, they went to great trouble to build an army that could obtain them. This was a classic case of military and political goals driving each other in the establishment of a polity.

The Maratha polity did not, however, become the basis of a nation-state, in the European sense, nor did it overturn the existing social order.[7] Perhaps the most instructive aspect of the rise of the Marathas was the extent to which they followed the pre-existing Mughal military and political system as they developed. This trajectory demonstrates two aspects of political and military development on the subcontinent at that time, though both of these observations could equally well apply more broadly in time and place. First, the Mughal system was effective in reaching its goals. While goals and means certainly mature in concert with each other, a successful imperial system, like that of the Mughals, usually indicates that a functional equilibrium between political claims and military capabilities has been found (if only temporarily).

---

[7] There is a considerable amount of Hindu nationalist writing that argues that Maratha power was, indeed, the basis of a real nation, presumably modern India. Shivaji's explicit adoption of Hindu religious sanction in support of his claims of kingship, and the Maratha struggle against the power of the Muslim Mughals, makes the Marathas a Hindu success story.

The second aspect of development on the subcontinent was that the rise of the Marathas was not the result of, nor did it produce, an intellectual or conceptual break with the past. From the military perspective, it appears that the Marathas arrived at a new system of tactics that could overcome that of the Mughals. The Maratha system could not, however, achieve the positive goals that the Mughal army could, the conquest and control of extensive territories. In order to accomplish that, they were forced to become more and more like the Mughals. They gradually acquired artillery, infantry, and a bureaucracy.

Artillery was critical for an army that intended to capture forts. Without artillery it was even difficult to enter into negotiations for surrender, since a defender knew that he stood a very good chance of successfully resisting a siege. Thus not only conquest, but also control of territory, required an army to maintain a credible artillery park. Artillery in turn slowed an army down and increased its financial burden on the government. The need for artillery by itself transformed the Maratha army, shifting it from a fast-moving raiding force into a slow-moving conventional force. Moreover, artillery required trained specialists and large quantities of materials to operate. Although artillery can be multifunctional, used for sieges and in the field, most of the cannon the Marathas acquired were too heavy and not accurate enough for the field. Maratha cannon were handicapped by inconsistent boring, weak carriages, and poor sights. These problems would all contribute to the defeat of the Marathas at the Third Battle of Panipat.

The introduction of infantry into the Maratha army also slowed it down. Musket-armed infantrymen were extremely useful in both sieges and the field, but the available weapons, and the training of both infantry and cavalry, severely limited their effectiveness. Muskets depended upon powder and shot to function. Since these could not be obtained reliably by foraging, a supply train was needed. The generally poor quality of the available muskets made them unreliable and slow firing, which in turn required thick lines of infantry to be able to stave off cavalry charges. This meant that large numbers of infantry had to be deployed to be effective, further raising the logistical burden. Poor training further exacerbated this problem, leaving infantry formations able to face only one direction. Although cavalry might in theory protect the flanks of such a cumbersome line, Maratha cavalry was not trained to do so.

Both the military and political requirements of an established, standing army and the shift in power at the Maratha court from the king to the prime minister, led to the creation of a bureaucracy staffed by Brahmins. In some sense the Brahmin class had always been important in the creation of the Maratha polity, since it required Brahmin creativity to invent a process whereby Shivaji could become a Hindu king. It was also not surprising that the growing institutional complexity of the Maratha court would draw in members of the educated class to manage things. The big difference in practice in the Maratha government, as opposed to the Mughal government, was that the bureaucrats were civil officials who received salaries, rather than lands, for their service. Brahmin bankers also became part of the extended social network of government officials, tied into the financial system necessary to supply the army and collect local taxes for the government.

The end of Mughal power

With the succession in 1720 of the Chitpavan Brahmin Baji Rao to his father's position of *peshwa*, the Marathas gained a truly astonishing leader, who was both bold and wise. The Maratha king was now a figurehead, but the Marathas were still gaining in power. Baji Rao demonstrated Maratha power, and the sharp decline of Mughal power, with his surprise raid on Delhi in 1737. After dealing a sharp defeat to the Mughal force cobbled together and thrown at him outside the walls of the city, the Maratha leader withdrew, evading another Mughal army that tried to block his retreat.[8] Nizam-ul-Mulk was then duly called back from his virtually independent kingdom in the Deccan to face Baji Rao again, despite his earlier failure against the Maratha *peshwa*.[9] Sadly for Nizam-ul-Mulk and the Mughal court, he fared the same as in his first encounter with Baji Rao. The Mughal army was maneuvered into an untenable position, surrounded, and forced to accept unfavorable terms.

Just as it seemed that Mughal fortunes had reached their nadir, a new threat arose from a resurgent Safavid Persia under Nadir Shah.[10] By the time Nadir Shah invaded the Mughal empire in 1739, he had already vastly expanded the Safavid empire beyond its earlier boundaries. He relied upon great mobility, mounting his musketeers and placing *shaturnal* on camels to allow his firepower to keep up with the cavalry. Kandahar (March 24) and Kabul (June 29) fell in 1738; the Khyber Pass was forced

---

[8] Richard Burn (ed.), *Cambridge History of India*, Vol. IV, London: Cambridge University Press, 1937, 403.

[9] Nizam-ul-Mulk had joined together with Maratha leaders hostile to Baji Rao in 1726 to attack the Maratha king while the *peshwa* was on campaign. Baji Rao returned and restored the situation. Nizam-ul-Mulk was maneuvered into an arid area and surrounded near the town of Palkhed. Although his artillery preserved his army from extermination when the Marathas attacked on March 11, 1728, lack of water forced Nizam-ul-Mulk to negotiate very unfavorable terms of surrender for himself. Burns, *Cambridge History of India*, 400.

[10] This account of Nadir Shah's invasion of the Mughal empire follows Burns, *Cambridge History of India*, 357–63.

on November 26, and Peshawar and Lahore fell in short order as he rode south into Mughal territory. The Mughal court's intelligence was so poor that the threatening letter Nadir Shah sent from Lahore was initially ridiculed. Once it became known that Kabul had already fallen, an attempt was made to place Nizam-ul-Mulk in overall command of the Mughal army. Nizam-ul-Mulk, and indeed all of the other regional powerholders, declined the opportunity, though they accompanied the Mughal army, commanded by default by the Great Mughal, Muhammad II, with their own troops.

In late February the Great Mughal ensconced himself with his army in a strong defensive position at Karnal. The Mughal army reputedly comprised 200,000 infantry and cavalry with 5,000 field guns exclusive of *shaturnal*, Nadir Shah's army some 125,000 cavalry.[11] Nadir Shah arrived in the vicinity of Karnal on February 22, obtaining, in sharp contrast to the Mughals, good intelligence of his opponent. The Mughal camp itself was clearly too strong to be assaulted directly, so Nadir Shah remained nearby without attacking, and on February 23 sent a detachment to cut off an approaching Mughal reinforcement army. The Mughal army got through to the Great Mughal's camp on February 24, but lost its baggage to the Persians. The commander of that army promptly turned around to retrieve his baggage, and ran directly into the Persian army. In a very one-sided rout, the Mughal general was captured, and his army destroyed. The Great Mughal fell back into his camp, but lack of supplies forced him to surrender to Nadir Shah.

Nadir Shah entered Delhi on March 20, 1739, taking control of a city with greater wealth than he had ever imagined. In territory, he formally annexed all the land west of the Indus, and the province of Kabul. He was also acknowledged as lord of all India. When he left Delhi on May 16, he carried not only tens of millions of rupees in cash and jewels, but also the jeweled Peacock Throne of Shah Jahan. Mughal prestige had been thoroughly destroyed.

Nadir Shah was assassinated in 1747, and Ahmad Khan took control of the eastern part of his empire. Ahmad Khan wrested Lahore, Kashmir, and Multan from nominal Mughal control in 1752, and Sirhind in 1757. He had even looted Delhi in January of 1757, before falling back to Afghanistan. In 1758, however, a Maratha army marched into the Punjab and captured Lahore from Ahmad Khan's son. This was actually the greatest extent of Maratha power into Hindustan and the north, and it was unsustainable. Ahmad Khan struck back in 1759, driving the

---

[11] For these numbers see Burns, *Cambridge History of India*, 360 fn. 1.

Marathas out of Hindustan by early 1760. In response, a Maratha army was dispatched from the Deccan to restore their position in Hindustan. It departed on March 10, 1760, with 20,000 Maratha cavalry, forty cannon, and Ibrahim Khan Gardi's 9,000 sepoy infantry trained to French standards. This formidable army was also, however, slowed down by a very Mughal-like host of camp followers, wives, and their retinues, all supplied by large numbers of elephants and other beasts of burden. Large numbers of other troops, Maratha and otherwise, joined up as the army marched toward Delhi, adding tens of thousands of soldiers, and some two hundred cannon, but also several times that number of camp followers, and many proud generals.

This unwieldy host, already riven with personal jealousies and incompetently commanded by Bhao Sahib, reached Delhi in late July. The arrival of the rainy season placed active military campaigning on hold, and intensified an ultimately futile round of intrigue and negotiation. When the rains stopped, Bhao Sahib advanced north from Delhi toward Kunjpura, a fortified position controlling a ford across the Jumna River, held for Ahmad Khan by his garrison of ten thousand men. Ibrahim Khan Gardi's heavy cannon bombarded the Kunjpura, which was then carried by storm. Ahmad Khan initially could not cross the river because it was still in flood, but while the Marathas were celebrating their victory, he stole a march on them, and forded the river at Baghpat, forty kilometers north of Delhi. Although he lost some men in the two-day operation, he was now between the Marathas and Delhi.

After their first attempts to drive Ahmad Khan back failed, the Marathas were forced to retreat north to Panipat. There, Bhao Sahib chose to make a stand, and entrenched himself in a solid defensive position with his cannon well emplaced. Ahmad Khan was not foolish enough to make a direct assault against the superior Maratha cannon, and set up his own fortified camp to wait things out. After more than two months of light skirmishing, Maratha supplies ran down, and they resolved to make a direct assault on the enemy rather than starve to death. The two sides faced each other over an eleven-kilometer front. Gardi's artillery on the left flank fired high and ineffectively, leaving him to prove the mettle of his troops by a bayonet charge. They forced back Ahmad Khan's right, and Bhao Sahib took advantage of this to charge the Afghan center. For some time it looked as if the Marathas might succeed, but Ahmad Khan threw his reserves in early in the afternoon and the tide turned. For several more hours the Marathas continued to fight hard, but then, late in the afternoon, they broke and a tremendous slaughter commenced. The Maratha army was annihilated, along with its camp followers. Ahmad Khan sacked Delhi on March 22, and then returned home.

Both sides were well provided with cannon and handguns at the Third Battle of Panipat, but where the Maratha cannon were dug in, and thus immobile, Ahmad Khan's cannon were almost exclusively *shaturnal* mounted atop camels. Thus, as the battle progressed, Ahmad Khan was able to keep his cannon in play, to very good effect, while the Marathas outran their artillery support. The Maratha infantry trained in European methods performed very well, but were only a small part of the Maratha army, and could have been easily outmaneuvered by Ahmad Khan's highly mobile army. In retrospect, the Third Battle of Panipat marked the limit of Maratha power in Hindustan as well as Ahmad Khan's. The Mughal court was now mostly irrelevant, accept as an occasional, and very limited, tool of political legitimacy.

What the Third Battle of Panipat made apparent was that conquest of the subcontinent required the ability to coordinate field artillery with either infantry or cavalry. From Babur to Nadir Shah and on to the British, gunpowder weapons were critical tools of empire. This continuity shows, however, that the arrival of the European military revolution was not very revolutionary with respect to the use of cannon and handguns. It was not technological change that led to social change on the subcontinent, but rather the political and social changes begun before the rise of British power, notably the increasing *zamīndār*-ization and regionalization of power, and the concomitant shift toward infantry, that enabled the fairly easy adoption of European military methods. It is the role of the British in exploiting those pre-existing trends to fuel their consolidation of centralized power that has retrospectively taken much of the credit for that transformation.

Plassey

The beginning of British rule on the subcontinent is conventionally dated to Robert Clive's victory over Siraj-ud-Daulah, the governor of Bengal, at the Battle of Plassey on June 23, 1757. Perhaps the most notable aspect of Clive's generalship in preparation for the battle was his intrigue with the commander of the governor's troops, promising support to make the commander governor in return for changing sides during the battle. Of only slightly less significance was that Clive disobeyed orders to provoke the battle. Clive was only one of what would be a long line of British commanders and political agents in Asia inclined to disregard orders to advance their own careers. Despite such poor discipline, the EIC and the British government were usually happy to accept the fruits of any such successful transgression.

Clive was not new to the subcontinent when he won at Plassey. He had served there earlier as an EIC clerk, distinguishing himself by capturing and holding the town of Arcot in 1751. This earlier conflict had involved a struggle between the sons of Nizam-ul-Mulk for control of Hyderabad, and a similar struggle between the sons of the governor of Arcot, with the British and French taking opposing sides in both contests. From the local perspective, the British and French were simply new players in the more general power struggle, though useful for the weaponry and tactics. Their larger struggle in Europe and America during the eighteenth century was not immediately relevant. But it would, in fact, be events in Europe that largely determined that it was the British, rather than the French, who would be left with a free hand to intervene in the crumbling Mughal empire.

Joseph François Dupleix, the governor of the French East India Company who took charge at Pondicherry in 1742, is responsible for first introducing the idea of hiring local mercenaries and training them in European-style infantry tactics. Dupleix had already spent twenty years at the French factory in Bengal before becoming governor, and was well versed in the political structure of the subcontinent. In order to advance French interests, he needed to create a credible military force, but as the head of a business organization, he needed to do so as cheaply as possible. Infantry was cheaper than cavalry, more plentiful, and easier to supply. With a small number of French officers, an infantry army capable of not only withstanding, but also overcoming elite native cavalry was created. The British quickly followed suit.[12]

Dupleix's initial successes over the British, a struggle he only reluctantly undertook because of British unwillingness to agree to a local truce, were undone by events in Europe. The Franco-British treaty of 1748 in Europe forced the French to return Madras to the British. But their rivalry on the subcontinent and engagement in local politics continued unabated. That same year, while Clive was succeeding in Arcot, Dupleix succeeded in putting the French candidate in charge in Hyderabad. Since Arcot was nominally under the control of Hyderabad, the French could reasonably argue that they had bested the British in the contest. The French not only continued their influence by securing control in Hyderabad again when their first candidate died, but also drove off a Maratha attack on Hyderabad. Trade, however, had suffered greatly after the 1748 treaty, and the company's directors sacked Dupleix for his military adventures, and in 1754 disposed of the majority of French holdings on the subcontinent.

As a result of Clive's victory at Plassey, the Great Mughal offered the civil administration of Bengal to the British. Clive was inclined to accept

---

[12] Hermann Kulke and Dietmar Rothermunde, *A History of India*, 3rd edn, London: Routledge, 1998, 221.

it, but he thought that only the British government, not the EIC, was capable of actually managing it. Prime Minister Pitt agreed with Clive's assessment, as well as his belief that Bengal would be the first step in a British empire, but he was concerned that tribute from Bengal would go directly to the king, thus providing the crown with a non-parliamentary source of income. Thus was born the extremely odd system by which Britain's Indian empire was administered by a private company for a century.

The British East India Company and the military revolution

It was not the British government, but the EIC that brought the European military revolution to India. But the EIC was a trading company that came into possession of political power in Bengal, rather than a political institution established for political purposes. There was therefore always a basic conflict between the company's responsibilities and its profitability. The British government used the EIC as a political buffer that allowed the sort of underhanded and ruthless acquisition of further territory that Parliament would not have easily accepted. Even so, Parliament did have oversight over the EIC, and did criticize it on several occasions for the means by which it acquired territory. It did not, however, force the company to return the land.

Whatever its political responsibilities, the EIC used its military to advance the company's interests, interests that, however, changed over time. It was clear to many of the company's leaders that their control over India was predicated on superior military means. When the EIC established its first foothold in Bengal, the subcontinent was in a near-constant state of turmoil as large regional powers struggled with each other for dominance, and local *zamīndārs* struggled against their overlords for greater independence. Long-term political stability required both a sweeping reduction in the armed force available to political powerholders, and the substitution of a new system that would allow those political powerholders to maintain their positions. Unlike the Mughal rulers, or even many of the regional powers, the EIC did not expect to offer military employment to local strongmen as a way of buying their loyalty, nor did they see an armed countryside as a potential source of military strength that might be tapped at need. As the EIC took over more territory and dismantled the military labor market by establishing a monopoly over armed force, the previous system of a heavily armed rural population disappeared.

With respect to the institutions of control, the British did not inject European political, social, or governmental practice into their rule and revolutionize Indian practice. The EIC adopted local practice in most things (excepting, quite significantly, for example, law). Thus the northern and southern systems as administered by the EIC were different. In the south, for example, Tipu Sultan had cut the *zamīndārs* out of his system in order to tax his subjects directly. This allowed him to build and maintain a European-style army that was very successful. His system was left in place when his territory was incorporated into the EIC's jurisdiction.

The major contrast between British and South Asian political structures was their respective focus on either the institution or the individual. The British were focused on the institution of the EIC, on enhancing the power of the state or governing apparatus as a persisting entity; South Asian rulers were focused on enhancing their own personal power. Significantly, although individual rulers were able to adapt European military methods, and improved their taxation and governing capabilities, they could not effect a political transformation into a system in which government functionaries were loyal to an abstract political apparatus. Thus, although the EIC adopted many pre-existing practices, resulting in very different administrative and tax structures in the north and south, the overall effect was to create a unified central government. Of course, the Mughal system had also maintained a central government and a unified empire, one that the EIC, in turn, subsumed and gradually transformed. This was really a question of politics and statecraft, not military technology or technique. The EIC's sepoy army was better trained overall than its opponents, and usually better armed, but these were not overwhelming advantages. Although the European military system changed South Asian military practice, it did not, by itself or as a proximate cause, revolutionize that practice or the social and political systems related to it.

FURTHER READING

Andrea Hintze, *The Mughal Empire and its Decline*, Aldershot: Ashgate, 1997.
Charnvit Kasetsiri, *The Rise of Ayudhya*, Kuala Lumpur: Oxford University Press, 1976.
Dirk H. A. Kolff, *Naukar, Rajput and Sepoy*, Cambridge: Cambridge University Press, 1990.
Hermann Kulke and Dietmar Rothermund, *A History of India*, 3rd edn, London: Routledge, 1998.
P. J. Marshall, *The New Cambridge History of India*, Vol. II, part 2, Cambridge: Cambridge University Press, 1987.
Kaushik Roy, *From Hydaspes to Kargil: A History of Warfare in India from 326 BC to AD 1999*, New Delhi: Manohar, 2004.
Jadunath Sarkar, *Military History of India*, Bombay: Orient Longman, 1970.

When Europeans first reached Asia, their guns were slightly more advanced than what was locally available. Nevertheless, European weapons were quickly adopted when their superiority was demonstrated. As more and better European weapons reached Asia, they too were adopted, and in some cases both gunners and guns were brought into the service of Asian governments. Indeed, some Asian rulers preferred to employ Europeans with their guns rather than train local forces as the cheapest and least politically costly way of increasing their military striking power. Many Europeans mistook this as a rejection of the technology itself.

The outcomes of European powers pushing more aggressively into Asia in the eighteenth and nineteenth centuries, exploiting their superior military technology, were very different in different polities. This was not due so much to the different cultures' attitudes toward technology, as to the different political environments that obtained there when European and American forces began to seek more substantial political and economic engagement, and to those foreign powers' changing designs upon their territories. Asians strongly resisted Western culture but accepted Western technology. Westerners then cast the resistance to Western culture as a rejection of technology and science, and, by extension, created the idea that the more Westernized an Asian government became, the more it was able to exploit military technology. Neither impression is correct, as a comparison of the various Asian powers in the nineteenth century shows.

The European and American colonial presence in Asia was in no way benign. Westerners went to Asia for two reasons, economic gain and cultural hegemony. These two goals were often, and continue to be, interlinked. European trade before the Industrial Revolution was mostly driven by European interest in acquiring Asian products like spices, tea, silk, or porcelain, among others. These early centuries of trade were also as marked by intra-European conflict over Asian ports, trade, and political influence, as by European–Asian conflicts. By 1763, for example, the British eliminated the French presence in South Asia, but they still had to conquer and govern the remains of the Mughal empire and all of the rising powers, like the Marathas, that had developed out of the general military and political fragmentation on the subcontinent. Handguns and cannon played fundamental roles in all of these conflicts. Westerners faced Asian armies that had undergone a similar military revolution to their own. Asian powers lacked access to sufficient guns to transform their armies fully, and only gradually undertook the cultural changes necessary to Westernize their military institutions.

After the Industrial Revolution, European trade with Asia shifted and indeed accelerated. European industry needed Asian raw materials to manufacture finished products, and Asian markets to absorb those goods. Asian materials also fueled European wars, with Bengali saltpeter supplying a large proportion of British gunpowder production. Asian man-power also began to support European conflicts, first within Asia, and then around the world. South Asian troops were used across the British empire, and communities of South Asian merchants still mark the British Commonwealth. In Southeast Asia, by contrast, the Chinese merchant community marks the remains of the Chinese influence that developed over centuries without imperial action.

European governments seldom gave the developing Asian polities the chance to absorb the fruits of Western science and technology. Asian colonies were, by design, supposed to enhance the economy and overall strength of the colonizing power. Western powers wanted, on the one hand, to sell manufactured goods, including technology, to Asian polities for profit, but also, on the other hand, to prevent those same purchasers from disrupting their economic or political relationships with the Western powers. Perhaps the best example of this was France's destruction of China's Western-style navy at Fuzhou in 1884, a force built under French supervision. Not surprisingly then, it was Japan, the only Asian power to have escaped most of the effects of imperialism, that was able to absorb Western technology and science quickly.

The Japanese reaction is frequently invoked by scholars making com-parisons, presenting, as it seems, the positive results of a rational evalua-tion of the value of all things Western. Unlike any other pre-modern Asian polity, Japan reinvented itself as a modern Western nation-state, and accrued all of the economic and technological benefits that accompanied such a change. As the second largest economy in the world at the begin-ning of the twenty-first century, this seems to vindicate the Western triumphalists who believe that real prosperity can only be achieved through the modern Western organization of society. This may or may not be true, but it has often raised the question of why Japan was able to modernize or Westernize as no other Asian polity. At the same time, Japan was the first Asian nation to wage an imperialist war against other

Asian polities in the twentieth century. Japanese exceptionalism is usually framed in terms of deep cultural differences (this is particularly attractive to Japanese scholars) rather than Japan's very different historical engagement with Western colonialism. Japan was not unique in its interest in and capability to switch to the European model, but rather it was unique in not being subject to direct Western colonization. That allowed it the time to absorb things Western.

Southeast Asia

Mainland Southeast Asia was squeezed between the powers of England and France, while archipelagic Southeast Asia was more subject to the brutal control of Holland, Spain, and, later, America. Myanmar (Burma), whose expansion to the west ran up against Great Britain's South Asian empire, was crushed in a series of three wars in the nineteenth century. The French built upon an eighteenth-century history of participation in Vietnamese affairs to take control of it in the middle of the nineteenth century, pushing China and Chinese influence temporarily out of Vietnam. Only Siam (Thailand) was able to balance the colonial powers to its east and west and salvage some vestige of independence. Meanwhile the Dutch ruthlessly exploited what is now Indonesia, and the Spanish did likewise in the Philippines. The United States entered this arena at the very end of the nineteenth century, belatedly and with some reticence. Its control over the Philippines was a product of its war with Spain, rather than a direct effort at colonization.

In all of these efforts, Westerners brought superior weaponry and training to bear on Southeast Asian governments in ways that prevented those authorities from controlling their territories. To the extent that many of those governments were no more benign in their treatment of their populations than were the Westerners, the resulting exploitative rule was not noteworthy. It is only in the current culture of the West that vicious exploitation of Asians by Westerners seems surprising. Yet if we look at the current, post-colonial use of cheap Southeast Asian labor, it is hard to discern much difference from colonial practice. The countries of Southeast Asia are now sovereign in the military and political sense of the term, but they must choose economic exploitation by foreigners (including, it must be pointed out, other Asians) or stagnation and poverty.

Burma (Myanmar)

The First Anglo-Burmese War (1823–6) was a direct clash between the expanding Burmese empire and the British Indian empire. Burma had been expanding at the expense of smaller kingdoms between Burma and India, such as Assam, Arakan, Manipur, and Cachar. The Burmese conquered Arakan in 1784, and proceeded to make heavy demands upon the local population for labor within Burma. These demands led some 10,000 Arakanese to flee to India in 1798; the Burmese regarded these refugees as their property and raided into India in attempts to get them back. Manipur and then Cachar were attacked in 1819, and Assam fell under Burmese control in 1822. British efforts to negotiate a treaty with the Burmese court stabilizing the border came to nothing. These negotiations were, however, somewhat disingenuous as the British had their own designs on the area.

A Burmese force directly attacked a British position in 1823, followed by Cachar, now under British protection, early the following year. Britain declared war in 1824, and quickly captured Rangoon, though the city itself was deserted. Burma's main settlements were organized around the river system, and it was precisely this transport network that allowed the British to bring in its navy, with its formidable artillery, reducing position after position. The conflict showed the irresistible power of Western artillery against native forts and settlements, but also the great difficulties of campaigning in an environment that made a large percentage of the British force sick, and in which the native population withdrew before the invaders. Local animosities did help, with Siamese (Thai) forces assisting the British, and most British successes coming in Assam, Arakan, and, to some extent, in Cachar. Continued British victories finally led to a peace treaty in 1826, leaving Britain in control of parts of southern and western Burma.

Despite this apparent success against Burma, the First Anglo-Burmese War was regarded for some time as a bungled mistake by the British, and the resulting territory a burden. Attitudes, at least about acquiring territory, changed over time, and by 1852 it was the British who initiated a second war against Burma. The Burmese court had attempted to stave off this war by making concessions to the British, but the British envoy managed to provoke a naval confrontation and commence hostilities. The British prosecuted the Second Anglo-Burmese War more skillfully than the first, and, after several bouts of hard fighting, the Burmese fell back to the north. The British then unilaterally annexed the lower Irrawaddy River valley in 1853, leading to the deposition of the Burmese king in favor of his brother.

Burmese independence was finally destroyed in the Third Anglo-Burmese War, in order to protect British influence from French encroachment. French colonialism in Vietnam (Indochina) presented the Burmese with the opportunity to play the foreigners off against each other, or, at the very least, to obtain weapons to strengthen their position against the

British. While the British were able to deflect these efforts diplomatically by putting pressure on the French, the threat remained, as did the possibility of conflict with China over parts of northern Burma. The Burmese court reasonably rejected a British ultimatum in 1885 that would have effectively made it a British puppet, but it was not prepared for the speed with which the British organized and launched their campaign to conquer the capital at Mandalay. A river fleet assembled in five days with 9,034 soldiers, 2,810 Burmese auxiliaries, 67 guns, and 24 machine guns, and immediately steamed up the Irrawaddy River to the capital. Burmese gun batteries were captured, in some cases by Indian troops in British employ. British infantry and naval bombardment broke through a series of strong points. The king surrendered soon after the fleet reached the capital. Some 1,800 cannon and thousands of handguns were captured, demonstrating that earlier Burmese efforts to upgrade their weaponry were not entirely unsuccessful. Britain made Burma a province of India in 1886.

Burma was separated from Indian administration only in 1937, and was overrun by the Japanese in World War II. The British recaptured it in 1945. Some Burmese fought for the Japanese, others for the Allies, and some for both. Burma regained its independence in 1948.

Vietnam (Indochina)

French missionary priests began French engagement with Vietnam, initially confining their activities to proselytizing in the seventeenth century, but shifting to more active political roles in the eighteenth. Pierre-Joseph Pigneaux de Behaine sided with Nguyễn Phúc Ánh (the future Emperor Gia Long), and personally lobbied the French court to support him. Pigneaux was, however, forced to raise troops in French-controlled India after the political turmoil in France rendered court support moot. With these forces, in 1788 he reached Vietnam, where Nguyễn Huệ and his Tây Son rebellion had unified the country and driven the emperor to seek help from the Qing dynasty in China. French assistance improved Nguyễn Phúc Ánh's navy, enabling it to defeat the Tây Son navy in 1792, the same year that Nguyễn Huệ died. This proved a turning point in Nguyễn Phúc Ánh's and French fortunes. By 1802, Nguyễn Phúc Ánh controlled the country and made himself Emperor Gia Long. China accepted this change in dynasties in 1804, by giving the state the name "Vietnam."

Despite the obvious connection between Catholicism and French military assistance, Gia Long's successors rejected both France and Catholicism. The Vietnamese court actually rejected the modernization that had allowed Gia Long to establish it, and sought a return to a more traditional society. This move was sometimes framed in Confucian terms, and consequently blamed on Confucian thought, but it had much more to do with power struggles within the court and society. French influence and modernization threatened many entrenched interests; those interests obtained sufficient political authority not only to block further advancement, but to reverse what had already been accomplished. Important segments of the elite had strong ties either to Chinese culture or to Buddhism, for example, from which they drew their legitimacy and economic control, and French influence directly challenged that. Unfortunately for the Vietnamese, the rejection of French culture and Catholicism directly, in turn, threatened French economic interests.

The pretext for direct French intervention was provided by the massacre of tens of thousands of Catholics, native and foreign. Having abandoned modernity, the Vietnamese were unable to resist a French expedition that landed in 1858. Like the British, the French were concerned to block Chinese influence, which was accomplished with the Franco-Chinese War of 1884–5. What we see in all of this is not the rejection of guns or military technology, but the rejection of Western culture for political and intellectual reasons. The French were willing to obtain influence and economic advantage by selling the Vietnamese modern weaponry; the Vietnamese could put off that influence only by rejecting the entire package. Vietnam would remain a French colony, French Indochina, through World War II (though it was briefly conquered by the Japanese), after which it was again divided between north and south. Several more decades of fighting freed Vietnam from French, and then American, dominance, allowing it finally to become a sovereign, united nation-state.

Thailand (Siam)

Like its eastern and western neighbors, Thailand was confronted by imperialism in the eighteenth and nineteenth centuries. Of course, it was a Burmese army that destroyed Ayutthaya in 1767, not a European one. Burma was only driven out in the 1790s. The Thai court was fortunate in its succession of monarchs and ministers, at least in so far as they understood very clearly the threat of European imperialism. While they were certainly pleased to see Burma subdued by the British, they knew that they might be next. Their response was logical: on the one hand, they directly engaged the West diplomatically, signing, for example, the Treaty of Amity and Commerce with Britain in 1826 (directly after Burma's defeat in the First Anglo-Burmese War), and on the other, they worked to modernize their country. Thai diplomacy was skillful, but probably the most important agreement that preserved Thailand as the only Southeast Asian country to avoid colonization was that between Britain and France. Those two imperial powers agreed to keep Thailand as a buffer between their respective colonies in Burma and Vietnam.

Thailand became a constitutional monarchy in 1932, and in 1941 invaded French Indochina. French land forces were outnumbered and less well armed than the Thai army, and quickly lost control of Laos. The French navy somewhat recouped this defeat at sea, but the French nevertheless conceded the lost territory in the subsequent peace treaty. This brief war, consisting of less than a month of actual fighting, demonstrated how far Thailand had come in modernizing its military. At the end of the year, however, it was once again an Asian power, Japan, which bullied Thailand. The Thai government was forced to concede the Japanese passage through its territory to attack Burma after several hours of fighting made it clear the Japanese army could not be resisted. Thailand's cooperation with the Japanese placed it on the losing side after World War II, but by shifting its allegiance to the United States it managed to avoid severe punishment.

South Asia[1]

The previous chapter discussed the introduction of the European Military Revolution to South Asia, and its ready adoption into the pre-existing system of warfare. This constituted a second gunpowder revolution in South Asian warfare. The British East India Company (EIC) gradually monopolized the military labor market and formed British-style infantry units filled with native, South Asian soldiers led by British officers. These units competed successfully against other South Asian armies, who adopted similar weaponry and styles of operation. Unlike the EIC, however, those other armies were subject to the vagaries of individual rulers, rather than institutions, and they were unable to sustain their operations against the EIC or any other South Asian power for more than the life of a single leader.

The EIC itself was an odd entity, what in twenty-first-century terms might be described as an "outsourced" or "privatized" conqueror for the British government. As it acquired more territory, and its commercial activities diminished in profitability, its main function was to insulate the British Parliament from the political problems of administering a colony. This was well understood and accepted: so, as long as the EIC was able to expand its territory and run it without requiring direct British government

---

[1] This section follows Kulke and Dietmar, *A History of India*, 224–57.

intervention, it was allowed to continue. That held true into the 1850s, when EIC armies finally conquered the Punjab, essentially completing its hold over the territories of the now captive Mughal emperor.

The 1857 Mutiny (or First Indian War of Independence, depending upon one's perspective) forced the British government to reassess its approach to running India. There were no contingency plans for a mutiny of the native army, that veteran force which had so recently conquered the Punjab and was so well trained in British military skills. While the native army learned to be British soldiers, however, the intellectual orientation of the EIC's officers toward those soldiers changed in the mid-nineteenth century. Where previous generations of EIC officers had practiced the "Asian" approach to understanding South Asia, stressing familiarity with local languages and customs, by the mid-nineteenth century the "Oriental" approach, which regarded all things Asian as inferior and backward, had taken hold. It was one of this new breed of British officers in India, men who kept a great distance between themselves and the troops, and treated their underlings with utter contempt, who mishandled his native soldiers and sparked the Mutiny.

Fortunately for the British, what the rebellious troops possessed in terms of battlefield skills, they lacked in strategic planning and political leadership. They turned to the Mughal emperor in Delhi, and the Maratha *peshwa*, neither of whom was capable of forging the many different communities of dissatisfied people into a real movement to overthrow the British, or to formulate a real strategy for doing so. The British turned to the Sikhs, newly conquered by the rebelling troops, for help. After the Mutiny was suppressed in 1858, the EIC was abolished.

Cannon and handguns were present on all sides in these conflicts. British victories over the Sikhs were hard fought, as were all the other conquests in South Asia. Sikh cannon firing grapeshot and canister inflicted substantial casualties on EIC armies, as did Maratha artillery. There was very little in the way of a technology gap, and certainly no reluctance on the part of South Asians to purchase or use the most advanced guns available. The greatest weakness of South Asian groups was their divided internal politics, but they were nevertheless capable of using guns in battle effectively, and in supplying them in the field. The EIC itself did not impose a unified system of revenue extraction on its South Asian territory, preferring, instead, to take over the pre-existing systems of conquered areas (if they were effective). Where it did change the local system, as in Bengal, the social effects could be profound. But it was not the particular nature of modern warfare that stimulated changes in government, whether by the EIC or a local ruler, so much as the increasing military and political competition between regional powers in the twilight of the Mughal empire.

Of course, it was Queen Victoria who came to rule India, assuming the title Empress of India in 1876. By that time, South Asian military man-power contributed to the extension of British imperial power outside of South Asia, though the Mutiny had shifted recruitment toward the Muslim and Sikh minorities. British colonial rule succeeded in creating a modern military, divorced from political or social change.

China

China's experience of Western colonialism was less severe than South Asia's, though the indignities that it did suffer were and are attributed to the Chinese military falling behind the West in technology. The Manchu rulers of the last Chinese dynasty, the Qing, were scapegoated for China's poor military performance, and as they formed the government from 1644 to 1911 some of that blame is surely justified. "Traditional" society or Confucianism is usually next in line on the list of reasons why China had so much difficulty fending off the West and then Japan in the nineteenth and twentieth centuries. There is considerably less truth to that argument. Successive Chinese armies and governments pioneered the use of guns in war, and sought out and incorporated new developments in firearms as they became available. However one might characterize late imperial Chinese attitudes to war, they in no way prevented the military from acquiring and deploying new weapons, or waging aggressive, expansionistic war.

It is not surprising that it was only in the nineteenth century that Western powers were able to make significant inroads into China. This was not due to rising Western capabilities, so much as to declining political vitality within the Qing court. The imperial system that had shown immense strength and reach in the late seventeenth and through-out the eighteenth century, declined rapidly, but not necessarily irrever-sibly, in the nineteenth century. Yet even in the nineteenth century, parts of the Chinese military including the navy adopted the latest Western weapons and tactics. Parts of the Qing army were fully modernized by the time the dynasty collapsed in 1911, an event precipitated by the discovery of a plan by junior officers within one of the provincial armies to overthrow the government. Clashes between major Chinese warlords in the 1920s often involved the full panoply of modern weaponry, from machine guns, to artillery, to train hospital cars. There was no appreci-able difference between Chinese and Western military technology.[2]

---

[2] For the warlord armies, including their capabilities and weaponry, see Arthur Waldron, *From War to Nationalism*, New York: Cambridge University Press, 1995, 53–71.

The great difference between China and any Western state in the late nineteenth and early twentieth century was that the Qing government failed, and it would take until 1949 for a stable, unified government to re-establish itself. Much of the political struggle for dominance and unity was fought on the battlefield with the machinery of modern warfare. Where that technology was limited, as it often was, this was due solely to the financial and logistical capabilities of a given army. The People's Liberation Army (PLA), that of the Chinese Communist Party, was hampered by poverty and limited access to heavy weapons. Consequently, it adopted tactics that allowed it to operate within these constraints. This was not by choice, or as a result of a resistance to advanced weaponry, but by necessity. That formative period for PLA strategy and tactics has, however, cast a long shadow over even current ideas of warfighting, and the importance of high technology on the battlefield.

In chapter 3, we left Ming dynasty China after it aided the Koreans in driving out a series of Japanese invasions of Korea. The Ming dynasty went into a general decline in the years that followed, with most of the successful and experienced generals from the 1590s dying off. Several that remained would be disgraced in the early efforts to repulse the rising Manchu threat in the steppe. As bad as the military decline was, the political collapse of the dynasty was far worse. Indeed, military decline was always reversible in good political times; it was in dire political environments that military reverses became mortal wounds rather than stimulants to reform. The late Ming dynasty suffered from a series of weak emperors, unwilling to overrule and actually command the bureaucracy. Without such leadership from the top, and hobbled by an institutional system designed to make the emperor crucial to the functioning of the government, factional politics quickly paralyzed the dynasty.

While the Ming government declined into arthritic senility, the descendants of the Jurchen Jin began to coalesce into a formidable political and military force. They were, of course, well acquainted with the Chinese imperial system, both from their own history and from regular contact with the Ming, and that provided them with a template on which to create their own government. They soon called themselves "Manchus" and began both to conquer neighboring steppe tribes and to incorporate them into a system of "banners." These banners served as military, administrative, and social units. The Manchu dynasty first called itself the Latter Jin, connecting it to the earlier Jurchen Jin dynasty, and then the Qing.

The requirements of state building led the Qing leadership to conquer cities and assemble a manufacturing base to support the war effort. Ethnic Chinese craftsmen did the majority of manufacturing work.

Ming efforts to control the Manchus were generally unsuccessful, with few Ming generals capable of fighting beyond the Great Wall. The Great Wall itself absorbed enormous numbers of Ming troops, as well as vast resources in weapons, material, and food. Few if any units were capable of offensive warfare, and few generals were willing to risk the political ramifications of military action. Success was no protection, since any victory could always be declared a defeat and a commander executed. Likewise, defeat could be declared a victory and an incompetent commander promoted.

Despite the crumbling military and political situation in the Ming, new Portuguese cannon were introduced and rapidly deployed. Not only direct siege warfare, but also the many battles associated with a siege involved large numbers of cannon and handguns. The Manchus recognized the superiority of the new Portuguese cannon, and made every effort to acquire not only the guns, but also the men capable of making and using them. In this they were successful, capturing Chinese artillerymen trained by the Portuguese. The Ming technological advantage was thus fairly short lived.

If the Manchus were not enough of a threat, a large number of rebel armies had sprung up within the Ming empire. These rebels made extensive use of cannon in their attempts, sometimes successful, sometimes not, to capture cities. Gunpowder was also widely used to mine city walls, often with disastrous consequences for the besiegers. On several occasions government armies almost succeeded in suppressing the rebels, but court politics seemed inevitably to intervene and either replace a victorious commander or countermand or undermine a working strategy. By the 1640s, these rebels were actually a threat to the dynasty itself. Ultimately, it would be a Chinese rebel army that would capture the Ming capital at Beijing, not the Manchus.

Beijing's fall to rebels placed the border generals holding the Great Wall against the Manchus in an untenable situation. The Manchus were just then shifting their strategy from one of making harassing raids through the Great Wall (the area to the Great Wall's north having earlier fallen to the Manchus), to a directed campaign of Ming conquest. The generals had already been ordered to fall back and defend the capital from the rebels, but before they could act on that, the city fell. Should they then follow those now pointless orders, or remain in place and hold the Great Wall against the Manchus? The Manchu army would have gotten through regardless, and the rebels were marching on the main Ming army positions along the Great Wall, so the Ming generals threw in their lot with the Manchus. The rebels were soon defeated and driven out of Beijing, but the Manchus then took over. The Ming armies, now part of the Qing dynasty, were sent in pursuit of the remaining rebels, and subsequently played a key role in the conquest of the rest of the Ming empire.

Ethnic Chinese units possessed the majority of cannon and handguns. The Chinese banners within the original Manchu system were mostly infantry and artillerymen, while the Manchu and Mongol banners were steppe cavalry. Former Ming army units became "Green Standard" troops, and brought their infantry and gunpowder expertise into the larger Qing military establishment. Here we see a shift from Ming to Qing military practice: where the Ming recruited soldiers, albeit, in theory, from military households, and trained them to use weapons, the Qing divided weapon skills ethnically, expecting certain groups to maintain certain skills particular to their background. The mature Qing military and political system continued the practice of preferring Manchu officers and officials for important posts, or at least pairing a Manchu with a Chinese official. Even after centuries of rule, the Qing ruling house would be concerned to maintain Manchu dominance within the government.

As much as the Qing leadership had appreciated the importance of cannon before they undertook the complete conquest of Ming China, the actual process of breaking through strongpoints and fortifications, and conquering numerous towns and cities, reinforced the absolute need for cannon in positional warfare. A siege train of Portuguese cannon was worth waiting for when taking a fortified position. Just as their Jurchen ancestors discovered, along with the Mongols, in the twelfth and thirteenth centuries, China could only be conquered through riverine naval warfare and frequent sieges. The former Ming forces recruited for these tasks did them well, and were left in control of much of southern China when the last Ming emperor was captured in Burma and strangled in 1662.

Unfortunately for the Qing court, those forces rebelled in 1673 when it was made clear to their commanders that they would not be able to hand their fiefs down to their descendants. It took until 1681 to crush the rebellion completely. One of the most telling problems in the initial stages of the suppression campaigns was the superiority of the rebels in the number of cannons. This was partly due to their earlier start on military preparations, and the Qing court pressed a Jesuit priest into cannon founding to make up the difference. Heavy cannon were decisive, and it was not until the Qing army manufactured and brought enough artillery to the battlefield that they were able to turn the tide against the rebels.

The resources of the imperial state allowed it to finance and supply armies and weapons on a large scale, but it was difficult to maintain high levels of training and preparedness. With the war in the south over, and Qing control over China strong, the attention of the court turned back to the steppe and Central Eurasia. Within China, state Qing banner units distributed at strategic points, supplemented by Green Standard troops, provided local security and enforced loyalty to the regime. The quality of these forces declined rapidly as they shifted to peacetime garrison duties and policing. It was very different on the steppe frontier, where the rising power of the Russians and the Zunghar Mongols engaged the Qing court and army in a century of ultimately successful campaigning.

Qing policy with respect to Central Eurasia was remarkably consistent over time, owing in large part to the extremely long reigns of the Kangxi (1662–1722) and Qianlong (1736–95; d. 1799) emperors. The Qing court's primary concern with the Russians was to stabilize their mutual border in order to avoid conflict, and to use the valuable trade with China as a lever to prevent them from supplying or otherwise supporting the Zunghars. The Kangxi emperor achieved this by capturing the Russian fort at Albazin in 1685, this time using Dutch, rather than Portuguese cannon, and destroying the fort before withdrawing. A second siege was required in 1686 to bring the Russians to the negotiating table; the Treaty of Nerchinsk was concluded in 1689. With the Russians out of the picture, the Qing court could concentrate on breaking up the Zunghar as a political force.

The Kangxi emperor launched two major campaigns against Galdan, the Zunghar leader, in 1690 and 1696, taking part in both.[3] The Qing army was limited in its range of operations by the cannon and other supplies it dragged into the steppe, though Galdan unwisely strayed within reach at Ulan Butong, about 320 kilometers from Beijing, on September 3, 1690, and suffered a serious defeat. Superior weaponry required a much greater logistic effort, and slowed armies down. The emperor himself missed the battle, having fallen ill earlier and returned to the capital. Galdan survived, however, and every effort was made to improve logistics and lure him within range. Lack of food forced Galdan east in 1695, and the emperor led a second expedition of three armies into the steppe. The Zunghar leader fled one army and ran into another at Jaomodo, suffering a second crushing defeat on June 12, 1696. He was poisoned the following year; this temporarily suppressed the Zunghar threat.

The Yongzheng emperor, son of the Kangxi emperor, was less successful in pursuing a military solution to the still dangerous Zunghar polity, and it was left to his son, the Qianlong emperor, not only to defeat the Zunghar Mongols, but also to wage a successful war of genocide. While

---

[3] This discussion of the Kangxi, Yongzheng, and Qianlong emperors' campaigns against the Zunghars follows Peter C. Perdue, *China Marches West*, Cambridge, MA: Harvard University Press, 2005.

the Zunghars struggled to build a state apparatus, complete with a fortified capital defended by cannon, the Qing government worked to harness its empire's growing economic power in order to extend the reach of its army into the steppe. Qing–Russian trade continued to hobble Zunghar state-building efforts, keeping the Russians from supplying the Mongols with arms or food in large quantities for fear of losing lucrative commerce with China. It was also very much in Russia's interests to prevent the rise of another major Central Eurasian power, one that might threaten its own interests in the region.

Handguns had, by this time, become a standard weapon used by both sides, though they were still of limited use in fluid cavalry encounters. The small cannon cast for use by the Qing army were often left behind after the initial stages of a campaign; once Zunghar forces were encountered or discovered, speed became critical to force battle on them. On at least one occasion, a Zunghar force was brought to bay and defended its static position with handguns. Firepower was desirable, but could only play a supporting role. Qing armies had great advantages in terms of logistic support, the ability to sustain campaigns year on year, and a very canny and careful diplomacy that isolated the Zunghars from other Eurasian groups. The Qing army was still operating at the absolute limit of its logistic reach, where it was difficult to support many troops, or to allow them to concentrate in very large numbers. The oasis towns of what is now Xinjiang province had extremely narrow surpluses, and most food and supplies had to be shipped from China's poor northwest. Limited supplies there, in turn, were supported by shipments from China's wealthier southern provinces.

Where the Chinese economy in the eighteenth century was just wealthy enough to support this sustained military effort in Central Eurasia, at least as long as a strong emperor was willing to insist on making the effort, the Zunghars had no such economic resources to support it. Trade, which was the lifeblood of most steppe polities, the only reliable source of wealth beyond subsistence, was increasingly constrained by Qing diplomacy. As the Zunghar leaders failed to obtain and distribute wealth, they lost the ability to attract and retain other steppe tribal leaders. Those disaffected leaders, in turn, could be attracted by Qing wealth, and turned against the Zunghars. The destruction of the Zunghars was based upon economic warfare, not firepower. Even so, the continued resistance of the Zunghars turned the Qianlong emperor's goal from subjugation to extermination. An outbreak of disease greatly aided this end: by 1757, 40 percent of the Zunghar population had died of smallpox; military efforts to kill every other Zunghar provided the other means to this genocide.

China, or more precisely the Qing empire, at the end of the eighteenth century was one of the largest empires in Chinese history. Unfortunately, the policies that had so effectively dealt with the steppe proved disastrous when applied to the European traders arriving on the southeastern coast. This was not evident until the nineteenth century, however, when increasing European aggressiveness and improving weaponry collided with debilitating Qing leadership failures. The Qianlong emperor had imposed his will upon the Qing government, forcing it, for better or worse, into military adventures that stretched its capabilities to the limits of pre-modern technology. Qing campaigns in Southeast Asia and Taiwan had mixed results, and made much less geo-strategic sense than the elimination of the Zunghars.

Most twentieth-century Chinese nationalist rhetoric focused on Qing military and political failures in the face of European, and belatedly, American, imperialism in the nineteenth century. The Qing court rejected Western attempts to establish diplomatic relations based upon the Western notion of equal sovereign states, though it had already concluded treaties with Russia that virtually did so. When the Qing court attempted to suppress the opium trade, having received no satisfaction from the English court when it demanded it be stopped, the British merchants induced their government to go to war over trading rights. The Opium War (1839–42) went badly for the Chinese. It was not just the superior weaponry the British navy brought to bear, including a steam ship, but the incapable leadership at almost every level of the Qing government and military. Despite the British seizure of crucial transshipping points for grain ships north, and the destruction of Qing units either attacking or defending against the British, the political settlement was out of all proportion to their real effects.

It is easy to attribute British success in the Opium War to their superior weaponry, and such a judgment is certainly warranted on the tactical level. But the inability of the Qing authorities to shift their strategy and tactics to adapt to British strengths demonstrates that the empire's failings ran much deeper than the slight technology gap with the West. The Kangxi emperor had persisted in his decision to retake all of southern China when it seemed as if the rebelling Chinese generals might even overthrow the Qing. The Qing court during the Opium War was incapable of responding to a difficult problem on its coast, though some local officials managed to produce excellent copies of European cannon and ships. Other European powers followed up on British advances with their own, broadening the scope and depth of trade between China and the West. A Second Opium War (1856–60) between China and Britain, supported this time by France as well, culminated in an Anglo-French force looting and burning the Summer Palace.

The result of this gradual opening of China to Western trade was an influx of Western technology and culture. Most of the Qing empire remained, however, both off limits and quite untouched by Western influence. It was primarily in the coastal cities, and along the export trade routes, that Western influence was felt. Christianity made its way into the interior, sometimes beyond even those trade routes, but the direct efforts of missionaries to change Chinese society often engendered fierce and violent reactions. Missionaries and their converts were always subject to violent attack, though this provided many convenient excuses for further Western military encroachment. To the Chinese, it seemed very much the case that Western military power had been deployed to force the twin corrosive elements of opium and Christianity into their society. They had much less of a problem accepting new technology, particularly military technology, and it became an imperative to improve their military fortunes in the face of Western aggression.

Western incursions may have damaged the Qing regime's crumbling authority, but it was the accumulation of dissatisfaction among the general populace that was the real threat to the dynasty's continued survival. Western governments were a problem, without being an existential threat. It is therefore not surprising that senior government officials did not pursue modernization with great urgency. Moreover, the sorts of changes that modernization would require, even in terms of control over government resources, threatened the entrenched interests of many powerful groups. Managing internal problems seemed much more critical to the survival of the dynasty. This view was vindicated by the Taiping Rebellion (1850–64), an event that nearly destroyed the Qing.

The Taipings drilled and formed regular army units, picking up cannon as their movement progressed. They managed to capture the great city of Nanjing with an artillery barrage accompanied by gunpowder mines under the walls, and ruled over much of three provinces for several years. Westerners were initially well disposed toward the Taipings because of their putatively Christian ideology and lifestyle. That interest cooled when they discovered that the Taiping leader considered himself the younger brother of Jesus Christ. Internal divisions and inept strategy vastly weakened the rebellion, though its initial success had itself been aided by similar problems on the part of the Qing government and military. New provincial forces turned the military tide. These new forces drew upon the highly militarized countryside, where towns and villages under gentry leadership had long armed and trained to protect themselves from bandits. This was also a sign of the impotence of the Qing government, which had ceded local control over society to the gentry. The central government's own armies proved mostly ineffective.

Yet the late nineteenth century did see progress toward the creation of modern military units, both on land and on sea, modeled on Western practice.[4] Qing China began to build a blue-water navy, and organize Western-style infantry units armed entirely with the most up-to-date weaponry. Chinese students went abroad to study at Western colleges and universities, as well as military academies. Political events were, however, outpacing the gradual incorporation of modern practices. Poor leadership continued to paralyze the Qing court, which desperately clung to the remnants of its prestige as successive failures against the West and then Japan rendered that covering more threadbare. The Qing court under the Dowager Empress Cixi saw itself in a weak position that could be maintained only by balancing regional powers against each other, and making sure Manchus held crucial posts in government and the military. This had the effect of further reinforcing the already deep-seated fissures in the empire. Most crucially, Cixi intentionally distributed power, rather than concentrating it at the center, leaving the empire functionally fragmented.

This fragmentation of power was exemplified in the Sino-Japanese War (1894–5), fought over control of Korea. The Japanese were able decisively to defeat the Beiyang army and navy of northern China, while the other regional armies and navies of China did nothing. Without a strong court, corruption and inept leadership persisted throughout the military and government. Yet the war was fought with modern weapons and ships, though the Chinese forces performed poorly. By the end of the nineteenth century, the Qing regime was running out of time. Despite obvious failures in its government and military, the regime could not reform fast enough to fend off outside military pressure. Unlike the Japanese, to whom we will now turn, Qing China did not have the opportunity to cast off its old government and reform itself before directly engaging the West.

Japan

Japan avoided the attention of the West until the middle of the nineteenth century because it was not known to possess any desirable products, and was outside the regular trade routes. Until well into the twentieth century, Japan was a relatively poor country on the fringe of Asia. It was mostly closed to the outside world since the early seventeenth century. This "closed country" policy, coupled with general peace, created a fairly static society in which everyone knew their place and could not move from it. As we discussed in chapter 2, arquebuses and other guns were not "given up" as part of Tokugawa rule. Indeed, even after the sword hunts of the 1580s

---

[4] See Ralph L. Powell, *The Rise of Chinese Military Power, 1895–1912*, Princeton: Princeton University Press, 1955.

that strove to disarm the commoners of all weapons, the *bakufu* was well aware, and accepted, that a fair number of arquebuses were available in rural villages to protect livestock from predators. Commoners could even wear the short sword, though not the longer one, well into the Tokugawa era. The state retained the power to draft commoners for warfare, though lacking large-scale warfare, this was seldom done; the samurai as a class were the only members of society required to maintain martial skills.[5]

Samurai culture had changed as a result of the demands of commanding non-samurai infantry armed with arquebuses or spears. Where beforehand samurai were rewarded only for witnessed acts of individual prowess, hopefully backed up with a severed enemy head, by the close of the Warring States period some samurai were being rewarded for their performance in command of infantrymen. Peace brought further changes, though Japanese society was not demilitarized. Wars between provincial lords were forbidden, as were fights between individual samurai. Self-control, discipline, and service, often in civil administrative positions, became the standard applied to samurai.

By the nineteenth century, the Tokugawa *bakufu* was showing signs of sclerosis, but this was not a critical problem in the absence of a real threat to the established order. The government was aware of the events taking place in China, and the encroaching West, without this spurring any urgent reforms. When an American squadron of ships arrived in 1853 demanding that Japan open up, it was then clear that the looming threat had finally arrived. This was not, of course, the first time a Western ship or a Western envoy to the Japanese court had reached the country, but all previous arrivals had been successfully turned away or ignored. The American squadron was under orders to get its way, and was sufficiently powerful to do so.

The crisis was now upon the Tokugawa *bakufu*, and it was soon apparent that not only was it not up to responding vigorously, but other provincial lords were. It was clear that a fundamental political and military reform was necessary. What was less clear was how that could be accomplished, what it should be, and how quickly it could, or should, be done. Although the Tokugawa *bakufu* had kept the peace for more than two centuries, it had done so officially as a military administration acting for the emperor, which delegated enormous powers and responsibilities to the provincial lords, particularly with respect to collecting taxes and

---

[5] Shinko Taniguchi, "Military Evolution or Revolution?: State Formation and the Early Modern Samurai," in Rosemarie Deist (ed.), *Knight and Samurai: Actions and Images of Elite Warriors in Europe and East Asia*, Göppingen: Kümmerle Verlag, 2003, 170 and *passim*.

maintaining troops. If Japan were to build a navy and army capable of defending the country from Western powers, financial and military power would have to be centralized. To make matters worse, even as the government was trying to decide how to modernize the military, the available technology kept advancing. This was a time of great and steady improvements in artillery and small arms in the West, and it was important to buy the latest weaponry.

Some provincial lords quickly moved to reform their forces and arm them with the latest weaponry. From 1862 to 1868 the *bakufu* first lost control of the political arena, and then lost all credibility as a regime. Regional forces, notably those of Chōshū, were able to defeat *bakufu* forces in 1866, leading to a further erosion of support for the central regime. These conflicts were fought with mostly modern weaponry, but the *bakufu's* system of calling upon provincial lords to form an army to crush insurrection was too slow and foundered on the reluctance of many lords to support the regime. The *bakufu* collapsed entirely in 1868. Using the obvious alternative political center of the emperor, the formerly rebel forces "restored" the Meiji emperor to actual ruling. This was symbolic, of course, and the emperor was really no more powerful than he had been under the Tokugawa. But Japan was now united politically under a vigorous, reforming government determined to modernize and strengthen the country.

Although the Japanese government was keenly aware of and resented the unequal treaties it had been forced to sign with America, Britain, and the West, there was little actual exploitation of Japan by foreigners. The main interest in Japan for Westerners was as a possible stopover point from America to China, or a place where ships in distress could land. Japan was thus able to complete the great social, political, economic, and military transformation that falls under the rubric of the "Meiji Restoration" unmolested. This entailed the adoption of Western practice in many facets of life, and the dismantling of the social and political structures of pre-Meiji Japan. Class divisions were explicitly broken down, and samurai privileges removed. A Western-style army and navy were created, as well as a Western industrial economy.

For some of the original reformers, the dismantling of social distinctions and other changes went too far. Saigo Takemori, who would become the leader of the Satsuma Rebellion, encapsulated the desire of many samurai both to transform Japan through the adoption of Western technology and to retain the existing social structure. Saigo was an exemplar of Confucian virtue as practiced in Japan by the samurai. He resigned or was forced from the government and military in 1873 mostly because he advocated invading Korea, but also in response to the changes being made to the position of samurai in Japanese society. Back in Satsuma the following year, people sympathetic to Saigo established a system of schools for soldiers who had resigned with Saigo in 1873. The curriculum focused on military training and the Chinese classics, but also included English, French, and German. The schools hired foreign instructors to teach some of these subjects.[6] Saigo and those like him were thus not xenophobic, or even against modernization of the military and economy; they simply believed that Japanese society could and should function in a certain way regardless of the technology in use.

Saigo and his comrades eventually rebelled against the Meiji government, and were quickly defeated by the new army. In defeat, he became the honorable, even apotheosized, symbol of what had been good in "traditional" Japanese culture. But views like Saigo's could not exist openly in the new Japan, and the government and military soon moved to adopt the imperialism of the West as its foundational ideology. Closed off from the possibilities of colonies elsewhere, Japan directed its attention to continental Asia. Here it was extremely fortunate in facing the disintegrating Qing empire and its lagging political and military reforms. It defeated Qing China in 1894–5, and took control of Taiwan, the Liaodong peninsula, and Korea (though it did not establish full control over the latter until after the Russo-Japanese War). Western pressure forced it to turn over control of the Liaodong peninsula to Russia in 1895, though it was not until 1898 that Russia was able to move in.

In 1904–5, Japan defeated Russia in Liaodong, and annihilated the Russian navy at the Battle of Tsushima Straits. This was the first major defeat of a Western (as much as Russia was ever considered "Western") power by an Asian power in a direct clash. Japanese military and economic development brought it into the ranks of world powers, though as an Asian polity it was seldom considered genuinely equal to Western powers. Japan turned to preying upon the rest of Asia like the Western powers, justifying its actions as necessary to lead Asia into the modern world following its example and, later, in driving out Westerners to keep "Asia for the Asians."

Some Chinese, Koreans, and Southeast Asians did admire Japan's modernization, and even attended school in Japan, but only an eccentric minority was drawn to Japanese culture. This was a serious problem for the Japanese, since their dreams of empire depended upon other Asian states actually wanting to be ruled by Japan. While these states wanted the Western imperial powers gone, they had no interest in simply replacing

---

[6] Mark Ravina, *The Last Samurai*, Hoboken: John Wiley and Sons, 2004, 193–4.

them with Japanese imperial rule. Japan's dramatic progress into modernity allowed it to join the West in oppressing Asia; it also allowed it to take part in World War II as a major power. And like the Western imperial powers, it lost its empire after that war.

Japan's defeat in World War II did not immediately end colonialism in Asia. The remnants of colonialism continued for decades in Southeast Asia, and the effects continue today. China was rid of the West once it was rid of Japan; it then took a further four years finally to resolve its internal political problems and unite politically on the ruins of the Qing empire. Ironically, the new Chinese state absorbed the Qing dynasty colonial adventures of the eighteenth century, all the while decrying Western colonialism. In South Asia, local groups, like the Muslim League, struggled to define their own polities while the British government tried to divide its colonial possessions up so as to fracture or diminish the power of any resulting states, and in so doing contributed materially to the strife that remains there today.

Colonialism was not needed to prove that Asian states were interested in Western technology; they had been importing Western technology, particularly military technology, long before the Western powers gained enough of a military and political advantage to advance their own interests against Asians by force. Nor, it should be said, was Asia able to throw off the control of Western powers only when it modernized its military. Asian emancipation, at least from Western domination, was the product of political development. Political consolidation and some degree of unity, if only among a ruling elite, were prerequisites for taking the political initiative against Western colonial powers. That political development had been progressing or was already mature before the West arrived, but it took some time to absorb the intrusion of Western powers into the political environment, adapt to it, and return to its previous development trajectory. Consequently, Western imperialism actually delayed technological progress in Asia, and temporarily slowed political development.

The varying degrees and rates of Western penetration of Asia were due not to Western technological progress, but to the varied stages of political activity in the respective Asian polities. As Asian polities developed, local conditions at certain times left them more and less vulnerable to military and political disruptions. Western powers inserted themselves into this power environment, throwing their support behind one or another local player in order to gain political and commercial influence. Western players often failed in their efforts, but these failures at such a great distance from their home country had few serious European consequences. By contrast, when these efforts succeeded, they could temporarily derail Asian development or permanently shift power from one group to another. The uneven and intermittent engagement of Western powers in Asia made it very difficult for local leaders to adapt to Western interference in order to overcome it, particularly when the Western powers actively sought to prevent that adaptation.

Japan, which had experienced the fewest direct effects of imperialism, progressed the fastest, consolidating itself politically, and laying a foundation for incorporating Western technology into its society. Other states have had to go through a painful process of disentangling Western culture from Western technology. The former is so tainted by its colonial associations that it has taken considerable political will to accept some of it, and to balance that against native cultural interests. The latter remains attractive, particularly in the military sphere. But then, new military technology has always been attractive in Asia.

FURTHER READING

W. G. Beasley, *The Rise of Modern Japan*, London: Weidenfeld and Nicolson, 2000 (3rd edn).

Rosemary Deist (ed.), *Knight and Samurai: Actions and Images of Elite Warriors in Europe and East Asia*, Göppingen: Kümmerle Verlag, 2003.

Peter C. Perdue, *China Marches West*, Cambridge, MA: Harvard University Press, 2005.

Ralph L. Powell, *The Rise of Chinese Military Power, 1895–1912*, Port Washington, NY and London: Kennikat Press, 1972 (first published by Princeton University Press, 1955).

Mark Ravina, *The Last Samurai*, Hoboken: John Wiley and Sons, 2004.

Nicholas Tarling, *Imperialism in Southeast Asia*, London and New York: Routledge, 2001.

Conrad Totman, *The Collapse of the Tokugawa Bakufu, 1862–1868*, Honolulu: The University of Hawaii Press, 1980.

Conclusion

Christianity (FOR CHRISTIANITY IS PLATONISM FOR THE "PEOPLE"), produced in Europe a magnificent tension of soul, such as had not existed anywhere previously; with such a tensely strained bow one can now aim at the furthest goals. As a matter of fact, the European feels this tension as a state of distress, and twice attempts have been made in grand style to unbend the bow: once by means of Jesuitism, and the second time by means of democratic enlightenment – which, with the aid of liberty of the press and newspaper-reading, might, in fact, bring it about that the spirit would not so easily find itself in "distress"! (The Germans invented gunpowder – all credit to them! but they again made things square – they invented printing.)

Friedrich Nietzsche, *Beyond Good and Evil*

India detonated a nuclear bomb on May 11, 1998, and a second bomb on May 13. Pakistan responded by exploding five of its own nuclear bombs on May 28, 1998. The Indian subcontinent had officially gone nuclear. China, of course, had exploded its own atomic bomb on October 16, 1964. North Korea tested a small atomic bomb on October 9, 2006. Japan, South Korea, and Taiwan are understood to be able to build nuclear bombs in a relatively short period of time if they choose to do so, and all possess the necessary skills to mount those weapons on missiles. Only the Southeast Asian states seem far from this technology. Twenty-first-century Asia thus exhibits a great variety of real and potential military capabilities that have no particular correlation to the social or political systems of the individual states. The presence or absence of nuclear technology and missiles is no guide to the nature of a polity or culture.

Quite obviously, the reasons for a given state's choices of military technology are based on a wide variety of factors, ranging from threats, real or perceived, to domestic and international prestige, to temporary political concerns. One would have to look to a state's military and political history to understand why and how it came to possess its current military capacities. As I argued in the introduction, the Western perception of Asia is informed by a lack of knowledge of Asian political and military history, and a consequent assertion of Asian military backwardness. Westerners have measured non-Westerners by their degree of Westernization, and equated Western culture with modernization and technological prowess. By extension, the possession of particular technologies, the artifacts of Western culture, implies some level of acceptance of Western culture and, particularly in the realm of technology, the superiority of the West. Technology has become the sine qua non of Western dominance, and the basis of modernity.

The artifacts of one culture are often eagerly sought after by other cultures, but they are only rarely understood or used in the same way. This causes a two-sided misconception. For the originator of a given technology or other cultural artifact, it is hard to imagine that acquisition of that item or knowledge does not necessarily imply the adoption of the culture that produced it. It is even harder to grasp the possibility that an artifact will be used and understood in a different manner than its creators intended. On the acquirer's part, it is often equally difficult to make the sort of intellectual and social changes necessary fully to exploit or reproduce the acquired artifact. A compromise is therefore reached, whereby a receiving culture makes some changes in order to use and reproduce something effectively, but without completely copying the culture of the originator. The originating culture, more likely than not, never really accepts that its cultural artifacts can be adopted without a wholesale acceptance of its culture.

This would all be a very abstract discussion, and one that seems very far from the question of whether or not gunpowder caused a military revolution in Asia, if it did not go directly to the issue of how technology is believed to affect culture. The basis of the European Military Revolution argument is that changes in technology caused changes in warfare that in turn caused changes in politics and society. More specifically, it is argued that the technologies in question, gunpowder, cannon, handguns, *trace italienne* fortifications, and so on, fomented not simply changes, but very specific changes necessitated by the objective nature of those inventions. If this were true, then anyone adopting those technologies would have to follow the same trajectory of development, and understand those technologies in the same way. What this book has shown, however, is that this is not true. Receiving cultures make compromises to adopt and adapt new technology. And, if we return to the example of nuclear weapons and missiles, it is clear that it is dangerous for Western nations to assume that Asian nations see these devices in exactly the same way they do.

Asia was not very far behind the West in military technology during the early modern period. That gap has substantially closed over the course of the twentieth century. The West, America in particular, still maintains a strong lead in most areas of military technology, though that lead may be less decisive in the field. An absolute superiority is no guarantee of functional superiority under limiting political and geographic circumstances. China, for example, might still be able to win a conflict with the United States over the independence of Taiwan because the United States might be unwilling to endure or inflict too many casualties. Strategy is most often a question of degrees of superiority, of the relationship of strength and cost to the value assigned to a goal, rather than a process of absolute determinations. Technology cannot, therefore, be an objective determinant of value, values, or power.

The Western perception of its military advantage over Asian powers during the period of European imperialism has confused the advantages of political will, strategic planning, an acceptance of money-losing colonies, and many other strengths, with technological superiority. European imperialism developed over decades and even centuries, failing in many instances, but usually managing to hold on to any successes. These gradual encroachments required local support to be possible and sustainable, often transferring large amounts of advanced Western technology to the colonized country. Rather than a clash of cultures or societies, Western imperialism was a sustained attack upon Asian regimes. Western powers bought influence from local powerholders with guns, and used guns to strengthen the military component of European-backed efforts to transform local politics. As so many battles in South Asia showed, however, European victories could be extremely close-run things. Great Britain's core strength was the ability to sustain battlefield setbacks politically, which South Asian regimes often could not.

By placing the technological cart before the political and social horse, Westerners have reassured themselves not only that they created the modern world, but also that as the developing world modernizes it will Westernize as well. If technology is not, as this book has argued, the guiding hand imagined by Westerners, and if even the military technology some have placed at the heart of the European transition to modernity was, as we have seen, Asian in origin, then the origin of modernity lies elsewhere. Europeans did not create a culture objectively superior to all others, and the West's global ascendancy in the twentieth century is likely a temporary circumstance. Asian history is just as relevant to any discussion of the current state of the world as European history, and certainly more important in understanding Asia. European history is not the master narrative of world history, or even modern history, unless one chooses to remain ignorant of everyone else's histories. Ancient Greek culture led neither to the invention of gunpowder or guns, nor to the invention of the atomic bomb.

Technology and revolution

In the introduction to this volume, I contrasted the wealth, maturity, and stability of Asia in the early modern period with the poverty, backwardness, and volatility of Europe, and used this to frame the introduction and development of guns. An alert reader no doubt saw that as an ironic reference to the reversed situation of the present day. This is also a warning to those who would imagine the current strength and dominance of the West to be something fundamental to the Western culture. Seen in the context of pre-modern history, the rise of the West is an aberration. This seems more certain at the beginning of the twenty-first century than it did a century or two ago; the return of Asia to a truly dominant technological and economic position may well take another century or so, but probably less than that.

Many of the basic technologies so important to the development of European modernity were invented in Asia. They were taken up by people trying to emerge from poverty and ignorance, and vigorously experimented on and exploited for all their benefits. The almost unimaginable improvements in European society took centuries to emerge, and they now form the basis for Western dominance of the world. We now face a world, however, in which Asian people are embracing mature Western technology as a means to emerge from poverty and ignorance, and to develop their societies. If that half of the world's population could reach even the current economic level of the West over the next century, the world would again be transformed both quantitatively and qualitatively.

The history of gunpowder and guns lies at the center of the transformation of Europe from the Middle Ages into modernity. But this is not the same as saying that it was the motive force propelling that change. The Military Revolution in Europe would not have been possible without the dramatic economic, political, and institutional developments that began in the sixteenth century at the latest, if not earlier. Yet the analysis of those developments, and their conflation with the changes in military practice wrought by the introduction of gunpowder and guns from Asia, has badly distorted our picture of Asian cultures and their histories. The subsequent political collapses of various Asian regimes, and the often successful exploitation of those times of chaos by European powers for their own imperialist or mercantilist ends, have confused a time of temporary European technological advantage with a permanent and fundamental cultural superiority. This confusion has arisen and persisted because of a profound Western ignorance of Asian history, and has been abetted by an injured Asian sense of weakness and exploitation in the wake of European imperialism.

Guns and gunpowder were invented in China, and gunpowder weapons revolutionized Asian warfare before Europeans arrived. Thus any argument about military culture or attitudes toward the military in Western versus Eastern societies based on the presumption that only the West could invent, develop, and deploy guns effectively is wrong. Asian states and empires fought enormous wars for centuries with astonishing violence and skill. Asians were just as eager to kill each other with the most effective available weapons as were Europeans. This is not a proud truth, but a lamentable one. Yet it also goes to the heart of the question of whether or not there was a military revolution, or more accurately many disparate revolutions, in Asia that matched the one in Europe. There was no substantial technological difference between these revolutions; the major distinctions were cultural and political.

By itself, a gun was no more than a curiosity. It was only when guns were produced in large enough numbers, used by trained military units, and supported by a supply system allowing sustained use in battle, that they became revolutionary. This is to say that it was political and institutional developments, not technology by itself, that turned guns into effective military instruments. Chinese institutions were the first to harness gunpowder to military use, and to mass produce it to make weapons. The fruits of these Chinese developments gradually spread to the rest of Eurasia where they were received in whole or part and adapted to local conditions. Guns became a Eurasian weapon, with improvements and practices circulating throughout the continent, and they were used differently, and effectively, in many different environments. There was indeed a military revolution in Asia, and it spread to Europe as well.

I have argued in this book that modern warfare was created, or at least first appeared, in China during the twelfth and thirteenth centuries. Many modernists might feel that this is simply the usual sort of theory of a pre-modernist, who sees nothing new in the modern period, and can always claim that every constituent of modernity existed at some time or place in the pre-modern world. What distinguishes the modern world is not each individual part, but how it all fits together. But Chinese warfare in the twelfth and thirteenth centuries contained not just a few parts of modern or early modern Western warfare, it contained them all together. Nor did it somehow lose or misplace that totality and reacquire it with the arrival of the West. European guns were only slightly better than what was available in Asia when the first wave of European merchants and missionaries arrived there.

Many places and regimes in Eurasia received the tools of early modern warfare from China, and spent considerable time absorbing this mode of war; it was only in Europe that the Chinese system was fully reproduced. This is not to say that Europeans knowingly copied China, only that it took the invention of systems and practices similar to those of China before European governments and armies began most fully to exploit the use of guns in war. Although it took Europeans some centuries to arrive at a military system close to that of China during the Song dynasty, the delay was not due to the slow development of guns in Europe. European governments first had to evolve their bureaucratic institutions to the point where they could support an army in the Chinese manner before political and military leaders (and in Europe these were not yet entirely separate in the early modern period as they were in China) could organize an army in the Chinese manner.

Where European and Western historians see the success of Western imperialism, and then its eventual collapse, an Asian historian could easily point to the utter failure of European empires within Europe. No European country was capable of achieving a lasting hegemony, let alone a unified empire, on the western edge of Eurasia. By contrast, the Mughals ruled over South Asia, and a succession of regimes ruled over the Chinese ecumene, for centuries. Why was Great Britain able to rule India after decades of effort, but not continental Europe? A relatively small number of British officials controlled a vast empire with the same technology that existed in Europe. Since the British did not have a decisive technological advantage over all the Indian contenders for power, it was clearly not technology that allowed the creation of a British empire in India. A political culture of empire pre-existed the British colonial enterprise; the British East India Company operated within that system and eventually took control of it. Similarly, European traders took over existing trade routes in South, Southeast, and East Asia, and connected them to Europe; they did not create them with their technology.

European colonies were often a transfer point for wealth from a given European government's budget, in the form of military and administrative expenditures, to that government's merchants. These transfers were acceptable because they provided an excuse to maintain a large military establishment, contributed to the dignity and glory of the state, and fed money, through the medium of corruption, back into the ruling class. Despite this, long after the rise of the West, Asia still possessed many of the world's largest and most developed cities, as well as much of its most advanced technology. Both in terms of economic strength and manufacturing capability, Asia was far in advance of the West. Until the second half of the nineteenth century the two largest economies in the world were

India's and China's. A century and a half later, it is as if Asia is taking up where it left off when Europeans interrupted it. The center of modernity is reasserting itself.

If the story of guns and gunpowder shows us anything, it is that Europeans did not invent the modern world. As Friedrich Nietzsche (1844–1900) blundered so revealingly in *Beyond Good and Evil* (1886) concerning who invented gunpowder and printing, it is Asian technology and culture that is at the heart of the European transition to modernity. Western hubris over its temporary dominance in the world since the late nineteenth century has allowed it to imagine that its deep intellectual orientations, inherited from the ancient Greeks and passed through the lens of the Enlightenment, demonstrate its inherent technological and cultural superiority. Yet none of the technologies that early modern Europeans pointed to as initiating or paradigmatic examples of the modern world was invented in Europe. There was a military revolution in Asia, and it was followed by a military revolution in Europe.

Index